QUALITY ASSURANCE
the route to efficiency and competitive
Third Edition

ELLIS HORWOOD SERIES IN
APPLIED SCIENCE AND INDUSTRIAL TECHNOLOGY

Series Editor: Dr D. H. SHARP, OBE, former General Secretary, Society of Chemical Industry; former General Secretary, Institution of Chemical Engineers; and former Technical Director, Confederation of British Industry

This collection of books is designed to meet the needs of technologists already working in the fields to be covered, and those new to the industries concerned. The series comprises valuable works of reference for scientists and engineers in many fields, with special usefulness to those industries developing a quality management system.

Published and in active publication

QUALITY ASSURANCE IN THE PROCESS INDUSTRIES
J.AZAMBRE , Directeur du Département Sécurité-Environment de TOTAL Exploration- Production, France and J.G. AUDOUSET, Ingénieur Conseil en Assurance Qualité, France
PRACTICAL USES OF DIAMOND
A. BAKON, Research Centre of Geological Technique, Warsaw, and A. SZYMANSKI, Institute of Electronic Materials Technology, Warsaw
NATURAL GLASSES
V. BOUSKA *et al.*, Czechoslovak Society for Mineralogy & Geology, Czechoslovakia
INTRODUCTION TO PERFUMERY: Technology and Marketing
TONY CURTIS, Senior Lecturer in Business Policy and International Business, Plymouth Business School, and DAVID G. WILLIAMS, Independent Consultant, Perfumery and Director of Studies, Perfumery Education Centre
QUALITY ASSURANCE AND COST CONTROL IN MANUFACTURE AND NEW PROJECT ASSESSMENT
M. DUNAUD, formerly in charge of all aspects of Quality Management in The General Delegation for the Armaments Industry, France
THE HOSPITAL LABORATORY: Strategy Equipment, Management and Economics
T.B. HALES, Arrowe Park Hospital, Upton, Wirral
MEASURING COLOUR: Second Edition
R. W. G. HUNT, Visiting Professor, The City University, London
LABORATORIES: Design, Safety and Project Management
Editor: T.J. KOMOLY, ICI Engineering, Winnington, Cheshire
PAINT AND SURFACE COATINGS: Theory and Practice
Editor: R. LAMBOURNE, Technical Manager, INDCOLLAG (Industrial Colloid Advisory Group), Department of Physical Chemistry, University of Bristol
DESIGN, CONSTRUCTION AND REFURBISHMENTS OF LABORATORIES Volume 2
R. LEES, Laboratory of the Government Chemist, London
HEALTH PROTECTION FROM CHEMICALS IN THE WORKPLACE
Editor: Dr P. LEWIS, Senior Executive, Occupational Health, Chemical Industries Association, London
CROP PROTECTION CHEMICALS
B.G. LEVER, Development Manager, ICI plc Plant Protection Division
FERTILIZER TECHNOLOGY
G.C. LOWRISON, Consultant, Bradford
REPROCESSING OF TYRES AND RUBBER WASTES: Recycling from the Rubber Products Industry
V.M. MAKAROV, Head of General Chemical Engineering, Labour Protection, and Nature Conservation Department, Yaroslav Polytechnic Institute, Russia, and VALERIJ F. DROZDOVSKI, Head of the Rubber Reclaiming Laboratory, Research Institute of the Tyre Industry, Moscow, Russia
ACCIDENTAL EXPLOSIONS: Volume 1: Physical and Chemical Properties
LOUIS A. MEDARD, formerly Head of the Laboratory in the French Government Explosive Branch
ACCIDENTAL EXPLOSIONS: Volume 2: Types of Explosive Substances
LOUIS A. MEDARD, formerly Head of the Laboratory in the French Government Explosive Branch
PROFIT BY QUALITY: The Essentials of Industrial Survival
P.W. MOIR, Consultant, West Sussex
COLOUR DYNAMICS AS A SCIENCE
ANTAL NEMCSICS, Professor at the Technical University of Budapest, Hungary
TRANSIENT SIMULATION METHODS FOR GAS NETWORKS
A.J. OSIADACZ, UMIST, Manchester
BASIC QUALITY ASSURANCE
M. REYNIER, Joint Chief of Quality Assurance Department, Societe Bertin & Cie, France and also President of Logical Quality Group of the MFQ (South-East), France
QUALITY ASSURANCE: The Route to Efficiency and Competitiveness, Third Edition
L. STEBBING, Quality Management Consultant
QUALITY MANAGEMENT IN THE SERVICE INDUSTRY
L. STEBBING, Quality Management Consultant
QUALITY MANAGEMENT FOR THE SMALL BUSINESS
L. Stebbing, Quality Management Consultant, UK and R.J. PENGELLY, Director RJM Business Analysts Ltd, UK
INDUSTRIAL PAINT FINISHING TECHNIQUES AND PROCESSES
G.F. TANK, Educational Services, Graco Robotics Inc., Michigan, USA

QUALITY ASSURANCE
the route to efficiency and competitiveness
Third Edition

LIONEL STEBBING F.I.Q.A., F.Q.S.A., S.M.A.S.Q.C.,
Quality Management Consultant

ELLIS HORWOOD
NEW YORK LONDON TORONTO SYDNEY TOKYO SINGAPORE

First published in 1986
Second Edition published in 1989
and reprinted in 1989, 1990, 1992 and 1993
Third Edition published in 1993
and reprinted and issued for the first time in paperback in 1994 by
Ellis Horwood Limited
Campus 400, Maylands Avenue
Hemel Hempstead
Hertfordshire, HP2 7EZ
A divison of
Simon & Schuster International Group

Printed and bound in Great Britain by
Hartnolls, Bodmin

Library of Congress Cataloging-in-Publication Data

Available from the publisher

British Library Cataloguing in Publication Data

A catalogue record for this book is available from the British Library

ISBN   0-13-109753-9   (pbk)

4 5   97 96

Table of contents

Foreword to the third edition

The success of the first two editions has shown that Lionel Stebbing has the right approach in expounding the principles and practice of quality assurance. He has been one of the pioneers in the field and it must be particularly gratifying to him that the concept of total quality has at last gained virtually universal acceptance.

He would be the first to say that he is still learning. As the complexity of industry has increased, and intensification of competition has demanded even higher standards, still greater emphasis has been placed on quality assurance, leading to refinements in its methodology and application.

A third edition of *Quality Assurance* is, therefore, timely.

D. H. Sharp
Series Editor

Foreword to the second edition

When this book was first published in 1986, it was Industry Year in Great Britain. This year marks the bicentennial of Australia, and the holding of the International Expo 88 here in Brisbane. The author has been living and working in Queensland for the past twelve months, so it is appropriate that the Foreword should come from 'down-under'.

Australian industry has taken to quality management as its key to industrial growth and its door to international markets. No longer is Australia just a great place to live, comfortable in its assured primary industry and mineral export markets. Australia is developing international business in a range of challenging markets—challenging because of the inherent quality in these markets, both in competing products and the expectations of the purchasers. A National Offsets Policy and long-term Partnership for Development Agreements with multinationals are focusing the demands of established quality practitioners upon Australian industry.

All these initiatives mean hard work for companies to grasp and integrate quality assurance, or upgrade their application of its principles into a whole quality management structure for their organizations. It takes people with the breadth of experience and skills of transfer of knowledge like Lionel Stebbing to bring quality assurance principles out of the page to you the reader.

It has been a privilege to have Mr Stebbing in Queensland, where he has been able to apply his skills directly to this State's quality upgrading. Now it is your turn to benefit by reading his words.

Peter Ellis
Director-General
Department of Industry Development

Foreword to the first edition

by Mr John Butcher,
Parliamentary Under Secretary of State for Industry

It is not too long ago that the 'Made in Britain' label was recognized and respected throughout the world as a virtual guarantee of unmatched quality and performance.

Today of course we have things rather less our own way on world markets, even though our industry continues to produce its fair share of outstanding products.

That is partly a reflection of the enormous intensification of world competition during the last 30 years. Japan in particular has demonstrated that the route to economic success is the pursuit of ever higher standards of quality by continually setting new standards of technological innovation, reliability and performance which have made her the biggest exporter of manufactured goods in the world.

Certainly it has become increasingly clear that we will only increase our own share of domestic and world export markets by matching that level of commitment and competing on every aspect of quality to the point where 'Made in Britain' is once again synonymous with the very best the world can offer.

This book can contribute to helping British management to meet that challenge at a time when quality is increasingly the key to improved competitiveness. I hope it will be widely read. And because 1986 is Industry Year, which is also concerned with changing attitudes towards and within our industry, the publication of Mr Stebbing's book could scarcely be more timely.

Preface to the second edition

The excellent reception given to the first edition of this book and the subsequent updating of the quality scene since its first publication have resulted in a need for the preparation of a revised and expanded edition.

Since the first edition, the international series of standards on quality systems has been ratified and published as definitive documents. Many national standards bodies, particularly in Europe, have adopted these as new revisions to their existing quality standards. For example, in the UK all four parts of the international standard have been issued without variation as BS 5750-1987 (parts 0, 1, 2, 3 and 4). It being agreed that the revision of BS 5750 should be identical with the ISO standards in the interests of international harmonization and international trade.

Other countries, particularly Australia, have endorsed the use of the international standards and have issued them as separate dual-numbered documents running concurrently with their own national standards on quality.

It is gratifying to see that we are approaching some form of harmonization with regard to quality systems and perhaps, in the not too distant future, the ISO quality systems standards will be applied internationally.

The second edition of this book, therefore, uses the ISO standards as the basic systems documents. Definitions, where these are applicable, are taken from ISO 8402-1986 (Quality—Vocabulary). Other definitions remain as for the first edition.

Chapters 4 and 8 have been expanded to give more information resulting from experience and some of the figures amended to reflect this. A chapter on management review has been added.

In closing I must express my gratitude to the many users who have helped me to improve this book by suggesting corrections and additions.

Lionel Stebbing
September 1988

Preface to the third edition

Since the publication of the second edition of this book in 1988, many more countries have adopted the ISO 9000 series of standards on quality and ISO standards have been issued on auditing and auditor qualifications. I have taken these into consideration in this third edition.

Generally, however, the standards defining quality systems do not address the subject of quality costs and, as the control of quality costs is an integral part of assuring quality and the prevention of failure, I have included a chapter on this subject. I have also included further information on the development and documentation of the quality system, particularly in relation to: the criteria for 'when' and 'how much' to document; the differing styles of second- and third-tier documentation; and information on implementation plans and some pitfalls to avoid.

The chapter on the role of quality circles has been expanded to include a number of problem-solving techniques.

Again I must express my gratitude to the many users who have helped me to improve this book by suggesting additions and corrections.

Lionel Stebbing
January 1993

Preface to the first edition

It is unfortunate that quality assurance continues to be misunderstood and I have written this book to try to dispel some of the myths and break through the mystique surrounding the subject and to present what I believe to be the soundest philosophy. It is a consistent and logical approach which, if implemented and practised in everyday activities with total support from senior management, can lead only to 'getting it right first time—every time'.

I appreciate that some may not totally agree with my philosophies and methods but I have found that they do achieve the desired results; therefore some may have to alter their thinking radically to accept these philosophies and methods. There are many interpretations but I am convinced that this is the right one. If a change of thinking is required, I would refer you to that great statesman Sir Winston Churchill who said:

> There is nothing wrong in change if it is in the right direction. To improve is to change, so to be perfect is to have changed often.

Perfection is difficult to achieve but one can get very close to it with constant practise. Quality assurance is a skill and with any skill, once one has learned it, one must practise it to be perfect. There are many individuals who have helped me practise my skills and these same individuals have taught me much.

It would be impossible to list them all but some must be mentioned: David who did not believe me at first but who became my greatest convert; the two Alans and one Allan who made great contributions in many areas; Odvaar who taught me to understand the Norwegian approach; Eric and Bob who gave me the Canadian view; Willem whose persistence made me go into print and Yamanouchi-san with whom I spent many delightful hours discussing the Japanese approach, not only with regard to the quality of the product but also regarding the quality of life.

No function can be said to be right unless it has been checked and confirmed, and without the assistance of Mike it would never have achieved its 'approved' status.

My wife Betty must receive the greatest appreciation. She painstakingly read and typed the final draft and gave me the encouragement and support that I needed when I felt I would never get it finished. Her remarks, after reading the final draft, were quite revealing: 'Very good but surely it is only common sense after all!'

Is it? I leave you, the reader, to decide.

Finally, my thanks must go to another David whom I regard as my frame-maker. I painted the picture and David framed it for me. He is my editor.

Lionel Stebbing
August 1986

Acknowledgements

The author wishes to acknowledge assistance and co-operation with the supply of information from:

British Standards Institution, Certification and Assessment Department, UK
Canadian Standards Association, Canada
Department of Trade and Industry, UK
ETRS-Stebbing, Australia
Institute of Quality Assurance, UK
National Society of Quality Circles, UK
Registration Board of Assessors of Quality Systems, UK
Standards Australia

Introduction

THE TOTAL PRESENTATION

Richard Wagner (1813–1883), the great German composer, when he prepared his music dramas (operas), was at pains to bring together all the relationships between the different art forms involved in presenting a music drama. In so doing, and before committing himself to paper, he gave as much thought to the words, scenery, costume and overall presentation as to the music, his intention being to create a complete sound picture. Wagner gave this philosophy the title *Gesamtkunstwerk* (complete art work)—a bringing together of all activities and functions so that none is subservient to the other and that each is planned, controlled and executed in a formal and systematic manner. (This is one reason why Wagner's music dramas do not transfer well to the small screen as they should be seen as a whole to appreciate the total presentation.)

Translated to the industrial scene, we would nowadays call this philosophy *quality assurance*. Perhaps the name is unfortunate as the word quality, in normal parlance, implies a subjective judgement. Quality, like beauty, is in the eye of the beholder. What is considered by one person to be of good quality, could be considered by another to be of poor quality, and vice versa. However, in the context of quality assurance, quality has a precise meaning. It is defined as:

The totality of features and characteristics of a product or service that bear on its ability to satisfy stated or implied needs. (ISO 8402-1986: Quality—Vocabulary)

It is, therefore, necessary to understand the requirements of the customer and what he or she means by quality if the product or service is to satisfy the stated or implied needs. In a consumer society the requirements of the customer can be identified only by market research, and information gained this way must be fed back to the finance, design and production departments for review for feasibility and implementation. In the case of major items, then the requirements must be identified by the customer in the form of detailed specifications.

In other words: What is the item required to do? What are its service requirements? What shape, size and colour are required? What is the expected service life and how is it to be disposed of when its usefulness has come to an end? The importance of the disposal of an item is often overlooked. Much will depend upon its size and complexity.

In the case of small consumer items, disposal should be comparatively simple, but for capital plant consideration should be given at the outset to its ultimate decommissioning and dismantling. Hence the definition of quality referring to the totality of features and characteristics of a product or service.

ASSURANCE OF QUALITY

In order to assure quality, it is therefore necessary first to ensure that all the requirements for the total presentation are known. In other words, the customer's requirements must be sufficiently detailed to be fully understood by the supplier so that there are no areas of doubt as to the service requirements.

This is the *sine qua non* of any quality system. The gathering together of all the information, the planning of all activities, and the detailing of precise instructions should all take place before any activity commences. Then the subsequent proper control of these activities becomes possible.

Quality assurance requires the total integration and control of all elements within a particular area of operation so that none is subservient to the other. These elements cover such aspects as administration, finance, sales, marketing, design, procurement, manufacture, installation, commissioning and even, as we have seen, decommissioning.

If all the elements of an operation are to be totally integrated so that none is subservient to the other, the role, or function, of each of these elements should first be established, and, as in Wagner's music dramas, there should be a director to bring it all together. Therefore, responsibility should be assigned for the establishment of requirements and the integration and control of all activities. Ultimately it is the senior executive of an organization who must accept responsibility for this direction and for the quality of the items or services produced by his or her company.

Quality assurance is, therefore, a management function which cannot be delegated. As will be shown, a properly constituted quality assurance department can produce a plan for action and a system to be followed but its implementation is a management responsibility.

Quality is not something that can be 'tacked on to' a manufacturing or service process: as we have seen, quality assurance is a philosophy of total integration of the business to achieve the required result.

Unfortunately, in all too many cases, this responsibility of management is not recognized and the central philosophy of quality assurance not appreciated. Attempts are all too often made by management to delegate the function to a department which is given a title containing the word quality, such as quality department, quality control department, quality assurance department, or even a combination of all three, quality assurance/quality control department. This latter title is usually abbreviated to QA/QC department, which will be seen to be a total misnomer.

Quality assurance has thus become a very misconstrued and misunderstood concept due, at least in part, to its unfortunate title which is at best misleading and, at worst, meaningless, when one considers its total implications. Perhaps Wagner's portmanteau title *Gesamtkunstwerk* would be better. At least it pulls away from the word quality which, unless the precise definition (such as that of ISO 8402) is known and appreciated—which it very rarely is—is the cause of much misunderstanding.

MYTHS AND MISCONCEPTIONS

It is important, before continuing further, to dispel some of the myths and misconceptions that surround quality assurance. The most popular misconceptions are that: it is very costly; it is bureaucratic; it is a massive paper generator; and that it places emphasis on correcting deficiencies after the fact rather than preventing defects from occurring in the first place. It is necessary to consider also the proper role of the department which is given such an unfortunate title and which seems to indicate that it alone is responsible for quality.

It is important, in the first place, to understand what quality assurance is not.

It is not quality control or inspection.
It is not a super-checking activity.
It is not responsible for engineering decisions.
It is not a massive paper generator.
It is not a major cost area.
It is not a panacea for all ills.

Now perhaps an explanation is due to qualify all the above statements.

It is not quality control or inspection. Although a quality system will include quality control and inspection, both these activities form only a part of a company's total commitment to quality. They relate directly to the control of the manufactured item or the service delivery. These two activities have no involvement in activities which occurred upstream beforehand, such as design, procurement, sales and marketing. They should be considered, therefore, only as one of the elements in the total presentation.

It is not a super-checking activity. In other words, the quality assurance department should not be responsible for checking everything done by others. For example, the quality assurance department should not be responsible for checking engineering documents and specifications for engineering content or checking welding procedures for metallurgical content, but there are some—in my view incorrect—quality assurance philosophies which do place the responsibility for these checking activities upon the quality assurance department. This cannot be considered either efficient or cost-effective. The responsibility for such checks should be on those who are sufficiently qualified and experienced to determine the efficacy of the activity under review.

It is not responsible for engineering decisions. In other words the quality assurance department should not have to make decisions regarding engineering activities—nor for that matter any decisions outside its own remit. The only people who can be responsible for engineering decisions are engineers; that is what they are trained and qualified to do.

It is not a massive paper generator. However, because such things as mill certificates, test certificates and third party certification documents in general have become regarded as being necessary to meet quality assurance requirements, a misconception has arisen that all such paper is the necessary requirement of a quality system. Such documents as mill certificates, test certificates, non-destructive testing certificates, are requirements to satisfy conformance to specifications. Specifications are engineering documents, not quality assurance documents.

Unfortunately, in many organizations, quality control or inspection activities are the responsibility of the quality assurance department and, consequently, the need for such documentation is seen as a quality assurance requirement rather than an engineering or production requirement.

Third party certification is also considered by many to be a quality assurance requirement. In the main third party certification is issued to identify that an item or service meets minimum requirements imposed by legislation. For example, safety and environmental standards which are rigidly imposed by government agencies on nuclear facilities and offshore drilling and production platforms are required to be certified by a regulatory body before commencement of operations. Such certification is a legislative rather than a quality assurance requirement.

However, a well-designed and fully implemented quality system will ensure and verify that the documentation and certification requirements are achieved in the most efficient manner. The responsibility for documentation and certification should not be placed on the quality assurance department, as has often been done in the past. Hence the stigma of it being a massive paper generator and a major cost area. This leads nicely into the next statement.

It is not a major cost area. As far as documentation and certification are concerned, quality assurance is not a major cost area. There are procedural requirements to support a quality system but, having said that, any self-respecting organization should have procedural controls in place in any event and should not have delayed their installation and implementation until the company has become so large and/or that control has been lost. It is a fact that many organizations have been in existence for many years before implementing a quality system. Initially, in these circumstances, the development and implementation of such a system can be quite substantial but the cost should be equated against improvements in efficiency, productivity and profitability. The best time to implement a quality system is at the inception of a company. Prevention is better than cure.

It is not a panacea for all ills. Quality assurance will not cure everything but it will go a long way towards getting things right first time, every time. We are all fallible creatures and we all make mistakes. The person who makes no mistakes makes nothing.

All activities, regardless of their nature, have some human input somewhere, sometime. The possibility of achieving perfection every time is, therefore, very remote but one should strive to achieve perfection most of the time. This can be achieved only by constant practice and continual updating of skills. The requirements for training to acquire new skills and to keep abreast of new technology, and for retraining where one has not participated in an activity for some time, will go a long way towards achieving perfection every time.

If quality assurance is none of those things then what is it?

WHAT IS QUALITY ASSURANCE?

It is cost-effective.
It is an aid to productivity.

It is a means of getting it right first time every time.
It is good management sense, and, most importantly:
It is the responsibility of everyone.

In the following chapters it is the intention to show how a well-developed, well-implemented and well-supported quality system can meet these five criteria of 'what quality assurance is' and to confirm that Wagner's *Gesamtkunstwerk* is, perhaps, a better title to describe the philosophy presently known as quality assurance.

1

The background to quality assurance

CUSTOMER–SUPPLIER RELATIONSHIP

The background to quality assurance is the customer–supplier relationship. The ultimate purpose of any quality system is to ensure complete satisfaction by the customer with the goods or services provided by the supplier. Thus, the customer–supplier relationship is an active rather than a passive one. The first step in this relationship is to determine the customer. Depending on the nature of the product or service, either the customer will, or should, provide a full specification of requirements, or the supplier, by market research and feedback from the market-place, will produce services or goods to a presumed customer requirement. Any quality system must, therefore, involve the customer, either directly or indirectly. Although this customer–supplier relationship may be regarded, at least partly, as external to the supplier's activities, the same philosophy applies internally within a supplier's workplace at each stage of the operation. The customer becomes the user or consumer of the next stage in the operational process and so a quality system applies through the whole complex of activities within any organization. Fig. 1.1 typifies this internal customer–supplier relationship.

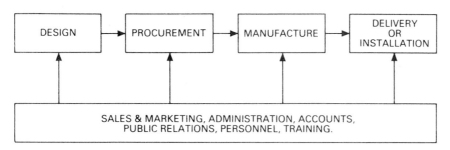

Fig. 1.1—Internal customer–supplier relationship.

HISTORICAL PERSPECTIVE

Often in the past, quality criteria were defined more by the experience of a supplier rather than by any specific requirements of a customer. The customer stated the need in broad terms and the supplier gave a service or manufactured an item which was considered would fill that need. It was only on completion that it was determined whether or not the service or item suited the customer's requirements.

Although that was many years ago, these practices did, to a certain extent, spill over into modern industry, the only improvements being that very basic objectives were conveyed verbally or framed into very sketchy procedures. In the case of a manufactured item, the inspector, who usually worked for and reported to the production department, had little idea of the full inspections required as insufficient data were given, due to inadequate information from the customer and lack of interface with the design or engineering department.

Many inspection results were accepted by the customer purely on the basis of his or her confidence in the manufacturer. However, the customer sometimes provided a little added assurance by having a representative at the manufacturer's works to witness some of the inspection and test points.

Sometimes defects were not discovered until manufacture was at an advanced stage, often leading to costly repair work and sometimes involving scrapping, with the inevitable schedule delays. In spite of frequent inspection, not all defects were detected and this resulted in the in-service failures with which we are all too familiar.

This was the system (or lack of system) largely practised until very recently and it is not surprising that customers often criticized the poor quality and delivery performance of their suppliers. This approach has seriously affected the ability to be competitive in both home and overseas markets. Indeed, recent experiences have shown that even now, these inspection practices are still very much in evidence.

In today's highly demanding environment of quality, together with the concern by customers and the costs restraints within a company, the emphasis must now be proactive rather than reactive. The question 'Have we got it right?' (quality control/inspection) must give way to 'Are we doing it right?' (quality assurance).

During recent years with design, manufacture and installation processes becoming increasingly complex and safety and environmental requirements becoming more stringent, the old inspection practices have been found to leave too many areas open to human error, notwithstanding the quality and extent of inspection coverage. Unfortunately, there is still the tendency to cling to these old inspection practices, which serve only to identify that an item or service is acceptable or unacceptable on a 'go/no-go' basis.

THE SYSTEMATIC APPROACH

A more appropriate approach is to look at methods which reduce the amount of inspection and testing activities. Each person in an organization should be responsible for the quality of the work he or she produces rather than relying on the activities of others subsequently to discover any faults.

The results of these old inspection practices leave much to be desired.

The current philosophy is to insist on objective evidence of quality rather than make assumptions by inspection, or accept a guarantee by a contractor or supplier, that the required quality does exist.

This objective evidence of quality must be seen to exist, not only in the completed product or service but in all activities which are involved in completing that item or service, e.g. administration, design, procurement, manufacture and installation. By controlling all those functions in a systematic manner there is a reasonable assurance that each activity is right before the next activity commences. This could be construed as the producer–receiver relationship, with each function within a complex organization being responsible for the quality of its own product.

This evidence of quality relates to all the activities concerned with the actual design, procurement, manufacture and installation of an item or the production of a service. These activities in themselves, if they are under control, will give the customer the product in a 'fit for purpose' condition and within budget and on schedule.

There are, however, many other functions outside these areas which indirectly affect the efficiency of achieving fitness for purpose. These include such functions as administration, market research, sales, finance, after-sales service and so on, which should all be included in the quality system. Thus not only is fitness for purpose achieved but it would be achieved in the most efficient and cost-effective manner. Inevitably such increase in efficiency must lead to increased profitability with all its attendant benefits. This philosophy of operating an organization is known as Total Quality Management.

OBJECTIVE EVIDENCE OF QUALITY

Objective evidence of quality is that which confirms that all activities within each of the functions of a service or manufacturing process and, in the case of large projects, site construction and commissioning, have been carried out in accordance with established working methods. These methods are identified in documents which are known as *procedures* and *job instructions*.

Procedures detail the purpose and scope of an activity and also identify how, when, where and by whom the activity is to be carried out. Emanating from such will be documents which will detail the results of these activities. A design process, for example, will produce a document such as a specification, a drawing or a data sheet. A procurement process will produce a document such as a tender package, purchase order or contract. An inspection or test process will produce a document such as a mill certificate, non-destructive testing certificate or heat-treatment certificate.

Job instructions direct personnel in carrying out a specific task. Job instructions do not necessarily produce documentation and, in such instances, can be audited only by watching the person involved carry out the task.

In manufacturing, evidence of procedures being followed, together with the documentation produced, provide the objective evidence of quality. Thus, procedures and job instructions, together with the methods for ensuring they work, make up a *quality system*.

THE NEED FOR AUDIT

Once procedures are established, how can it be ensured that the procedures are being implemented and are effective? What takes the place of inspection in the old system of operation? The answer is a compliance audit.

What is an audit expected to prove?

An audit is undertaken to indicate whether a procedure or job instruction is working satisfactorily. It readily highlights non-conformances and should lead to action being taken to correct them and prevent their recurrence.

The requirement for quality audits is determined by management; therefore, management responsibilities should be recognized as such and integrated into the management system.

It is a management decision to implement audits, and in order for an audit to work effectively, the group concerned with undertaking audits must have the organizational freedom to oversee the development, implementation and maintenance of the quality system. In this context, the word 'group' can imply as few as one or even a part-time activity, depending on the size and nature of the organization.

As has already been stated, for the sake of convenience, this group is usually given the title 'quality department'. This is perhaps unfortunate as quality assurance is a philosophy which should be practised throughout an entire organization and should not be regarded as the responsibility of just one department. To secure the required authority, organizational freedom and independence, it is essential, therefore, for the quality manager to report directly to senior management. The ISO quality system standards actually refer to the quality manager as the 'management representative', thus emphasizing the importance of the position. This is the *sine qua non* of any effective quality system. Any attempt to place the so-called quality assurance department within, say, the process or production department, indicates that management has not appreciated the philosophy of quality assurance.

Experience has shown that, in most cases, where quality assurance has been ineffective, this has been largely due to an incorrect 'chain of command'. The organization for quality will be covered in greater detail in Chapter 6.

THE NEED FOR PROCEDURES

It follows that in order to assess and report any procedural non-conformances within any discipline or department and to obtain positive corrective action, it is imperative that all personnel within the quality assurance department are adequately qualified and experienced and are accepted and respected as such. The department should not be regarded as a policeman but as a guide, philosopher and friend.

To implement a quality system and to assess and report shortcomings within the system, the quality assurance department must have bases upon which to work. These bases are the written procedures which should indicate 'what' is required or is to be controlled; 'who' is responsible for ensuring that the requirement is met or that the control is carried out; and 'how', 'when', 'where' and possibly 'why' it is controlled. In addition, the procedures should describe how quality and safety requirements will be accounted for.

As well as taking account of quality and safety requirements, it is also important that procedures indicate how interface problems between departments or disciplines can be avoided. The procedures which involve an interface between departments, disciplines or functions must, therefore, have the approval of all those groups directly concerned. A procedure should be written by the main department, discipline or function concerned, in consultation with the quality assurance department, to ensure that all relevant quality and safety requirements are included and that the document is capable of being audited. The methods and techniques of auditing will be dealt with in greater detail in Chapter 16.

2

Principles, philosophies, standards and procedures

In a complex field such as quality assurance, full codification in the form of national standards or codes of practice is virtually impossible. Various aspects of the discipline have, however, been so covered. As mentioned in the Introduction, the definition of quality as used throughout this book is that of ISO 8402. Other national standards and codes of practice have been produced, mainly to give guidance on quality systems and their levels of application.

THE QUALITY SYSTEM LEVEL

When reference is made to a particular quality level, in many instances this refers to sampling inspection percentages. However, the reference to a quality system level carries an entirely different meaning.

In the main, quality system standards are issued to cover three parts, levels, or categories, of application, as follows:

Level 1 covering design, manufacture and installation.
Level 2 covering manufacture and installation.
Level 3 covering final inspection and/or test.

There are, as with most things, exceptions to the rule. The nuclear industry, for example, has only one level, which is equivalent to Level 1 described above, whereas the Canadian Standard Z299 has four levels, but in all cases Level 1 includes activities and functions relating to design, manufacture and installation.

There are two types of quality assurance standards: industry-related standards and general standards.

Industry-related standards are those developed by purchasing bodies to enable suppliers to meet the quality requirements of a particular industry. These are normally produced as an aid to government procurement or in industries where there is an important and overriding safety requirement. Examples include defence, aerospace and nuclear industries.

General standards are those issued by national bodies to give guidance to industry in general on quality system development. They are normally for guidance purposes only but are becoming increasingly prevalent as a contract requirement.

Regardless of the country of origin or the industry connotations, the differences within these standards are, in the main, quite small.

COMPARISON OF QUALITY ASSURANCE STANDARDS

Fig. 2.1 identifies a number of the standards which address the criteria applicable to quality systems. Each standard is unique in its own way, yet, if the contents of each are evaluated, common factors are found.

AUSTRALIA	(AS 2990 Quality systems for Engineering and Construction Projects
	(AS 3901 Adoption of ISO 9001.
	(AS 3902 Adoption of ISO 9002.
	(AS 3903 Adoption of ISO 9003.
CANADA	(CAN3 Z299.1 Quality Assurance Program—Category 1.
	(CAN3 Z299.2 Quality Assurance Program—Category 2.
	(CAN3 Z299.3 Quality Assurance Program—Category 3.
	(CAN3 Z299.4 Quality Assurance Program—Category 4.
INTERNATIONAL	(ISO 9001 Model for quality assurance in design/development, production, installation and servicing.
	(ISO 9002 Model for quality assurance in production and installation.
	(ISO 9003 Model for quality assurance in final inspection and test.
UK	(BS 5750 Quality Systems.
	(Part 1—Adoption of ISO 9001.
	(Part 2—Adoption of ISO 9002.
	(Part 3—Adoption of ISO 9003.
	(BS 5882 Specification for a total quality assurance programme for nuclear power plants.
USA	ANSI/ASME NQA-1 Quality Assurance Program Requirements for Nuclear Facilities.

Fig. 2.1—Some typical quality system standards.

A basic list of 25 functions, which could be considered to represent the typical criteria for a Level 1 quality system, has been used as a norm and from it a comparison table compiled (see Fig. 2.2). Each of the numbers beneath the standards refer to the applicable section of that standard. This table does indicate common ground with regard to procedural requirements, but what it does not identify are the areas of *emphasis*. For example, BS 5882 and ANSI/ASME NQA.1 place much more emphasis on design control than do the other standards. Both BS 5882 and NQA.1 are quality systems relating to nuclear power plant projects. The other standards place their emphasis more on manufacturing.

	AS 2990	ISO 9001*	Z299.1	BS 5750.1*	BS 5882	NQA–1
Quality system	2.1	4.2	3.1	4.2	1	11.2
Organization (management responsibility	2.2	4.1	3.2	4.1	2	11.1
Audits	3.21	417	3.5.21	4.17	18	11.18
Quality system documents	2.3	4.2	3.5.3	4.2.	1	11.2
—manual	2.3	4.2	3.3	4.2	1	11.2
—inspection & test plans	3.6	4.2	3.5.6	4.2	11	11.11
Manufacturing control (production)	3.13	4.9	3.5.13	4.9	9	11.9
Planning (contract review)	3.1	4.3	3.2.2	4.3	1	11.2
Design control	3.2	4.4	3.5.2	4.4	3	11.3
Documentation & change control	3.3	4.5	3.5.3	4.5	4 & 6	11.4 & 6
Control of inspection, measuring & test equipment	3.4	4.11	3.5.4	4.11	12	11.12
Control of purchased products & services	3.5	4.6	3.5.5	4.6	7	11.7
Incoming inspection	3.7	4.10	3.5.7	4.10	10	11.10
Purchaser-supplied products (free issue)	3.19	4.7	3.5.19	4.7	NSI	NSI
In-process inspection	3.8	4.10	3.5.8	4.10	10	11.10
Final inspection	3.9	4.10	3.5.9	4.10	10	11.10
Sampling (stastical methods)	3.20	4.20	3.5.20	4.20	10	11.10
Inspection status	3.10	4.12	3.5.10	4.12	14	11.14
Identification & traceability	3.11	4.8	3.5.11	4.8	8	11.8
Handling & storage	3.12	4.15	3.5.12	4.15	13	11.13
Work instructions	2.4	4.2	3.5.3	4.2	5	11.5
Special processes	3.14	4.9	3.5.14	4.9	9	11.9
Preservation, packaging & shipping	3.15	4.15	3.5.15	4.15	13	11.13
Records	3.16	4.16	3.5.16	4.16	17	11.17
Non-conformances	3.17	4.13	3.5.17	4.13	15	11.15
Corrective action	3.18	4.14	3.5.18	4.14	16	11.16
Training	2.2	4.18	3.2.6	4.18	2	11.2

* Includes a requirement for servicing.
NSI = Not separately identified.

Fig. 2.2—Quality system standards—comparison table.

Many major projects (such as an offshore platform or petrochemical plant) have a large design content and require design controls just as much as does the nuclear industry; therefore one must extract the design elements from the nuclear standards.

On the other hand, with the remaining elements of a project, namely procurement, manufacture, installation and commissioning, the requirements can be adequately covered by using such standards as BS 5750 or CAN3 Z299 as a basis.

From this it will be seen that no single standard fits any industry completely; therefore, it is necessary to adapt what is already available. The word *adapt* is used with great emphasis. When buying a suit 'off the peg', unless one is of average build it never fits properly and will need to be adjusted in the right places. Similarly, no industries are 'of average build'; they are all unique in their quality system requirements and, therefore, existing standards need tailoring.

INDUSTRY COMPARISONS

Figs 2.3, 2.4 and 2.5 show comparisons between offshore, nuclear and aerospace projects. One vital area which does not apply in the nuclear and aerospace projects, and is unique to an offshore project, is the fabrication site. By the time a module or jacket leaves the fabrication site it has got to be right. If it is not 'right' and faults are discovered when installed offshore, quite apart from losses due to schedule delays and production shortfalls, repairs offshore can cost fifteen times as much as onshore repairs.

Although fabrication sites, in the main, utilize purchaser-supplied materials and equipment, they require in-house controls just as much as a manufacturer but with a different emphasis—more towards receiving inspection, special processes, traceability, and the like. As an example, Fig. 2.6 gives an indication of differing procedural requirements throughout a major project.

PROCEDURES

In the background to quality assurance (Chapter 1) reference was made to a procedure. It is now worth while to look briefly into the preparation of a procedure.

Format

All procedures, to be effective, should be consistent in their presentation. As with any type of document, uniformity of presentation is of paramount importance; therefore guidelines should be formulated for the preparation of procedures. In other words, there should be a *procedure for writing procedures*. All procedures should carry the same contents list, although the number of sections within a procedure may differ from company to company, according to requirements, but as a minimum there should be three sections, i.e. 'Purpose and Scope', 'Actions' and 'Documentation'. The development of the procedure is dealt with in detail in Chapter 9.

Procedure-writing responsibilities

The need for a procedure has to be identified by a responsible person within an organization. Usually, when formulating a quality system, this need will be determined by senior

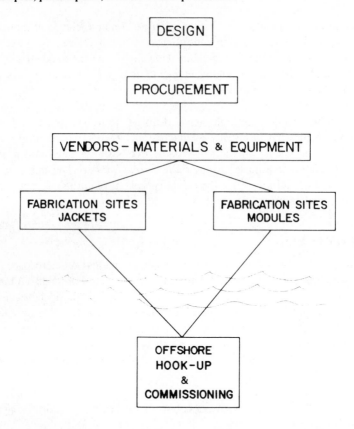

Fig. 2.3—Offshore industry.

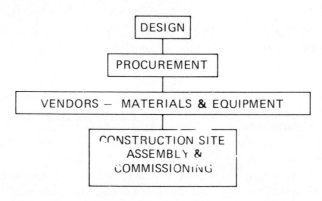

Fig. 2.4—Nuclear industry.

management, taking into account the activities of the organization concerned. The establishment and implementation of procedures can be undertaken only by personnel who are familiar with the activities and functions to be controlled. Unfortunately, in practice, the

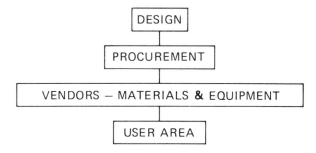

Fig. 2.5—Military/aerospace industries

quality assurance department tends to be given the sole responsibility for procedure writing, whereas it could be said that the only procedures which can be effectively written by the quality assurance department are those relating to auditing, corrective action and auditor qualification and training. The proper practice is for the quality assurance department to be instrumental in recommending procedural requirements in consultation with the department or discipline concerned.

Once the procedural subject has been determined, and an author delegated to carry out the work, the procedure should be written utilizing the agreed format.

QUALITY MANUAL, SYSTEM AND PLAN

Before a quality system can be established, there must be agreement on what that system is intended to achieve. It can be seen from Fig. 2.6 that a design contractor places a different emphasis on certain in-house controls than does, say, the fabrication site mentioned earlier. Therefore a company's requirements together with all regulatory requirements, should be established and documented.

At this stage it is worth while identifying the differences between a manual, system and plan. Fig. 2.7 identifies by diagrammatic means those differences but these will be dealt with in greater detail in Chapter 10.

Quality manual

A quality manual is usually defined as a 'document setting out the general quality policies, procedures and practices of an organization'.

The word 'general' is important in this definition. A quality manual is usually the first indication a prospective customer receives of a company's approach to quality assurance. This document should set out the company's intentions. It is generally accepted that it should contain: a policy statement; authority and responsibilities; organization; system element outlines; and a procedures index. It should not, however, contain detailed procedures. Not only would their insertion make the document a very costly item but updating would be a continual problem. Procedures can be amended without affecting the element outline in the manual and should be made available at the point of use. The actual development of the quality manual is described in Chapter 8.

	Design	Procurement	Manufacture	Installation and Commissioning	Operation and Maintenance	Decommissioning
1. Quality system	0	0	0	0	0	0
2. Organization	0	0	0	0	0	0
3. Audits	0	0	0	0	0	0
4. Quality system documents	0	0	0	0	0	0
—Manual	—	—	0	0	0	0
—Inspection and test plans	—	—	0	0	0	0
5. Manufacturing control	0	0	0	0	0	0
6. Planning (contract review)	0	0	0	0	0	0
7. Design control	0	—	*	—	—	—
8. Documentation and change control	0	0	0	0	0	0
9. Control of inspection, measuring and test equipment	—	—	0	—	—	—
10. Control of purchased items and services	—	—	0	0	0	0
11. Incoming inspection	—	0	0	*	*	—
12. Purchaser-supplied items	—	—	0	*	*	—
13. In-process inspection	—	—	0	0	—	—
14. Final inspection	—	—	0	0	0	0
15. Sampling	—	—	*	0	0	0
16. Inspection status	0	0	0	—	—	—
17. Identification and traceability	—	—	0	0	0	0
18. Handling and storage	0	0	0	0	0	0
19. Work instructions	—	—	0	0	0	0
20. Special processes	—	—	0	0	—	—
21. Preservation, packaging and shipping	—	—	0	0	0	0
22. Records	0	0	0	—	—	●
23. Identification of non-conformances	0	0	0	0	0	0
24. Corrective action	0	0	0	0	0	0
25. Training	0	0	0	0	0	0

0 = Requirement.

* = Requirement in some cases.

— = No requirement.

Fig. 2.6—Procedural requirements through the project phases.

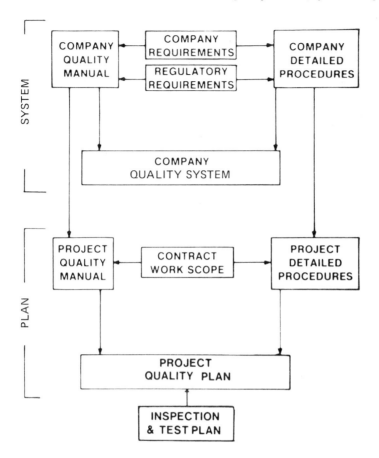

Fig. 2.7—System/plan.

Quality system

Referring to ISO 8402, a quality system is defined as: 'The organizational structure, responsibilities, procedures, processes and resources for implementing quality management'.

We have seen that the manual describes the intent, i.e. what is to be done. The procedures detail not only what but who, how, when, where and possibly why. Thus, the manual plus the supporting detailed procedures comprise the company's quality system.

Quality management

Referring to ISO 8402, quality management is defined as: 'That aspect of the overall management function that determines and implements the quality policy'.

Quality plan

Referring to ISO 8402, a quality plan is defined as 'a document setting out the specific quality practices, resources and sequence of activities relevant to a particular product, service, contract or project'.

When the company's quality system is applied to a given project or contract there is invariably the requirement for some form of adjustment or modification to suit that particular project or contract work scope. This adjustment or modification can take the form of either additions to, or reductions in, the corporate system.

For example, a contractor who can have an involvement in all activities from design through to installation has to develop a system to cover all these functions. This contractor, however, may win a contract for design only, in which case he or she will extract only those procedures relating to design and 'front' them with a manual unique to that contract. This manual plus the supporting procedures becomes the project quality plan (see Chapter 10).

Project quality plan

Before leaving this subject, we need to touch briefly on who defines project quality policy. There are a number of ways a customer can set up a project management team (PMT), for example:

Customer PMT—where the customer will actually manage the project utilizing his or her own staff and resources.

Integrated PMT—where the customer, together with a main contractor, will manage the project, utilizing staff and resources from both areas. In other words, pooling resources and assigning the best person to a given job.

Contractor PMT—where a contractor is given the responsibility for managing the project.

Detail design contractor with project management responsibilities—where a contractor is engaged to undertake the design of a given plant or structure and will manage the procurement, manufacture and installation.

In the case of customer PMT, the project quality requirements will be established by the customer and imposed upon all main contractors who will, in turn, develop their own quality plan in accordance with their scope of work.

In the case of an integrated PMT, the project quality requirements will be established by the customer/contractor but in all probability the emphasis will be based upon customer philosophies. Again, the main contractors will be expected to develop their own quality plans in accordance with those requirements related to their scope of work.

Where a contractor is employed to manage a project, the quality requirements will be identified by the customer and the contractor will develop a project plan which will be reviewed and probably approved or agreed by the client, prior to imposing it on all subcontractors.

Similarly, where a detail design contractor has been engaged not only to undertake the design but also to manage the project, then this design contractor will develop the project plan and impose it on all subcontractors.

3

The penalties of inadequate procedures

THE REINVENTION OF THE WHEEL

Experience has shown that, all too often, the simple failure to learn from past mistakes and to profit from expensively acquired experience can lead to inefficient operation and expensive reworking—particularly in industries engaged in project work. In the absence of a proper corporate quality system each new project becomes a 'one-off', leading in popular parlance to the 'reinvention of the wheel'.

Invariably at the start of any new project or contract one goes through the agonizing activity of developing and implementing project or contract procedures. In the absence of a corporate system this activity starts from scratch without being able to identify problem areas which have been encountered previously. Communication is partly to blame for this but, in the main, the problem lies in the absence of a uniform system of working which is regularly reviewed, has senior management support and which is utilized on every contract.

The results of this 'reinvention of the wheel' soon become apparent. The start of a project or contract is usually the most unproductive, inefficient and unprofitable period and the same problems manifest themselves later on.

Experience has shown that the following statements and questions are frequently made or asked:

'Why didn't you specify ...?'
'Who approved it?'
'Why wasn't I included in the distribution?'
'Who authorized that change?'
'Where is the documentation?'
'I can't read it!'
'That is not my responsibility!'
'Why did we buy from those people?'
'Who inspected that?'
'I didn't have an up-to-date specification!'
'We never had time!'

'But we have always done it that way!'

All of these need never have been said. Let us take each in turn.

Why didn't you specify ...?

This is a question often asked during the later stages of a project or contract when the material and/or equipment received is incompatible with service requirements.

A typical example is equipment intended for sour-service use being received only to be found later to be unsuitable for such service. The consequences of this are:

—equipment to be reordered to the correct specification
—additional cost
—schedule delays.

This situation has arisen because either one, two or all of three things occurred:

(a)   Service conditions were not known at the time of specification development.
(b)   The specification was either not checked or not checked properly by competent personnel.
(c)   The design engineer was not sufficiently knowledgeable or experienced.

In condition (a), the service requirements should have been identified at project start-up or as soon as possible thereafter.

Remedy—Develop and implement contract review or design criteria review procedure at early design stage, so that all are aware of the details of the contract work scope.

In condition (b), the specification should have been checked by appropriately qualified and experienced personnel using approved checklists.

Remedy—Develop and implement a design validation procedure during the design stage, which will identify who is responsible for checking the appropriate documents.

In condition (c), the design engineer should have been suitably qualified and experienced.

Remedy—Develop sufficiently detailed job specifications and implement in-house training schemes to cover any shortfalls in an employee's experience.

Who approved it?

One of three things has possibly happened here:

(a)   There is no approval signature.
(b)   The signatory is unknown and possibly unauthorized.
(c)   Signature is not legible.

Each condition should have been identified during the design state.

Remedy—Develop and implement a design document approval register, with sample signatures, at project start-up. This should be a fundamental requirement of any document validation procedure and should be identified and established during the early stages of a company's establishment or project start. Those responsible for approving documents should have their signatures registered, as is required, for example, in banking, in which registered signatures are required to prevent unauthorized individuals drawing from the account. A document validation approval register will act in a similar manner.

Why wasn't I included in the distribution?

This question could be countered with the question: 'Should you have been included in the distribution?' Too many times distribution lists are developed which include personnel who have no involvement in the activity. If, however, the answer is 'yes', then the document distribution procedure is either non-existent or is not being adhered to.

   Remedy—Develop and implement a document distribution list which will form part of the document control procedure.

   Keep document distribution to an absolute minimum.

   All distribution lists should be developed from the 'need to know' rather than the 'want to know' situation. We all like to see our name in print, it makes one feel important, but do we really have an input into the document? It should be a management responsibility to formulate distribution lists and these should be compiled as early as possible.

Who authorized that change?

This goes hand in hand with 'Who approved it?' Changes to documents should receive the same attention as the original documents.

   Remedy—Develop and implement a document change control procedure which will interface with the validation procedure.

Where is the documentation?

Material or equipment has been received without the supporting documentation (test results, material analyses, and the like). What happens now? The material/equipment has to be quarantined pending receipt of documentation, thus taking up storage space and possibly delaying construction. This situation has probably been caused by the supplier/manufacturer not having completed the documentation at the time of inspection, or shipment, but being instructed probably by unauthorized personnel to ship the material/equipment and send on the documentation later.

   This is short-sighted policy as it can cause only delay and frustration and may lead to incorrect material being release for use.

   As material/equipment received without documentation cannot be used until the documentation is received, the supplier should accept responsibility for storage as the shipment is not complete without the necessary documentation. The contract on the supplier should make this clear.

   Remedy—Ensure in procurement packages the requirement for documentation to form an integral part of the contract. Also instruct inspection personnel not to release any items without the specified documentation, and then support that instruction to the full.

I can't read it!

Obviously an illegible copy of a document which has found its way into project records. This again results in frustration and delay.

Unauthorized copying of documents may be the cause here. This is a common problem, as it is so much easier to borrow a document and copy it oneself rather than go through the procedure of obtaining an authorized copy.

Remedy—Set up and implement a strict document control system which identifies responsibility for document reproduction. This system to specify method of document reproduction; identification of documents; authority and approval.

An officially reproduced document can be identified with the words 'official copy' using red ink (or such other colour which will not reproduce in its original colour). Any document not carrying such identification should be regarded as unofficial and treated accordingly.

Recently, machines capable of copying in colour have been introduced thus presenting problems with unofficial copying. In such instances, the problem can be overcome by utilizing embossing pincers on which is etched some form of identification. As yet no company has produced a copying machine capable of reproducing an embossment.

That is not my responsibility!

A very good excuse and in many instances perfectly valid. A well-written job specification will identify a person's responsibilities and reporting routes.

In too many cases a job specification states in great detail the major responsibilities relevant to the position, only to be invalidated by an appended statement such as 'and other responsibilities which may from time to time be delegated by your supervisor'.

This is an 'escape clause'.

Remedy—Make job specifications clear and concise. When responsibilities are assigned over and above those indicated, then an amendment should be made to the job specification in writing. This is a safeguard, not only to the employee but also to the supervisor.

Why did we buy from those people?

Perhaps the recipient of the material or equipment knows something about the supplier which has not been communicated to the purchasing body. This statement would be made only if there has been some bad experience with the company concerned.

When assessing a possible supplier (a subject which will be dealt with later) all information should be made available.

Remedy—Ensure that procedures take into account previous performance in vendor assessment. This means there must be a system to update vendor records with information from project or contract groups.

Who inspected that?

The inspector gets the blame in this case, but was it really his or her fault? Obviously an item has been received which is not considered by the recipient to be acceptable. Does the recipient have the correct information to make such a judgement? Perhaps the specification was wrong or perhaps the item was released without being controlled. There are many possibilities. Do not be too quick to pass judgement. It is very easy to blame the inspector ... or the night shift!

This leads naturally into the next statement.

I didn't have an up-to-date specification!

Those who work, or have worked, in an inspection environment will have some sympathy with anyone who has to make such a statement. One cannot always blame the inspector for not having up-to-date documentation. Many are often instructed to inspect an item against a specification to be made available to them by the vendor. Therefore, one is reliant upon the vendor to supply all up-to-date information, but one really does not know whether it is up to date or not. This is a difficult situation to be in!

Also, the inspector can be given very sketchy information in the form of a fax, telex, letter or telephone message, from which he or she may be expected to carry out a responsible inspection. If the inspector complains, he or she may be reprimanded for nit-picking.

Remedy—Verify that the inspector is supplied with sufficient up-to-date information to carry out the inspection properly. This will be influenced by an effective and well-implemented document control procedure.

The inspector should be given the responsibility to determine whether he or she has sufficient, and up-to-date, information to carry out the task. If he or she suspects shortcomings, then support should be given in delaying the inspection until sufficient and correct information is received.

A personal experience is given to illustrate the point. During his early days in industry, the author was called upon to carry out an inspection assignment on equipment with which he was not completely familiar. It was a case of obeying orders as the job description included the 'escape clause' referred to above.

The equipment in question was for a hospital in Mexico and, the author having recently returned to work after undergoing an appendectomy, his supervisor considered he had the most recent applicable experience.

He was instructed to obtain all relevant information from the supplier—which he did.

The inspection was duly completed and the equipment released for shipment, only to be rejected upon arrival at the hospital in Mexico. The question asked was inevitable: 'Who inspected that?'

Naturally a very searching examination was held to determine what had gone wrong.

The information given by the supplier was, as far as he was concerned, correct. He had supplied the equipment in accordance with the purchase order and the inspection confirmed this. However, the investigation showed that the information given in the purchase order was incomplete. The equipment should have been supplied to an earlier catalogue reference description so as to interface with the equipment already installed at the hospital. The supplier had provided the latest type, which was not what was required, but had in effect been ordered.

In this instance, it was not a case of an up-to-date specification not being available but of the correct specification not having been used.

This incident led to an analysis of what had gone wrong and what should be done to prevent a recurrence of the situation. Evidently there was a lack of information in the contract documents, probably brought about by insufficient liaison with the engineering function and no independent check had been carried out on them.

We never had time!

This statement is particularly significant—usually made when the 'pressure is on'. One never has time to put it right when it happens, yet one always manages to find time for rectification later on when costs have escalated tenfold. This is surely not very efficient or cost-effective!

An effective and well-supported quality system would have gone a long way towards preventing the occurrence of the problem in the first place. 'Getting it right first time every time' is the maxim to adopt.

It has been quoted that the cost of maintenance work on an offshore platform amounts to approximately £10 million per annum. One could ask how much of this could be saved by 'getting it right first time'.

But we have always done it that way!

By thoroughly examining an activity it is almost always possible to find a much more efficient and cost-effective method of doing it. Probably most of us have never taken the trouble to find out whether a particular activity can be undertaken more efficiently. Regardless of technological advances within a particular industry, the ability to assure quality has not kept pace. As has already been said, there is still a tendency to cling to these old methods of working, whereas companies should be looking at more efficient methods of achieving the desired quality. When reviewing current activities, a veritable Pandora's box of problems may be opened up.

Malpractices, inefficiency, duplication of activities, corner-cutting and high rework costs are just some of the shortcomings that can be uncovered.

Personnel may see their jobs at stake and this can result in lack of co-operation, with the subsequent difficulties in implementing a quality system. Management must be firm and fair when committing itself to such a course.

When this list of statements and questions is examined, it should become apparent that the majority could have been procedurally controlled during the early stages of a project or contract.

COMMUNICATION AND CO-OPERATION

Communicating the problems, which have been experienced on previous projects or contracts, is of paramount importance, yet all too often it is not done. This may be due, in part, to the fact that at the end of a project or contract the team is disbanded and separated. No one person is aware of the totality of problem areas. The quality manager is probably the ideal person to highlight these areas and to monitor the recording of such problems in corporate records. The corporate quality system should then be revised to eliminate recurrence on future contracts. This, of course, can never happen without top management and company dedication to quality.

The customer can also play a very important part by debriefing the contractors at project completion. All too often problems are encountered, either during subsequent stages of a project or even after commissioning, which are not communicated back to the contractor, nor probably on to the subcontractors. This does not refer to major problems which are well advertised, but to those lesser problems which may result in unnecessary repair and maintenance costs, with possible production stoppages (which may well go towards the £10 million maintenance costs for offshore platforms referred to earlier).

This is an example of active customer–supplier relationship referred to at the beginning of Chapter 1.

It would be very difficult to quantify how many times one is greeted with: 'Quality assurance! What do we need that for? We have never had any problems. Our structure, facility, equipment, or whatever, has been operating for the past x number of years and is still operable.'

This may well be true but has anyone ever been advised what has been involved to keep it there and to keep it operating?

It is only recently, in what has become a very highly competitive world, that customers have begun looking more closely into quality costs. They now have the time and information to equate costs against previous project or contract performance and, in some cases, relate these costs with contractors' activities. The tender lists for new projects or contracts are a lot shorter than they used to be. If contractors fail to pre-qualify, they should look inwardly and start asking questions.

If it was necessary, in two words, to state the requirements of a successful quality system, the first would be 'communication'—which has already been stressed—and the second would be 'co-operation'.

It will become apparent in later chapters how much reliance is placed upon communication and how much dependence upon co-operation. The outcome can result only in cost-effectiveness, increased productivity, enhanced profitability and competitiveness, and go a long way towards 'getting it right first time, every time'.

4

Setting up and developing the appropriate quality system

THE RESPONSIBILITY FOR QUALITY

The senior executive of any organization is responsible for two things—the efficiency of the organization and the quality of the goods or the services which that company offers.

In the larger business organization, he or she will ultimately be responsible to the shareholders for the efficient running of the company and its profitability. In the smaller business organization, where the senior executive may well be the owner of the company, he or she will have a responsibility to the company's employees, to his or her own family and, in all probability, to the bank manager for the viability of the company.

FIRST CONSIDERATIONS

Any organization, large or small, whether privately owned or not, can remain viable only if it continues to give the service(s) or to produce items which the customer wants and at a price the customer is prepared to pay. There are, therefore, two things which must be considered when embarking upon the development and implementation of a quality system.

First, there is the need to satisfy customer requirements by supplying these services or producing items which are fit for purpose, within budget and on schedule. Second, there is the need to supply these services or items in the most efficient and cost-effective manner. These can be accomplished only by introducing effective management systems, in addition to those of a quality system standard.

The need to satisfy customer requirements

Satisfying customer requirements can be achieved by developing and implementing a quality system utilizing the criteria given in the appropriate general quality system standard, such as the ISO 9000 series. The requirement to implement a quality system to an industry-related quality system standard will, no doubt, have already been demanded by the purchasing body for that industry and will be a contractual obligation. There are, however, many instances where customers, other than those in safety-related industries, are demanding compliance with an appropriate quality system standard.

In any event, there are difficulties in meeting imposed requirements as most quality system standards are open to interpretation and misinterpretation. It is, therefore, recommended that, initially at least, any organization embarking upon a quality management system should use the available quality system standards as guidance documents only. Indeed, it may well be prudent to develop the quality system independently of the quality system standards, verify its implementation and effectiveness by audit and then determine with which standard the system complies.

The development of the appropriate quality system will be dealt with in detail later.

The improvement in overall business efficiency

The criteria of the quality system standards are, primarily, directed at producing items and services which are fit for purpose. There are, however, many other functions in addition to those specified in the quality system standards which contribute to the overall business efficiency of an organization, such as administration, secretarial, accounting, market research, maintenance, after-sales service and public relations. Shortcomings in any of these areas can lead to loss of business. Satisfying customer requirements and improving overall business efficiency are generally considered to be the two main reasons for implementing a quality system. There are, however, a number of other objectives which could be considered, such as:

— to increase customer confidence
— to enhance the company's corporate image
— to improve employee participation and morale
— to achieve registration as a quality-assured company.

PUBLIC RELATIONS

In the widest sense, quality assurance should apply to the whole business activity not just to the project or service. In particular, this applies to what is nowadays called 'public relations' or PR. Just as most management systems are applied common sense, most PR is, in reality, just old-fashioned courtesy and 'good manners'. It is an area in which all too many 'quality-conscious' organizations fail. The items they produce or the services they give can be of the highest quality yet, for example, if that organization neglects to keep the customer informed of delays due to unforeseen circumstances, then that customer becomes agitated and with good reason. He or she expects to be informed of the reason for the delay; common courtesy demands it. Communication is of the utmost importance. In the most common of situations when a bus or train is late, or fails to arrive, the traveller is most upset in being kept waiting without being advised of the reason for the delay or when transport is expected. A short communication by transport staff advising the reasons for delay puts the traveller's mind at ease. While he or she doesn't arrive at the destination any earlier, the psychological advantages of keeping the traveller informed are great.

The same thing applies to the late delivery of items or the start-up of a service commitment. Keeping the customer informed shows that the organization has the customer's interests at heart.

Management should also appreciate, but rarely does, that perhaps a company's most important members of staff are the receptionists and telephone operators, the links with the outside world. It is frustrating, and all too common, to be connected to an extension, via a switchboard, and to have the extension remain unanswered with the caller left 'high and dry'. In such circumstances, the operator should be instructed to intercept the call and offer an alternative connection. Many large and reputable organizations fail to adopt this practice.

The reception area is another case in point. There are many instances on record where a visitor to a company is kept waiting, or worse ignored, while the receptionist finishes a private telephone conversation or is engaged in idle conversation with a colleague. Similarly, keeping a visitor waiting is bad manners.

Such malpractices can have only an adverse effect on the overall business efficiency of an organization and the elimination of these practices should, therefore, be included in any system designed to increase the effectiveness, profitability and competitiveness of a company. A company must always be regarded as 'good to deal with'.

THE COST OF QUALITY

All companies employ someone to be responsible for the accuracy of its financial transactions and, generally, that person occupies an executive post. That person is usually aware of the cost associated with such matters as absenteeism, holidays and down-time, and will be obliged to present a complete financial statement of the implications of these matters to the authorities and, where appropriate, to a company's shareholders. Only rarely does an organization employ an executive of equivalent level who is responsible for quality yet, in many instances, a company's quality costs can be equal to, or even exceed, the profit margin of that company. Quality costs are the costs of putting things right and generally are not totally recognized.

When an analysis is made of all associated costs, the result can be quite substantial. It should, therefore, be a requirement of every senior executive to realize what these costs are. The requirement to keep a detailed analysis of an organization's financial affairs is required by legislation yet, where the costs associated with putting things right are concerned, this is usually given scant attention.

The subject of quality costs, identification, assessment and control is dealt with in detail in Chapter 5.

THE QUALITY EXECUTIVE (THE MANAGEMENT REPRESENTATIVE)

In most manufacturing organizations and, indeed, in many service organizations, there is a department that has been given the responsibility for quality and, as has already been stated, this department is given a variety of titles all bearing the word 'quality'. Although responsible for the control of the quality of the completed item or service, in many instances this department has no responsibility for verifying that all activities which preceded the manufacturing or process function were correct.

Companies should look towards the total integration and control of all activities. Such integration and control cannot be achieved by a department responsible solely for quality control or inspection, as the result will be only an increased activity in inspection and/or testing, which, in turn, increases the costs of putting things right.

George Bernard Shaw wrote in his play *John Bull's Other Island*:

> There are only two qualities in this world, efficiency and inefficiency; and only two sorts of people, the efficient and the inefficient.

This statement has a great deal of truth in it. Efficiency is what every senior executive should be aiming for. The inefficient person is often inefficient because he or she is not happy with the work. That person is probably unsuited for the task being undertaken and management has not identified the problem. We are all fit for some purpose and we are all capable of undertaking some task or other efficiently. The problem lies in determining the task for which the individual is best suited.

Proper training can do much to increase efficiency, yet all too many companies do not recognize the fact.

Continuing with Bernard Shaw's definition, it could well be that quality assurance should be regarded as efficiency assurance. This being the case, then the responsibility for determining the efficiency of an organization must be with someone much higher in the management structure. It is necessary, therefore, when developing and implementing a quality system to appoint, preferably in an executive position, a person who is to be responsible for co-ordinating and monitoring the system. The appointed person should have management capabilities and will be expected to be a guide, philosopher and friend. It is also essential for this quality executive to be able to communicate at all levels. Knowledge and experience of the industry are essential requirements, as are the understanding and application of management systems. A knowledge of efficiency techniques would be an added advantage. This person, once appointed, would in effect represent the senior executive and would determine, with other management representatives, the functions to be controlled to achieve the required fitness for purpose.

ACHIEVING ACCEPTANCE OF THE QUALITY SYSTEM

As we have seen, an effective quality system involves all departments and functions. Such a system can be developed only with the full participation and co-operation of all concerned, all of whom must have the opportunity of helping to shape the system. A system that has been thoroughly discussed and agreed is much more likely to be accepted and implemented than one that is imposed—whoever does the imposing! It is worth while expending a great deal of time and effort in obtaining this co-operation and acceptance. It is necessary, therefore, for the respective department and/or discipline heads to be involved in determining the applicable system level. This can be achieved, in the first instance, by forming a working party, which should comprise representatives from all the departments and/or disciplines concerned.

SETTING UP THE WORKING PARTY

The responsibility for the formation of the working party should lie with the person who has been appointed to the quality executive position, and that person should essentially represent the senior executive of the organization and have independence of action. All quality system standards, regardless of country of origin, place great emphasis on this point and, in general, the criterion is that the person so appointed should preferably be independent of all other functions. ISO 9001 states:

4.1.2.3 Management representative
The suppler shall appoint a management representative who, irrespective of other responsibilities, shall have defined authority and responsibility for ensuring that the requirements of this International Standard are implemented and maintained.

In the case of large organizations, this independence is comparatively easy to achieve and the quality assurance department will operate as a totally autonomous group. With small organizations, however, it is not possible to achieve this independence economically and it is in such instances that the *function* rather than the *person* should be defined. This will be dealt with in greater detail in Chapter 6.

The working party should be chaired by the senior executive of the organization, with the quality executive acting as the co-ordinator. This working party should include representatives from all the major departments and/or disciplines and these representatives should be, preferably, heads of departments and/or disciplines. Where this is not possible, then the representative should be given power of attorney to act for the respective head.

ESTABLISHING THE APPROPRIATE QUALITY SYSTEM

The objective of the working party is to establish the appropriate quality system applicable to the organization concerned. Before this can be done, experience has shown that it is usually necessary for certain actions to be taken, such as:

— to define responsibilities and lines of communication within each department or discipline;
— to establish interdepartmental interfaces;
— to verify and agree the activities and functions that are to be procedurally controlled;
— to communicate to all employees the reasons for, and the benefits to be obtained from, the implementation of a quality management system.

Taking each in turn:

Define responsibilities and lines of communication within each department or discipline
In many organizations, a person's responsibilities are not clearly defined. There is a tendency to appoint someone to a given position and then to delegate additional

responsibilities to that person as he or she becomes more proficient and experienced. As time goes on, this person reaches supervisory or management status purely by taking on these additional responsibilities and then, when things go wrong, it becomes exceedingly difficult to identify the cause or the source of the problem.

All responsibilities should be documented in the form of a job description, which should include as a minimum:

(1)   the title or description of the position
(2)   the grade or level of the position
(3)   the reporting structure of the position
(4)   whether or not the position carries any supervisory responsibilities
(5)   the primary authorities and responsibilities of that position
(6)   the knowledge and experience required to fill that position
(7)   the output requirements of the position.

Experience has shown that job descriptions are generally task related, do not address quality requirements and ignore authority statements.

Fig. 4.1 gives an example of a typical format for a job description.

The activity of developing job descriptions will involve liaising with all employees, and when the individuals are questioned on what they believe to be their responsibilities there will inevitably be duplications and overlaps. There could well be instances of activities not being completely covered as the demarcation lines had not been sufficiently clear and explicit. This in itself is, in the author's experience, the cause of so many so-called quality problems.

It is to be understood, however, that in many processes or operations there needs to be a handover period when responsibilities may be shared; such as in chemical manufacture, when a new process should be handed over from 'development' to 'production'—or, as discussed later, when different departments need to co-operate. It is important that the precise takeover point be agreed and laid down; otherwise 'the baton may be dropped'.

The exposure and elimination of the duplication of activities is a sensitive area and must be done with care and consideration, otherwise it could well lead to ill feeling and resentment among employees who feel that their jobs are in jeopardy. This must not happen!

In addition to documenting job descriptions, it is advisable to formulate a promotion or career progression chart, which will tie in with the relevant grade or level of any given position. This information should be available to all employees and it will help in giving them a sense of belonging, which will inevitably lead to a greater responsibility to the company and will ultimately achieve the efficiency required to produce the items and/or services fit for purpose and right first time, every time.

Once job descriptions have been documented it will be possible to formulate organization charts for each of the departments concerned. These charts will enable each grade, or level of employee, to understand and accept where their position is located within the hierarchy and to whom each person reports.

Establish interdepartmental interfaces
Organization charts can be established for individual departments and/or disciplines but

TITLE:	Here would be inserted the appropriate title for the position.
POSITION LEVEL:	Here insert the appropriate grading related to the position.
REPORTS TO:	Here would be inserted the person's immediate supervisor's position.
SUPERVISES:	Here would be inserted any supervisory responsibilities.
PRIMARY AUTHORITIES & RESPONSIBILITIES:	Here would be inserted the primary authorities and responsibilities relating to the position, together with any interdepartmental interfaces.
KNOWLEDGE AND EXPERIENCE:	Here would be inserted the minimum qualifications and experience required adequately to undertake the requirements and responsibilities of the position.

Fig. 4.1—Typical job description.

they will not achieve the integration of the total system if they are developed in isolation. No department can work in isolation. There is always the need to liaise with others. For example, sales must liaise with design, production (process) and finance. An organization chart which identifies these interfaces should, therefore, be developed. Where interfaces are established, then of course these would be documented in the appropriate job specifications and procedures.

This detailed organization chart will ultimately identify the primary positions and reporting routes of the company.

Verify and agree the activities and functions that are to be procedurally controlled
This activity will eventually determine the effectiveness of the system, and an in-depth consideration of what needs to be controlled is essential. The quality system standards can give useful guidance in this instance. There are many national standards in prominence but that which is gaining the greatest acceptance is the International Standard (ISO) 9000 series.

This series of standards relates to design/development, production, installation and servicing of a product but can act as a useful guide to any organization embarking upon the development and implementation of a quality system.

The total activities or major activities of the organization should first be listed. If a company is engaged in the design, manufacture and installation of a product, then each activity within each of these three major elements should be itemized. For example, the control of design would cover such activities as:

(a)   establishing design parameters
(b)   detailing the design
(c)   design checking
(d)   design approval
(e)   control of design changes
(f)   development of specifications
        and others.

The control of manufacture would cover such activities as:

(a)   incoming inspection
(b)   in-process inspection
(c)   non-destructive testing
(d)   final inspection
        and others.

DOCUMENTING THE QUALITY SYSTEM

When all the major activities have been identified, then a brief outline describing what is done to control these activities can be documented. These outlines assist in determining the procedural requirements and they will also be utilized in the formation of the quality manual should such a document be required.

The typical quality manual given as Appendix A to this book contains system element outlines for all the requirements of ISO 9001. It will be noted from these outlines that many subsidiary activities are involved which should be controlled by means of procedures.

Therefore, the outline for design control as a system outline can now be done. Similar outlines should be developed by each department concerned, including the quality assurance department itself.

The eventual responsibility of the quality assurance department will be:

(1)   to verify the implementation and effectiveness of the quality system;
(2)   to identify any deficiencies within the system;
(3)   to verify that corrective action has been taken to correct deficiencies and that action has also been taken to prevent a recurrence;
(4)   to verify that personnel operating in the quality assurance function are adequately trained to carry out their activities.

Fig. 4.2 sets out the system element outlines that would be required to meet the criteria of the various levels, categories or parts, of the quality system standards. It is to be understood that these should be used as guidelines only, as there could be many activities related to a given system level which an organization need not implement. The two prime examples are 'purchaser-supplied products' and 'sampling schemes'. Many organizations do not receive free-issue products, neither do they require sampling schemes. Therefore, if they do not apply they need not be considered.

	LEVEL 1	LEVEL 2	LEVEL 3
1. Quality system	X	X	X
2. Organization	X	X	X
3. Audits	X	X	X
4. Quality system documents			
—Manual	X	X	
—Inspection and test plans	X	X	X
5. Manufacturing control	X	X	
6. Planning (contract review)	X	X	X
7. Design control	X		
8. Documentation and change control	X	X	X
9. Control of inspection, measuring and test equipment	X	X	X
10. Control of purchased items and services	X	X	X
11. Incoming inspection	X	X	X
12. Purchaser-supplied product (free issue)	X	X	
13. In-process inspection	X	X	
14. Final inspection	X	X	X
15. Sampling	X	X	X
16. Inspection status	X	X	
17. Identification and traceability	X	X	
18. Handling and storage	X	X	X
19. Work instructions	X	X	X
20. Special processes	X	X	
21. Preservation, packaging and shipping	X	X	
22. Records	X	X	X
23. Non-conformances	X	X	X
24. Corrective action	X	X	X
25. Training	X	X	X

Fig. 4.2—Comparison between quality system levels.

A control should not be implemented purely because it is addressed in a quality system standard. The criteria for the control of an activity or function must, therefore, lie in the aspects of default. What must be taken into consideration is the result of a deficiency in relation to the risk and cost involved, not only in rectification but in the cost of developing and implementing a procedure to control the activity itself. The more controls one implements the greater the cost—but to what effect?

Consider this analogy. In the era of the hour-glass figure, Edwardian ladies were wont to make use of an undergarment known as the corset. The tighter this garment was drawn the more waspish the figure and, in times of heat or stress, the poor suffering female was apt to faint. The same could be said of an over-controlled quality system. The more procedures imposed, the more bureaucratic the system becomes and the economics of the system are defeated. Consider, therefore, the word CORSET, and when identifying whether or not an activity should be controlled one should question, in the event that the activity should go wrong, what would be the:

COst of putting it right?
Resources required to put it right?
Safety implications should it go wrong?
Environmental impacts should it go wrong?
Time involved in putting it right?

If the answer to one or more of these questions is 'substantial' then one should develop and implement a procedure to control that activity. If, on the other hand, the answer to all the questions is 'minimal', then it is possibly more economical to correct a deficiency whenever it occurs rather than spend time, effort and money in developing a documented procedure to control an activity that will seldom be defective.

The determination of the activities to be controlled, and the methods by which they are to be controlled, is the most important step in the development of a quality system and must be treated with great care.

If a procedure doesn't do anything, or if it is uneconomical to operate, or if it gets in the way, or if it produces unnecessary documentation, it is best forgotten!

Having documented the system element outlines, the next step is to develop a procedures index. If the system element outlines of the quality manual in Appendix A, Part 2, are examined it will be seen that each system outline will result in a number of activities. These activities would then be listed and indexed for procedural control.

All procedures should carry a document number as the procedures themselves will eventually form part of the company's document or library system.

A numbering system should be developed, which will identify the procedure to the department that implements it. Such procedures should not be annotated as being quality system documents. A typical numbering system would be as follows;

XYZ–DE–001

where XYZ represents the company's initials, DE represents the design and engineering department and 001 represents the document number. The title of the document would also be indicated, for example:

XYZ–DE–001 Design Validation.

Procedures that are to be implemented by more than one department are normally of an administrative nature and could, therefore, be identified as:

XYZ–ADM–001 and so on.

Once an index has been developed, it should always be updated. If it is found that a particular procedure is no longer relevant and can be discontinued, the number allocated to that procedure should be declared obsolete and not used again, with the procedure index being annotated accordingly.

After the system element outlines and the procedures index have been developed it will be possible to identify responsibilities for the authorship of procedures.

The procedure index can be used also to identify those procedures which already exist and those which have to be written to complete the total system. The exercise of reviewing existing documentation may well highlight the existence of duplicate or similar documents and possibly documents which are obsolete. This presents a good opportunity for reappraisal and a 'spring cleaning' session.

In essence, if an organization carries out a design activity, the eventual quality system must be 'level 1' or 'part 1'. If, however, no design function is carried out, or if the company utilizes existing or proven designs, the quality system will be 'level 2' or 'part 2'. If there is a requirement only for inspection and/or test, the quality system will be 'level 3' or 'part 3'. Typically it would be expected that a service organization would implement a 'level 2' or 'part 2' system. However, this could be open to discussion depending upon one's definition of 'design'.

APPLICATION TO SERVICE INDUSTRIES

The various quality system standards might at first glance appear to be applicable solely to manufactured items and it may seem that service organizations could find them very difficult to apply. This is certainly not the case.

If the 25 criteria of a typical 'level 1' quality system are analysed, it will be seen that many of them relate not only to manufacture but also to service industries. For example (referring to Fig. 4.2), every organization, regardless of the field of work in which it operates, would require to implement the following system elements:

(1) organization
(2) audits
(3) quality system documents (manual/work instructions)
(4) planning
(5) documentation and change control
(6) control of purchased items and services
(7) records
(8) identification of non-conformances
(9) corrective action
(10) training.

These are the author's *Ten Essential Elements* of a quality management system.

Even a cook, when making a cake, carries out activities which can be directly related to a quality system standard. The various activities in cake-making are identified in Fig. 4.3. It will be seen from this simple process of cake-making that 14 out of a possible 24 'level 2' activities are covered. One could ask the question: 'What happens if the cook undertakes to make a cake to his or her own recipe?' Would this be classified as a design

1.	Organization	Who makes the cake
2.	Planning	Decide type of cake to suit the occasion (wedding, birthday, etc.)
3.	Work instructions	Recipe
4.	Document control records	Recipe library
5.	Control of purchased items	Ingredients—preferred brands, most economical source
6.	Manufacturing control	Mixing, blending, forming
7.	Control of measuring and test equipment	Scales, spoons, jugs, etc.
8.	Special process (heat treatment)	Baking
9.	In-process inspection (non-destructive testing)	Fork test, skewer test
10.	Protection and preservation of product quality	Storage/freezing
11.	Completed item inspection and test	Eating
12.	Control of non-conforming items	Consult the *Something went wrong—what do I do now?* cookbook* (material review board)
13.	Corrective action	Rework cake into a trifle
14.	Training	On the job training by parent or cookery lessons

* Bear, John and Marina (1970) New York: Harcourt Brace Jovanovich Inc.

Fig. 4.3—Quality assurance in making a cake (level 2).

activity and thus become a 'level 1' system? The author thinks not as the control of such a 'design' is based on proven culinary practices. There are others, however, who would disagree!

This example is always popular at training courses. At one such course a delegate made the statement that corrective action had been taken but there was no evidence of any action taken to prevent a recurrence of baking an inedible cake. One can only conclude that such action would be to replace the cook!

IMPLEMENTING THE QUALITY SYSTEM

The final stage is the implementation of the system. This will involve the co-operation of all concerned and, to obtain this co-operation, all employees must understand the reasons for implementation.

Communicate to all employees the reason for, and the benefits to be obtained from, the implementation of a quality management system

This is best done by holding a series of 'awareness' talks, or seminars, starting with senior management through all levels to junior personnel. No one should be left out. Co-operation is usually more easily obtained if these 'awareness' sessions are conducted *before* procedural controls are documented but *after* the quality manual has been written and approved. In this way all employees can prepare, and possibly highlight, problem areas which exist because of inadequate controls. By this means, personnel can be made to appreciate that they are part of the system and that it will work to their benefit only if they co-operate.

The 'awareness' sessions, then, have the best impact if they are introduced after the quality manual has been written and approved. The manual should give supervisory staff, in particular, the broad outline of the system within the area of their own involvement.

The requirement for a regular review of the system should also be emphasized, and this review should include the results of internal quality audits. The word 'audit' may frighten some staff as they may expect to be supervised continuously and suspect that management is adopting the 'Big Brother' attitude.

It should be made clear to them that audits are carried out primarily to verify the adequacy of the system and only secondarily to verify compliance with instructions. It should also be emphasized that each individual is responsible for the quality of work produced and that reliance for quality cannot be placed on others subsequently to confirm that the required quality has been reached. 'Right first time, every time' should be everyone's goal. This is the prime goal of any quality system, whatever its level.

IMPLEMENTATION PLAN GUIDELINES

Experience has shown that acceptance of the quality system will not be satisfactorily achieved unless due consideration is given to the following:

1.   Aim first to implement the quality system elements where one stands to achieve the best results in the short term. The elements found generally to be deficient in nost organizations are:
     —planning (contract review)
     —document control
     —training
     —purchasing
     —calibration of inspection measuring and test equipment.
2.   Seek agreement from all concerned on the development and implementation time-table.
3.   Set achievable dates but build in flexibility.
4.   Once agreement has been reached, ensure that all employees know what their authorities and responsibilities are.

5. Conduct staff briefings as early as possible but ensure that follow-up activities are undertaken within two weeks otherwise commitment from employees will wane and it will be considered to be a 'nine days wonder'.
6. Permit ample time to monitor implementation and to review and revise documentation as necessary.

COMMON CAUSES OF IMPLEMENTATION SET-BACK

It has been found that, generally, where management has experienced a set-back in the implementation timetable this has been due to one or more of the following reasons:

1. A too ambitious or inappropriate timetable has been set.
    Remedy—Re-draft and agree a revised timetable.
2. A lack of management commitment and support.
    Remedy—Management re-education with, perhaps, the involvement of third party sources.
3. Conflicting priorities.
    Remedy—Management to review and reassign responsibilities.
4. Too much time spent on unproductive or unnecessary activities.
    Remedy—Conduct progressive audits and evaluate the criticality of activities utilizing the 'corset' analogy.
5. Too much paperwork.
    Remedy—Revise documentation and evaluate distribution, again utilizing the 'corset' analogy.
6. Employee resistance.
    Remedy—Re-education/retraining with, perhaps again, the use of third party sources. All employees must be involved in the system development and implementation.

With regard to third party involvement, it is to be understood that bringing in a third party is always a sensitive issue. If an 'outside expert' is brought in this must be very carefully handled so as to ensure co-operation of those most affected. Bringing in an outside consultant is an expensive operation and management must justify the cost.
    In summary, therefore, the essence of a quality system is simply:

Say what you do.
Do what you say.
Record that you have done it.
Audit for effective implementation.
Feedback and improve.

COSTS AND BENEFITS

Developing and implementing a quality system will cost time and money. It is difficult to give estimates of costs, as these will depend on the size of the company and the complexity of its operations, whether or not any form of system exists and on how many procedures are to be written and implemented. It would obviously be helpful if records of existing quality costs can be made available in order to enable an evaluation to be made of savings when the system is in full operation.

Initially, there will be outlays related to: the time taken by the working party in establishing the requirements; the time taken in writing procedures; and the costs involved in the 'awareness' sessions. In a sense these costs can be regarded as capital expenditure and amortized against the substantial savings made in such areas as: revisions to engineering documents; rework on faulty items; scrap reductions; and others.

These costs have been plotted in a general format on the graph given in Fig. 4.4. It will be noted that, after the initial, in effect, capital expenditure, the cost declines rapidly and the costs associated with maintaining the system should remain reasonably level. The savings made due to the implementation will rise initially and then remain effective so long as the system is implemented.

A case history

To illustrate savings which can be made, and again drawing on the author's experience, an example relating to a design project may be used. Design is a service and there is no real tangible item on which its costs and benefits can be quantified in terms of reduced reworking, loss of production, or other factors.

In one particular project for a petrochemical pipeline design, the client imposed upon the design contractor the requirement to implement a 'level 1' quality plan. (As a project is being discussed, the quality requirements are referred to as a plan.) The contractor was not conversant with the requirements and so it was necessary to develop and implement the required controls.

The contract was for six months' duration, involving 15 design engineers. This presented a good opportunity to analyse quality costs, particularly as a similar project undertaken some time previously could be used as a cost basis for comparison.

During the previous project where 15 engineers were also involved, 650 design documents (drawings, specifications, data sheets) were produced and, on average, each document was revised three times. Each revision was found to take, on average, two hours. The total time spent on revisions, therefore, was $650 \times 3 \times 2 = 3900$ hours.

During the later project where the 'level 1' plan was implemented, it was found that the time spent on development and implementation of the plan was initially six weeks using three personnel, with intermittent subsequent involvement by one person to verify the implementation and adequacy of the plan.

The initial work-load was accordingly 720 hours. Verification of the implementation and adequacy of the plan took 2 days per week for 22 weeks, amounting to 352 hours, making a total of 1072 hours.

It was found that, at the end of the project, revisions had dropped by half, resulting in a saving of 1950 hours. To this should be added the reduction in time spent by the document reproduction department and the document control centre. The overall gross saving approached 2300 hours, giving a net saving of 1228 hours, when the costs are discounted.

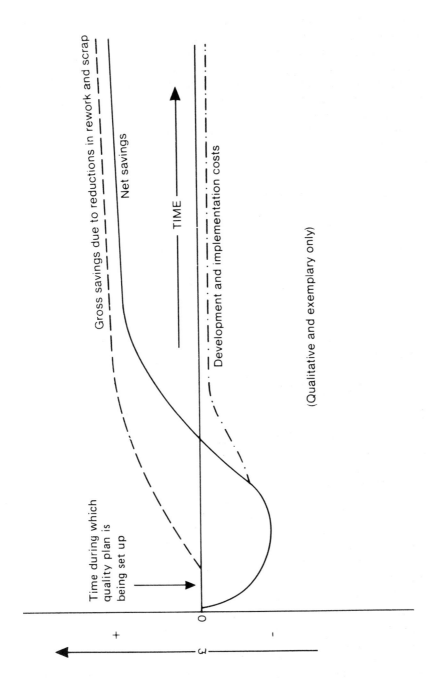

Fig. 4.4—Cost-effective graph.

When this was related to the total engineering budget of 14,400 hours, this represented a saving of approximately 9%, which may be considered a very good return for a first-time effort.

Implementation of the same plan in subsequent projects has reduced revision costs still further, thus placing this contractor in a much better competitive position than others who do not operate proper quality systems.

It should also be taken into account that development costs for the quality plan will be considerably reduced for future similar projects, provided that the lessons learned are properly assimilated and recorded in corporate records, so eliminating 'the reinvention of the wheel'.

5

Quality costs—identification, assessment and control

QUALITY COST DEFINITION

In the previous chapter a case history was presented which illustrated how savings were made as the result of implementing a quality system. However, such savings can be measured only if one has the baseline information from which to evaluate performance.

In general, most organizations do not measure quality costs explicitly since such costs are not required for the development of financial profit/loss statements, although they can have a significant effect on the profitability of a company. In the absence of a quality cost audit system it is extremely difficult for such organizations to determine effectively where such costs arise and how they can be controlled or reduced. Also, because there is no statutory requirement to collect and report on quality costs, the definition of what constitutes a quality cost can be many and varied.

Generally, quality costs can be allocated to three distinct costing centres, as follows:

—prevention costs
—appraisal (or inspection) costs
—failure/rectification costs.

It is worth while examining in detail how such costs are derived. Quality costs can be defined as the difference between the actual total inclusive costs of carrying out a service, or manufacturing and selling an item, and the costs which would obtain if there had been no failure during any part of the process. In other words, the costs associated with someone, somewhere, not getting it right first time.

It could be argued, however, that the costs of prevention and appraisal (inspection) are part of the total process costs and would be incurred in any event; which means that only the failure/rectification (and loss of future business) costs would be the difference between actual costs and those that would have been obtained if there had been no failures.

This argument could hold water if management has eliminated all unnecessary preventative and appraisal measures but, in a badly planned and managed situation, a large amount could be spent on prevention and appraisal yet still result in high failure/rectification. As quality becomes established, costs of prevention and appraisal should be minimized but a company must know what these costs are in order to achieve an opti-mum goal. In setting up the quality system management will incur costs initially during the planning stage and later in the implementation, maintenance, review and improve-ment stages. The costs incurred in such instances would be construed as *prevention costs*, in other words, the allocation of the necessary resources to prevent failures from happening.

In any quality system there always will be the requirement for an independent check or supervision during some part of the process. Complicated activities will need, at some stage or other, to be reviewed or checked by a peer or supervisor in order to ascertain that the process has been carried out correctly. The identification of, and the requirement for, such reviews or checks will be a management decision which should be made during the planning and development stage of the quality system.

There will ultimately, however, be costs incurred in carrying out these reviews and checks, and these are known as *appraisal costs*. *Failure/rectification costs* are those associated with failure to meet specified requirements and the resulting rectification or corrective action. These costs can be related to both internal and external activities: *internal*, where failure of some part of the process occurs *prior* to transfer to the cus-tomer, i.e. during the producer/receiver activity; and *external* where there is a failure to conform to requirements *after* transfer to the customer.

Prevention costs

These are incurred to reduce the costs associated with the failure, rectification and/or appraisal of the manufacturing or service process and would normally be related to:

— the activities of: planning and implementing the quality system; developing the quality system documentation; checking and approving such documentation and distributing or communicating the information contained within the documentation;
— the activity involving the verification of the entire quality system, i.e. the internal quality audit;
— the subsequent management review of the entire system;
— the assessment and verification of suppliers' organizations;
— the costs associated with training and education, which will include the development, implementation, operation and maintenance of in-house and external training pro-grammes;
— the costs related to developing and implementing quality improvement programmes, such as quality circles, performance measurement, problem solving, statistical process control, and others.

Appraisal costs

These are the costs incurred in verifying the conformance of the product or process to requirements and would normally include:

— verifying that purchased items are in conformance with requirements;
— checking and verifying the manufacturing or service activity throughout the process and then, finally, confirming the quality of the completed work—for example,

analysing and reporting of verification results, which are conducted after confirming that the activity has been satisfactorily accomplished;
— the costs associated with the storage of records as required to confirm the quality of the items or service.

Failure/rectification costs

These are the costs associated with 'getting it wrong' and, subsequently 'putting it right'. Internally, these can include such things as scrap; corrective action; re-verification and down-time.

Failure costs can also arise externally when faults are discovered after transfer to the customer and will include such things as: the time spent in dealing with customer complaints; concessions; corrective action; liability claims. Intangible costs, such as those associated with the loss of future sales and possible damage to the corporate image of the company, should also be considered under this heading. Damage to the corporate image of a company can result in the loss of either individual customers or a failure to attract potential new customers, thus reducing the company's market share. Quality costs under this heading can be, at the very best, only an estimate but nevertheless they should be considered as such costs could well amount to a considerable proportion of the total. Where such damage to a company's reputation does occur, then, of course, corrective action must be taken to overcome it.

ESTABLISHING A QUALITY COST DATA BASE

Once having verified the costing areas, it will be necessary to establish a method of collecting, segregating and accounting for such costs. There are, therefore, a number of steps to be taken to achieve a satisfactory quality cost data base, as follows:

1.   Identify all quality cost activities.
2.   Segregate the activities into prevention, appraisal and failure/rectification.
3.   Establish a system to record the costs associated with prevention, appraisal and failure/rectification.
4.   Develop a suitable accounting system which will allocate the costs to the applicable activity and facilitate prompt retrieval of the information for regular review and analysis.

Let us take each in turn.

Identify all quality cost activities

This is a management exercise where a determination must be made of the means required to meet the objectives of the quality system. Management must decide: where supervision is required, including by whom; when and where a verification/inspection activity is to be carried out, and by whom; what documentation is required to be checked, and by whom; when management audits are to be carried out, and by whom.

ISO 9001 (clause 4.1.2.2, 'Verification resources and personnel') requires that:

The supplier shall identify in-house verification requirements, provide adequate resources and assign trained personnel for verification activities.

At the end of the day the purpose of a quality management system should be to increase prevention and so reduce appraisal and failure/rectification activities.

Segregate the activities into prevention, appraisal and failure/rectification costs

This is as its title suggest. Having identified the who, how, what, when and where of a quality cost activity the decision should then be made to determine under which category each activity will be recorded. For example:

— Planning, process reviews, auditing, training, and quality improvement would fall under the category of prevention.
— Document checking and approval, receiving inspection, in-process and final inspection, and record storage would fall under the category of appraisal.
— Scrap, corrective action, reinspection, down-time, complaints, recall, warranty claims, public liability, and loss of future business would fall under the category of failure/rectification.

Establish a system to record the costs

This step will require the development of a reporting system which will accurately record time spent on quality cost activities *vis-à-vis* process activities. This may well mean establishing a time-sheet recording method with suitable alphanumeric costing codes which will allot the activity to a specific cost centre, for example:

— suffix A to an action could indicate a prevention cost
— suffix B, an appraisal cost
— suffix C, a failure/rectification cost.

These codes could be subdivided to indicate a specific action within the cost centre category, for example:

Prevention
— A1 could indicate quality management planning
— A2, procedure development
— A3, internal quality audits
— A4, quality training;

Appraisal
— B1, supervision
— B2, incoming inspection
— B3, document checking and approval
— B4, final inspection
— B5, record storage;

Failure/rectification
— C1, scrap

— C2, rectification
— C3, customer complaints
— C4, warranty claims;

and so on.

To put this in greater perspective and using a hypothetical situation, there could be an instance where an internal quality audit was carried out on a specific contract (the contract number being 89024), in which case the cost code would be:

89024–A3

or, perhaps, a document had to be revised due to a drafting error, in which case the cost code would be:

89024–C2

Whatever system is used, there will very probably be a requirement for management to promote an awareness campaign to put forward the benefits of such a costing system to the workforce. There is the possibility of negative attitudes from some employees who may see time recording in such detail as a threat. This must not be allowed to happen as the co-operation of all concerned is imperative.

In the author's experience, most negative attitudes towards quality cost accounting emanate from upper and middle management who, in the past, have not had to record time expended on any particular task. In this respect an attitudinal change is paramount. The system developed must, therefore, be simple to operate. Again, drawing on the author's experience, the failure of time-recording systems is normally due to the complexity of the documentation and the intricacies of the coding system.

In addition to a system for recording time spent on *quality cost activities*, there should also be a system which will allocate consumables, where used, to the respective costing category. For example, travel and accommodation expenses may be incurred in dealing with a customer complaint, in which case these should be charged to the failure/rectification cost under the appropriate code. If such costs were incurred in our hypothetical case then they would be charged to 89024–C3. The same would apply to communication expenses such as telephone, telex and facsimile. There may be some classes of costs which could be extremely difficult, if not impossible, to isolate and allocate to the user's department or function, such as new equipment or special test instruments. Such expenditure should be regarded as a capital cost and amortized over several years.

Develop a suitable accounting system

The development of a suitable accounting system could well be the most difficult part of the entire quality cost exercise. It will, inevitably, place an added responsibility on the accounting department and will, of necessity, require that department's utmost co-operation. The addition of quality cost codes, in addition to the standard cost codes, almost certainly makes computerization of the accounting system imperative. Such a system should facilitate immediate retrieval of information for analysis purposes. By setting up a quality cost register, it should be possible to produce a system to extract the relevant information from the data base and, by developing the appropriate software, assemble the data in the form required.

ANALYSIS OF THE QUALITY COSTS

Financial control of any business requires the appropriate methods of allocation and analysis of costs. The same applies to the control of quality. However, quality costing information is not produced to satisfy financial auditors and conflicts may arise between the requirements of auditors for corporate financial information and the requirements of management for quality cost information.

From the point of view of quality management, what will be demanded by the accounts department is a consistency of assessment rather than strict accuracy, so that trends can be discerned. Loss of reputation, and therefore of future business, cannot be assessed accurately but it is vital to have general agreement that the allocation of costs, although arbitrary, is fair and reasonable. Such cost could be referred to the working party finally to approve (see Chapter 4). Unfortunately, very few accountants are good at this sort of exercise—it goes against their training. It may be necessary, therefore, for the accounts staff, or a section of it, to be exposed to quality management education.

While on the subject of quality cost assessment, it is worth while mentioning that surveys carried out by a number of research organizations have revealed that for every customer who complains, nine will not complain but simply take their future business elsewhere. On the other side of the coin, however, a satisfied customer generally tells only four others. This represents a large imbalance between the recording of satisfaction versus dissatisfaction. These survey results could be used as a basis when allocating a cost to loss of reputation and subsequently the loss of future business. Providing, of course, that customer complaints are documented and reviewed. The best advertisement is a satisfied customer.

In many instances, unfortunately, customer complaints are 'hushed up'. Management does not hear of them and is therefore not aware of their total implications.

Quality management will need financial information in order to balance the three quality cost elements of prevention, appraisal and failure/rectification. The most productive way of investing money is in prevention. Appraisal costs offer less return on investment as such costs do not prevent failure, they only identify failure. Nevertheless, there will always be the need for some appraisal activity, if only to ensure the quality of the item or service before its release to the customer and to minimize rejection after delivery. Failure/rectification costs are unplanned and must be considered as a loss of resource resulting in a reduction in profit.

It is vital, therefore, that all information pertaining to quality costs be readily and quickly available, in the right format and at all levels of management and supervision if it is to be used effectively.

COST OPTIMIZATION

The major purpose for developing a quality costing system is to optimize these costs effectively. An essential element of such optimization must be in the analysis of the quality cost data which must, in turn, rely on the accurate and prompt production of the costing information.

In the analysis of the data, due consideration should be given to the utilization of alternative methods. For example, in cases of sporadic failure, analysis of the situation might well reveal that rectification costs are insignificant compared with possible prevention costs. In such an instance, therefore, it is likely to be far more economic to rectify the deficiency as and when it should occur, rather than to develop and implement a system for prevention. Such a decision can be made only in the light of all possible information.

There are, of course, a number of caveats. One could not accept sporadic failures if safety is involved. Here the 'CORSET' analogy would come into play.

A finished product (item or service) does not normally come into existence as the result of a single activity; there are usually a number of intermediate processes involved before handover to the customer. The identification of a failure cost in any of these intermediates may result in additional appraisal measures being taken, with limited beneficial results. It is often found that the causes of high quality costs are not the result of the failure of a given process but the result of deficiencies elsewhere. The ultimate aim, in such instances, should be to discover those processes in which preventative measures are weak. In other words, to trace the problem back to its source and eliminate the cause.

REPORTING QUALITY COSTS

The purpose of any reporting system is to give the recipient information. Corrective action, where necessary, should be taken by the recipient and progress monitored. Action should be taken also to prevent a recurrence of the problem.

The responsibility for quality cost reporting is usually divided between the quality and accounting functions but the collection and processing of the information is best left to the accounting function as this, being an independent service, usually enhances the credibility of the figures.

The publication of the figures is, again, best left to the accounting function but it should not be done in isolation. Other functions, particularly the quality function, should be actively involved in the planning of the format of the reports and the selection of the quality cost categories.

The format for presenting the quality cost information should be agreed. The reports should be easy to read and should be designed to communicate the pertinent information to the appropriate people. Reporting formats can be many and varied and can take the form of tabular structures, graphic information, bar charts, and Pareto diagrams. Examples of these various formats are given in Figs 5.1, 5.2 and 5.3.

The information contained in these reports can be utilized to promote quality awareness throughout the entire organization. With the aid of attractively designed and presented graphic information the quality costs results could become discussion points at all personnel levels.

Such information could show time lost due to the occurrence of failure and improvements in the reduction of failure costs. There is also the opportunity to promote awareness by all personnel towards reductions in quality costs. A number of organizations have adopted the concept of the *100-day club* which encourages employees to strive for error-

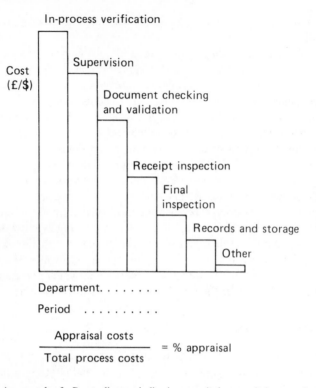

Fig. 5.1—An example of a Pareto diagram indicating appraisal costs relative to a given period.

free work for 100 days. At the end of that time, should the employee succeed, then the name of that employee is entered on the 100-day club register. One can then progress towards the 125-day club and so on. The concept of striving for 100 days of error-free work is not as easy as one would imagine. 100 days constitutes 20 working weeks, which is approaching 6 months. In any event, a responsible competitive attitude is fostered which can do only good for the company and its workforce. A similar concept is utilized very effectively in the safety field—the time during which there is no reportable accident.

Ultimately, quality cost data, if recorded accurately and categorized constructively into its various elements, will provide management with the information needed to make impartial and intelligent decisions on where, and in what strength, to attack the problem areas to meet corporate requirements. An analysis of the data will permit management to concentrate on those area where control of such costs can have the greatest effect on the profitability of the organization. By forecasting the effects of changes in any one area, logical decisions can be taken to deploy personnel to the best advantage in order to make the most practical investment and thus enhance the profitability of the company.

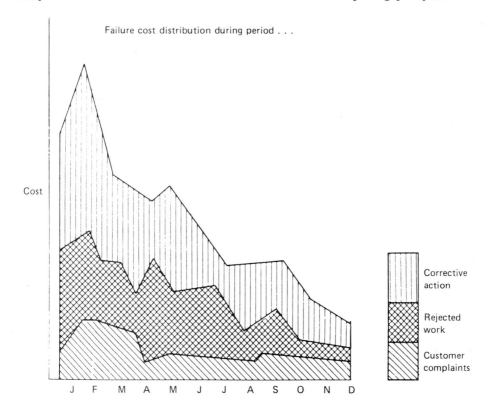

Fig. 5.2—Typical failure cost analysis.

QUALITY COSTS FOR PERIOD . . . .
Detailed analysis in hours by department

		Department			
Code	1	2	3	4	5
A1	6.5	6.5	4.1	8.6	2.4
A2	13.3	4.9	2.8	16.4	8.2
A3	4.0	2.0	3.5	4.5	2.0
A4	5.0	–	2.0	2.0	–
A	28.8	13.4	12.4	31.5	12.6
B1	8.0	6.5	5.5	8.5	3.8
B2	5.0	–	–	2.0	–
B3	1.0	1.5	2.0	3.0	2.5
B4	–	1.0	–	–	–
B	14.0	9.0	7.5	13.5	6.3
C1	–	–	–	–	–
C2	0.5	1.0	1.7	–	1.8
C3	–	2.0	–	3.4	–
C4	–	–	–	–	–
C	0.5	3.0	1.7	3.4	1.8
		Summary			
A	28.8	13.4	12.4	31.5	12.6
B	14.0	9.0	7.5	13.5	6.3
C	0.5	3.0	1.7	3.4	1.8
	43.3	25.4	21.6	48.4	20.7

Fig. 5.3—Quality cost table by hours.

6

The organization for quality

THE IMPORTANCE OF ORGANIZATIONAL FREEDOM

As will be seen from the quality assurance standards comparison table in Fig. 2.2, all the standards place great importance on organization. ISO 9004 makes the following comment:

Quality responsibility and authority

Activities contributing to quality, whether directly or indirectly, should be identified and documented, and the following actions taken:

(a) General and specific quality responsibilities should be explicitly defined.
(b) Responsibility and authority delegated to each activity contributing to quality should be clearly established; authority and responsibility should be sufficient to attain the assigned quality objectives with the desired efficiency.
(c) Interface control and co-ordination measures between different activities should be defined.
(d) Management may choose to delegate the responsibility for internal quality assurance and for external quality assurance where necessary; the persons so delegated should be independent of the activities reported on.
(e) In organizing a well-structured and effective quality system, emphasis should be placed on the identification of actual or potential quality problems and the initiation of remedial or preventive measures.

Organizational structure

The organizational structure pertaining to the quality management system should be clearly established within the overall management of a company. The lines of authority and communication should be defined.

Australian standard AS 2000 makes the following comment:

The primary responsibility of a 'management representative' is to ensure that the requirements of the Standard are implemented and maintained. A further purpose is to establish an official channel of communication between the customer and the supplier; this is particularly relevant in medium-sized and large organizations. The 'management representative' should also act as a focal point for co-ordination and resolution of quality matters.

While the supplier may select any competent member of staff to fulfil this role, the management representative (often referred to as 'quality manager') should possess authority consistent with responsibility for the quality system extending throughout the company. Where the management representative has other responsibilities these do not absolve responsibility for maintaining the integrity of the quality system and its effective use. To provide freedom of action and independence necessary for effective execution of these duties the management representative should report directly to senior executive management.

Canadian Standard Z299 makes the following comment:

> In developing an organization and assigning responsibility and authority, suppliers should recognize that Quality Assurance Programs are interdisciplinary and involve most of the organization. Many elements and activities at all levels in organizations are involved. Unless responsibilities for quality are fully acknowledged and understood by all, including top executives and shop workers, full compliance with the Standard (Z299) cannot be achieved. Also, persons assigned responsibility for assurance of quality should be aware of, but free from, the pressure of cost and production, and be given the necessary authority to perform their roles effectively.

Norwegian Standard NS 5801 makes the following comment:

> The requirement that the contractor's manager for the quality department shall have organizational freedom usually implies that he has an independent position in the organization, with direct responsibility to the top management and is not charged with other quality influencing functions.

All other standards make very much the same comment. However, what does it all mean?

QUALITY IS THE RESPONSIBILITY OF EVERYONE

It has already been determined that, ultimately, it is the senior executive of an organization who must carry the responsibility for the quality of the items or services produced. The senior executive alone, however, cannot undertake every activity necessary to produce these items or services, unless of course it is a single-person organization. There must be delegation of activities and in this delegation there must be the confidence that the employees are qualified, experienced and capable of carrying out the task for which they are employed. A certain amount of confidence is obtained at the initial interview but the confidence is sustained only if the employee continues to carry out his or her tasks in an efficient and effective manner. The senior executive cannot monitor all employees' performances on a continuous basis, therefore the confidence in the employees is maintained by the quality of the work produced.

The quality of work produced should not be determined by 'others'. There should be a fundamental requirement that every one within an organization is initially responsible for the quality of the work produced, and the assurance of quality should be practised by all personnel in their daily activities. The Australian Leo Buring (1876–1961) is quoted as saying:

> If everyone had to put his name on his day's work, the world would be a better place.

This applies equally today as it did then.

As this quality assurance should be a company wide philosophy, then every department must organize itself so that the work produced is not only correct but, more importantly, correct first time.

This concept could be depicted as an umbrella which protects the organization from the 'rain' of problems which could descend upon it. Fig. 6.1 shows such a concept. Beneath the umbrella are the various elements of a typical 'level 1' organization.

Each of these elements will require procedures and instructions to cover all the critical activities and functions within that element. Within each of these elements there should, however, be some means of verifying that the work carried out is, in fact, correct first time.

THE INDEPENDENT CHECK

Initially, of course, all employees should verify the quality of their own work by means of a self check. The accuracy of the work can then be confirmed as necessary by a controlling check carried out by a person suitably qualified but not directly involved with the activity.

What has to be determined is who is to be responsible for controlling and checking the accuracy or quality of the work within each of the elements. In each case the responsibility for this can lie only with personnel who are familiar with that work if the check is to be effective but, in order to obtain an unbiased result, the check should be carried out by personnel not actually engaged in that activity. Checking is an activity in itself and should also be procedurally controlled.

If this checking function is to be effective so that no activity goes forward to the next activity in an incorrect manner and the check is to be carried out only by suitably qualified and experienced personnel, then:

— Design documentation can be properly checked for technical detail and accuracy only by design engineers.
— Procurement documentation can be properly checked only by personnel familiar with procurement activities.
— Manufactured items can be properly checked only by personnel familiar with the specification requirements.
— Installation activities can be properly checked only by installation engineers.

These requirements are, basically, only a follow-on from finance, where the accounting function of any organization is checked, albeit a requirement by legislation, by qualified accountants.

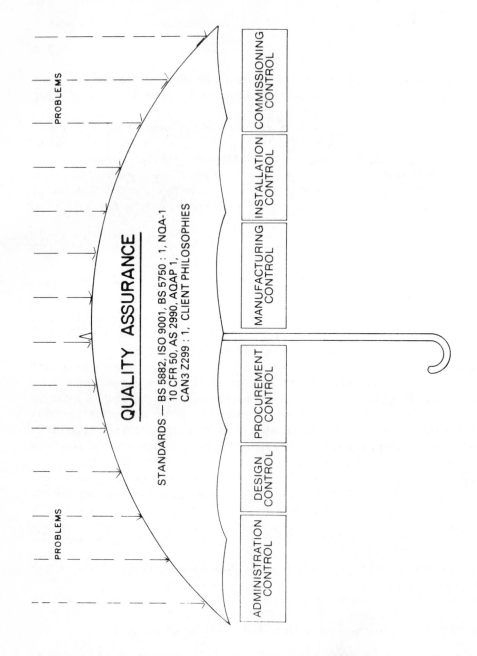

PROBLEMS

PROBLEMS

QUALITY ASSURANCE

STANDARDS — BS 5882, ISO 9001, BS 5750 : 1, NQA-1
10 CFR 50, AS 2990, AQAP 1,
CAN3 Z299 : 1, CLIENT PHILOSOPHIES

| ADMINISTRATION CONTROL | DESIGN CONTROL | PROCUREMENT CONTROL | MANUFACTURING CONTROL | INSTALLATION CONTROL | COMMISSIONING CONTROL |

Fig. 6.1—The quality assurance umbrella.

Even those engaged in simple unskilled trades such as 'housekeeping' activities contribute indirectly to the eventual quality of an item or service and their activities should be similarly controlled and checked, as necessary.

THE ROLE OF THE QUALITY ASSURANCE DEPARTMENT

Referring once again to Fig. 6.1, the quality assurance department would actually be located within the umbrella and would be responsible for:

(1) verifying, by audit, that the quality system requirements are being followed throughout the organization and that effective procedures and job instructions are being implemented by all departments and/or disciplines;

(2) verifying that those responsible for controlling and checking an activity have done so in a systematic manner and that there is objective evidence available to confirm such;

(3) ensuring that all procedural non-conformances are resolved;

(4) ensuring that fundamental working methods are established and that fully approved procedures are developed to cover them and that all departments and personnel are aware of, and have access to, current versions of these procedures;

(5) verifying that all procedures are regularly reviewed and updated as necessary;

(6) determining and reporting the principal causes of quality losses and non-conformances;

(7) determining, with senior management, where improvements are required and, where necessary, recommending the corrective action.

By taking these actions a step further, it follows that the quality assurance department verifies that the organization is effectively implementing the quality system which, as has been determined, has been developed by management under the direction of the senior executive in conjunction with our quality assurance executive. The quality assurance executive and the department under that executive, therefore, acts as the eyes and ears of the senior executive in determining that the company is operating in the prescribed manner and, should any problems arise, these can be dealt with effectively and efficiently.

Continuing with the umbrella analogy, the quality assurance department would, during verification activities, identify 'leaks' should these occur and would be instrumental in verifying that these 'leaks' are patched up by the appropriate department or discipline to prevent further 'leakage'. These 'leaks' could occur anywhere—over administration, over design, over manufacturing, and others. Hence the requirement of all quality assurance standards that the person responsible for quality should be preferably independent of other functions.

THE RECOMMENDED ORGANIZATION

The recommended organization for a 'level 1' company is shown in Fig. 6.2. This places the quality assurance function as a 'staff' function directly responsible to the managing director.

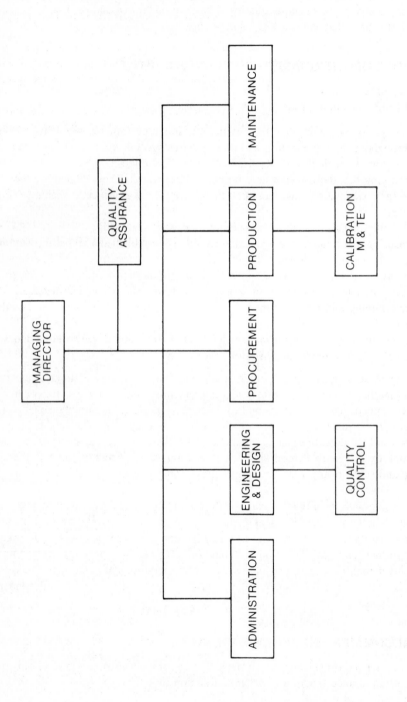

Fig. 6.2—Recommended organization for 'level 1' company.

The quality control department is shown as reporting to engineering and design; the reasoning for this is explained later. In a 'level 2' company, where there is no engineering or design activity, then quality control could well report to production.

This reporting structure, where quality control reports to production, may well be anathema to some as it could be argued that, where there is a conflict between schedule and quality, then the quality control manager could well be overruled by the production manager.

In the author's experience, there have been instances where, in an organization which had a reporting structure where quality control reported to the production manager but with no quality assurance department to keep a watchful eye on events, every Friday became a battle between the chief inspector and the production manager. The production manager would tour the manufacturing facility to determine which items were ready, but not released, for shipment. The fitness for purpose requirement was secondary; his philosophy being 'if it's wrong on delivery let the customer put it right and back-charge the rework costs to us'. Unfortunately, senior management also appeared unconcerned as they made no effort to support the chief inspector who wanted to delay shipment until the item was found to be correct. There was no commitment to quality by the works director; therefore there was no quality assurance representative to determine the implementation of, and adherence to, procedures. In fact, at that time there were very few recognizable procedures.

The prospect of receiving a large contract from the military, with a contractual requirement to implement a quality system, soon made senior management see the error of their ways and, with a little assistance from the author, a suitable system was developed, which included reorganization, so that responsibility for quality was placed on every department. The recommended organization did, needless to say, upset many senior personnel, but the Friday battles instantly disappeared.

The organization chart in Fig. 6.2 also shows the calibration of measuring and testing equipment as being the responsibility of the production department. This again may not be standard practice but surely it should be!

The production department should be responsible for the quality of its own work and should not rely on inspectors to determine subsequently whether the required quality has actually been obtained.

The production department will use measuring equipment to confirm sizes, tolerances and generally to control activities; then why should it not be responsible for the calibration of the equipment which it uses? The quality assurance department should be responsible for verifying that this calibration is carried out at the specified times and to the correct procedures. If discrepancies are found then the production department must take the necessary corrective action and prevent a recurrence. If subsequently there should be a recurrence of the discrepancy, then senior management would be required to resolve the matter.

Where a company places responsibility for the control of the measuring and testing equipment on the quality control or inspection department, the reason given, either implicitly or explicitly, is that the production department can not be trusted to do it properly. This lack of confidence in a vital part of the organization certainly implies a failure to appreciate the whole ethos of quality assurance.

As was indicated in Chapter 4, the smaller company may not be able to support economically a separate quality assurance department. In such circumstances, the function of quality assurance could well be undertaken by others not directly involved with the activity.

TYPICAL (THOUGH NOT RECOMMENDED) ORGANIZATION

Figure 6.3 identifies a typical company organization where there is no identifiable quality assurance function.

In this type of organization, the quality control department is responsible for the control of hardware and has, in all probability, been given an auditing function which many companies associate with quality assurance, hence the title QA/QC department.

In this organizational structure one must question who is to be responsible for verifying that the QA/QC department is itself working to procedure. Also, in such an organization, it is doubtful whether the other departments or disciplines—design, procurement, installation, and others—will accept this QA/QC department as the senior executive's representative. Experience has shown that, generally, this type of organization has not been found to be effective, neither does it demonstrate a company's total commitment to quality.

How then can the smaller company deal with this situation?

The quality assurance function can still be identified as in Fig. 6.2 but the verifying activity can be undertaken by others in the organization who are familiar with, but not directly responsible for, the activity under audit. This will mean, however, that the quality assurance function can co-opt others to act as the senior executive's eyes and ears, provided of course that such co-opted personnel are suitably trained and experienced. Alternatively, verification of compliance could be undertaken by a third party source.

Figure 6.4 shows a suitable organization for a quality assurance department within a 'level 1' company.

As has been mentioned many times, it is the senior executive who is ultimately responsible for the quality of the items or services which the company produces, and for the efficiency and cost-effectiveness of the total organization.

In a more direct manner, Fig. 6.5 shows how the umbrella concept operates.

QA/QC A MISNOMER

It has been established that, to be effective, the checking of an activity should be carried out by personnel who are familiar with, yet not directly responsible for, the activity.

Let us now analyse this further and, by so doing, determine that a quality control department cannot effectively be responsible for verifying the implementation and adherence of the quality assurance philosophy.

In essence, any type of checking activity could be equated with inspection. The accountant who checks the books is, in reality, inspecting them.

The design engineer who checks a design document is, in reality, inspecting it.

The buyer who checks procurement documents is, in reality, inspecting them.

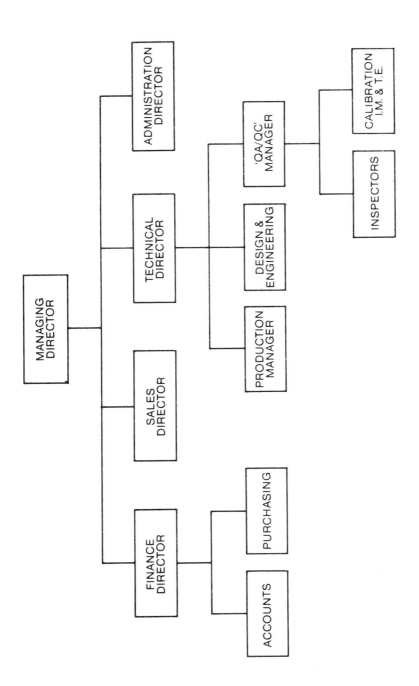

Fig. 6.3—Typical (though not recommended) organization of a 'level 1' company showing the possible location of the person responsible for quality.

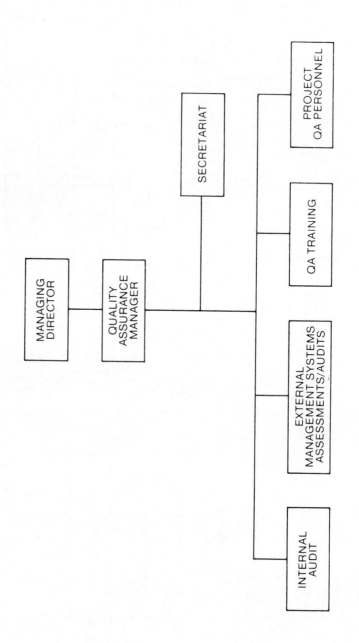

Fig. 6.4—Quality assurance department organization.

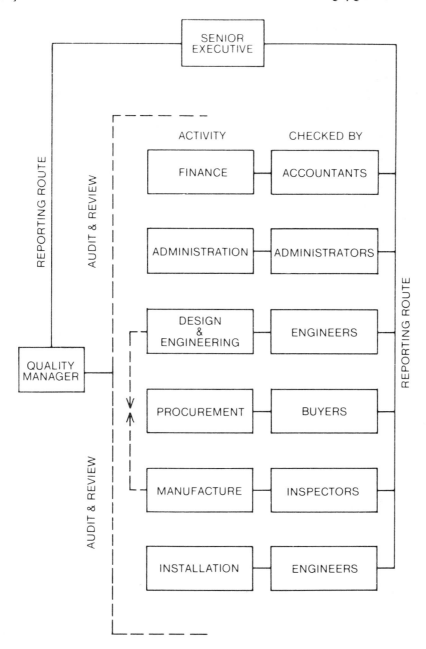

Fig. 6.5—The checking functions.

Yet none of these 'inspectors' reports to the quality assurance manager. It is therefore illogical that, in the majority of organizations, the person who checks hardware, which is an inspection activity, should report to a manager of a department which is designated as QA/QC.

If the function of hardware inspection is analysed still further, it will be determined that the inspector carries out a check against a specification. Specifications are developed by engineers, therefore the inspector is acting for the engineer, and should preferably report to that person. Hence the organization as shown in Fig. 6.2.

Inspection or quality control could, therefore, be considered as the continuation of the engineering function, which is, as has been identified, just one activity within the total quality assurance philosophy.

As with a change of government, the change of an organization's senior executive could lead to a change of administration. This change could affect the attitude towards quality. If the quality assurance representative is of executive status, then this change in attitude will be minimized. If, however, the quality assurance representative is well down in the hierarchy, as in Fig. 6.3, the effects of such a management change could be disastrous.

The requirement for the quality representative to be preferably independent of other functions should now be well appreciated.

7

The policy statement

DECLARATION OF INTENT

Any declaration, such as a bill passed by Parliament, trade agreement, social contract or similar pronouncement, becomes valid only when signed by a person, or persons, in the highest authority. Similarly, any quality system can be considered to have 'teeth' only if signed by the highest authority in an organization.

It will, of course, be necessary to formalize the intent of a quality system into a document which is generally given a title such as 'quality manual' The actual development and contents of a manual will be dealt with later, but there should be a signed declaration issued by the chief executive which signifies commitment to the documented quality system. As with any declaration of intent, it can be considered to be effective only in its actual implementation.

There are many instances, in all walks of life, where agreements or declarations of intent have been signed in all good faith but have been found not to be worth the paper they are written on, due to lack of implementation, caused by either the inability of the signatories to enforce the agreement or perhaps by a change in administration.

At least, in the quality-conscious company, the senior executive, in conjunction with the quality assurance executive, will have been instrumental in the development and implementation of the quality system and should, therefore, be familiar with its contents. The senior executive should, if totally committed, therefore have no hesitation in signifying this commitment by appending his or her signature to such a declaration of intent. This declaration of intent is generally known as a policy statement.

ISO 9001 (clause 4.1.1, 'Quality policy') requires that:

> the supplier's management shall define and document its policy and objectives for, and commitment to, quality. The supplier shall ensure that this policy is understood, implemented and maintained at all levels in the organization.

This means that management should develop and define its policy, objectives and its commitment to a quality system in a documented statement. This statement should be published and made available throughout the whole organization. In order to ensure that this policy is understood, an element of training will be required.

The policy statement

The signed policy statement should give all employees and potential customers an initial indication of that company's intentions towards quality and the benefits expected from it. In order to determine the effectiveness of the quality system, the customer could and, in the case of government agencies, very often does undertake an assessment or audit to verify that what is documented actually happens in practice. Similarly, the senior executive maintains confidence in the implementation and effectiveness of the quality system by means of internal quality audits which are carried out by an independent function— normally the quality assurance department.

A company's commitment to quality can be judged initially by the strength of the signed policy statement and, subsequently, by management's attitude as a whole and, therefore, by the extent to which it is actually put into practice. The policy statement, therefore, could be defined as:

> A signed declaration issued by the chief executive of a company signifying that company's commitment to a given quality system.

In the author's experience, a policy statement carries much more psychological weight if it is issued on the company's official headed paper. In this format, it can then be used as a 'stand-alone' document in a variety of situations such as sales promotion, employee awareness, and others. It would be management's responsibility to ensure that this policy is understood, implemented and maintained at all levels of the organization. It is not uncommon, and indeed strongly recommended, for such a statement to be prominently displayed throughout the company. In fact, in the author's experience, many companies issue this statement on a small printed 'tent' card, which is displayed on the desks of management and supervisory staff, thus serving as a constant reminder of the company's commitment to quality.

The general statement

In addition to the policy statement, it is useful to expand on quality responsibilities in the form of a general statement. The general statement could, therefore, be defined as:

> An amplification of the policy statement issued to include quality responsibilities.

There is no good reason why both statements should not be combined but, in the author's opinion, the combination of the two could detract from the impact of the policy statement as described earlier.

These two documents will eventually be included in the quality manual (should such a document be required), the formulation of which will be dealt with in the next chapter. Examples of both the policy statement and the general statement are given in Appendix A, Sections 1.1 and 1.2.

8

The quality manual

The quality manual was touched upon briefly in Chapter 2, where it was described as a document setting out the general quality policies, procedures and practices of an organization.

WHY A QUALITY MANUAL IS NEEDED

In addition to the fact that most quality standards indicate that due consideration should be given to the development of such a document, there are a number of very good reasons for its production.

It is a very good management 'tool' to keep employees aware of their responsibilities within the quality system; it can thus become a suitable training document.

Its use can reduce the 'learning curve' due to employee turnover and can thus assist in the continuity of events in such cases.

It can, if well written, become a useful addition to the 'sales aids' of an organization, as it will outline a company's intentions with regard to satisfying the customer by producing items and/or services which are fit for purpose.

The use of a manual as an effective training document has been proved on many occasions during the author's experience.

There are many major purchasers who require proof of the effective implementation of a quality system by a supplier before the supplier is included in the bidders' list. The quality system is usually related to the appropriate level of a quality system standard.

A case history may be of some interest. There was one particular supplier who was at a loss to fulfil the requirement of Canadian Standard Z299.3:1978 (Quality Verification Program Requirements) but was anxious to be included on the bidders' list for a major contract soon to be let. The author was engaged as a consultant to this supplier. One of the major problems encountered by this supplier was in the requirement for inspection. It was his understanding of the Standard that he would be required to engage an additional person as an inspector, as the Canadian Standard Z299.3:1978 clearly stipulated:

The use of competent persons for inspection other than those performing or directly supervising the work being inspected.

With a staff of only twelve personnel this apparent demand for extra staff would increase production costs and seriously affect competitiveness. However, it was pointed out that, to meet the requirements of the Standard, it was not necessary to engage any more staff as in no instance does the document state that the supplier shall have a separate or independent inspection group. It is quite satisfactory for the inspection to be carried out by another member of the workforce, provided he or she has the knowledge and ability to do so, and provided the person performing the inspection was not directly involved in the work.

This inference that the Standard called for the recruitment of special staff was a major misinterpretation of the requirement of the standard and indeed, even today, the ISO 9000 requirement for independent verification personnel continues to be misinterpreted by many companies. This misinterpretation is a throw-back to the early days of quality systems when many major purchasers insisted that their suppliers had independent inspection/quality control departments. Old habits die hard!

The supplier eventually developed and implemented a 'level 3 quality verification program' which met the requirements of the Standard and which was assessed and approved by the buyer, with the end result that this supplier not only attained the bidders' list but was also awarded a contract.

A few months later, on a follow-up visit, it was found that a different shop foreman had been appointed. The supplier advised that this had not really affected productivity as the quality manual, together with the relevant procedures, enabled the new foreman to assume his position with the minimum of training and indoctrination. The 'learning curve' had been considerably reduced and, in just this one instance, the initial cost of developing and implementing the quality system had been more than recouped.

THE SHOP WINDOW TO QUALITY

The quality manual could be described as a company's shop window to quality. It is to the company as the display window is to a store. The items in the store window will indicate to a prospective customer the nature and quality of the merchandise the store has for sale and, in order to appreciate the totality of its stock, the customer will venture inside and purchase whatever it is that is required.

Similarly, the quality manual describes a company's intentions towards satisfying the fitness for purpose criteria and the prospective customer, as for the merchandising store, can venture inside the company and verify that company's commitment to quality by auditing the system.

The quality manual, therefore, states in general terms the methods used by a company to assure quality. It is, as has already been indicated, a document of intent, describing 'what' is done to assure quality. The detailed procedures, which should be available at the activity locations, will describe, in addition, the 'who', 'how', 'when', 'where' and, possibly, 'why' of an activity.

MANUAL FORMAT AND CONTENTS

There is no defined format for a manual; the presentation of the document is a matter of personal choice. Initially, it is up to management to determine whether such a document is required and, if so, for what purpose.

The purpose of the document will determine its format and content. If the manual is required for internal purposes only then no doubt it will take on an entirely different format from that required for registration purposes. The registration bodies would expect a document to comply with the appropriate part of the quality system standard and would expect such a document to address all the elements of the standard indicating those elements which are applicable and those which are not.

In the author's experience, those manuals which have been developed by companies purely for second or third party registration purposes are generally nothing more than a regurgitation of the requirements of the standard and have very little bearing on the quality system of the company. It is important, therefore, to determine at the onset what the document is to be used for and the form it is to take. In any event it should be designed so that it is easily updated.

The format as discussed in this chapter is that generally accepted throughout industry and an example of a typical manual is given in Appendix A.

As described in Chapter 4, all activities and functions which require to be controlled should be collated into system or procedure outlines. These outlines describe in general terms what is required to control a given activity, and it is these outlines which form the basis of a quality manual.

As a guide it is recommended that a manual comprises three sections, as follows:

(1) Company quality policy:
— policy statement
— general statement on quality objectives
— statement on quality assurance authority and responsibility
— details of company and quality assurance organization
— statement on the manual amendments, reissue and distribution.
(2) System element outlines:
— outlines of system elements addressing the applicable criteria of the company's quality system.
(3) Procedures index:
— an index of the company's procedures.

Let us take each in turn.

Section 1   Company quality policy
This section should be devoted entirely to describing the company's commitment to quality and would include the following:

(a) The policy statement, which has been described in detail in Chapter 7.
(b) The general statement in quality objectives, which also has been described in detail in Chapter 7.

(c)   A statement on the authority and responsibility for quality assurance. This would
      detail the organization for quality as related to the requirements of the company
      but, wherever possible, it is to be emphasized that the person appointed should have
      the necessary authority and responsibility to ensure that the company's quality
      system is being implemented and adhered to by all concerned. Such responsibility
      will normally mean that the person so appointed should be of management status
      and should be preferably independent of other functions. The quality assurance
      authority statement will describe this, and a typical statement covering such author-
      ity would read as follows:

Authority and responsibilities

Department and Discipline Managers
With regard to quality, all Department and Discipline Managers shall be responsible for:

(1) the quality of work carried out by all personnel within their respective depart-
     ments or disciplines;
(2) verifying that approved procedures are adopted within their department or
     discipline and that any necessary complementary procedures are established,
     implemented, reviewed and updated as required;
(3) ensuring that all staff are adequately qualified and experienced in their relevant
     discipline to perform the duties of their position in a satisfactory manner;
(4) ensuring that all staff are familiar with company procedures and have ready
     access to them.

Quality Assurance Executive (Management Representative)
(1) The Quality Assurance Executive is the final authority and represents the Com-
     pany on all quality matters pertinent to the quality system as established by
     customer requirements, regulatory requirements and company quality policies
     and procedures. The Quality Assurance Executive reports directly to the Man-
     aging Director.
(2) The Quality Assurance Executive has the primary responsibility to structure
     the quality system, which will involve all company departments and/or disci-
     plines in a focused effort to ensure compliance with quality requirements.
(3) Specifically the Quality Assurance Executive is involved in areas such as:
     — drafting company policy on quality;
     — setting company quality objectives;
     — reviewing the organizational relationships as they affect quality and devel-
       oping proposals for improvement;
     — determining and reporting the principal causes of quality losses on non-
       conformances;
     — monitoring the company's quality system to determine where improvements
       are needed and recommending, as necessary, the appropriate corrective ac-
       tion.

(d)   The details of company and quality assurance organization normally comprise organization charts which show:
      — the company organization with departmental/discipline reporting lines; this chart should be developed to show the relationships, interfaces and hierarchical structure of the various departments or disciplines;
      — the quality assurance organization with its independence from other functions.
      Typical charts for both company and quality assurance organizations are as Figs 6.2 and 6.4.

(e)   The statement on amendments, reissue and distribution should indicate how amendments to the manual are dealt with. It should also indicate what is done to control the distribution of the manual.

Controlled and uncontrolled conditions
Manuals, as for most other documents, are issued under *controlled* and *uncontrolled* conditions.
   Controlled conditions imply that the document is given a serial number and allocated to a specified person. The recipient of the manual acknowledges receipt and is provided automatically with amendments and reissues.
   Uncontrolled conditions imply that the document is issued for information purposes only and so will not be updated. It is in a company's interest to keep 'controlled' documents to a minimum. One should establish a 'need to know' rather than a 'want to know' distribution list. A typical statement on amendments, reissue and distribution is given on p. 90.

Section 2   System element outlines
This section should contain brief outlines of the primary functions of the company's quality system as determined by both company and customer requirements.
   It should include the controls to be exercised on those aspects of the function which have an effect on quality to ensure conformance to customer requirements. The system element outlined should not only reflect current quality policies but should also take into consideration the requirements of national and international standards and regulations related to quality assurance systems, such as AS 3901; BS 5882; BS 5750.1; ANSI/ ASME NQA-1; NS 5801 and CAN3 Z299.1.
   Unless the company is very small with few functional controls, the inclusion of detailed procedures within a manual is to be avoided. There are three very good reasons for this:

(1)   Procedures are dynamic documents and are continually under review. Experience has shown that a procedure cannot be considered to have attained its full 'maturity' with regard to content, acceptability and affectiveness until it has reached revision 4. If procedures are included in the manual updating becomes a very costly and laborious process. If, however, procedures are kept separate from the manual, then any procedural amendments would be an independent exercise which would have no effect on the outlines in the manual.
(2)   The majority of the recipients of a manual would not generally be concerned with

Amendments, reissue and distribution

The XYZ Company Limited's Quality Assurance Department reviews this manual periodically with other departments and disciplines to reaffirm its adequacy and conformance to current requirements of the XYZ Company Limited. The maximum period for review of the manual is once yearly.

Amendments to the manual are made as required to reflect the current quality system. The amendments are made by replacement of the applicable page(s). Each amended page is identified by amendment number and date of amendment.

Amendments are numbered consecutively until such time as a new edition incorporates all such changes. When changes affect a considerable number of pages, and in any case after not more than ten amendments to one edition, the manual is reissued. Editions are identified in alphabetical order. Each edition cancels and replaces all previous editions and amendments.

The amendment list indicates all the amendments to the latest edition of the manual.

A complete list of quality manual holders, together with the amendment records, are retained by the . . . (here would be inserted the department responsible for the function, i.e. Quality Assurance Department, Document Control Department, Library, or others). Amendments and new editions of the manual are automatically distributed to all registered holders.

It shall be the responsibility of all registered manual holders to update the manual assigned to them and to destroy obsolete copies of all amended pages.

---

the detailed aspects of a given activity or the technicalities of its operation. Detailed procedures would, therefore, be just additional pieces of paper for which they will have no use.

(3)   Procedures are proprietary documents which have taken a great deal of time and effort to produce. They are for company use only and should not be made freely available to third parties. Procedures should generally be made available only to those who are to implement them.

There is, of course, the inevitable exception to the rule. When procedures are developed to meet certain customer requirements, the customer will invariably wish to review them to determine their compliance with certain contract conditions.

To illustrate points (1) and (2), the author during one particular consultancy was requested to review the company's quality manual, which at that time was a bulky document of 140 pages. The manual contained, among other things, a very detailed procedure covering the auditing of the quality system. As this was the most detailed document in the manual, it was evident who was responsible for quality in that organization—certainly not the senior executive as he appeared to leave all such matters to his quality manager.

The manual was issued under 'controlled' conditions to 44 individuals and that particular procedure was at revision 3. The procedure itself comprised nine pages; therefore a great deal of unnecessary paper (in fact almost 1200 pages) had been distributed to personnel who had no direct responsibility for auditing. Most of the recipients of the manual were not involved in the auditing function and would not therefore need to know the techniques but only to know that auditing was in fact carried out.

An outline of the auditing function is all that should have been required in the manual, the detailed procedure being made available to those who had a responsibility for auditing. It was later established that, apart from the quality manager, all others who had some responsibility for auditing were neither recipients of a 'controlled' copy of the manual nor did they have an up-to-date copy of the procedure.

What however is even more enlightening was the number of manuals issued under 'controlled' conditions. Of the 44 copies, ten were distributed to customers, the remaining 34 being issued to members of staff. The total workforce of that company was only 130, which meant that 26% of the workforce were on the 'controlled' distribution list. One can only assume from this that the 'want to know' rather than the 'need to know' philosophy prevailed. The responsibility for updating the manual, in this case, must have approached a full-time occupation. Generally it should be necessary to issue manuals under 'controlled' conditions only to management and perhaps supervisory staff. They, in turn, should be made responsible for keeping their staff informed of the manual contents.

The outcome of this consultancy resulted in the redevelopment of the manual, which became a much slimmer document of just 37 pages, with the 'controlled' distribution reduced to seven. The procedures were made available at point of use.

The system element outlines should follow a logical sequence and should cover all aspects of the relevant criteria of the company's quality system.

Whereas the outlines should logically follow the same sequence as the quality standard with which it is intended to comply, this can present a problem when supplying items or services on an international basis, and to countries where ISO 9000 is not the norm, as the majority of standards do not apply a uniform index. The need for a formal presentation of documents is a *sine qua non* of any quality system, yet nations do not practise what they preach when it comes to interchangeability of quality standards. The adoption by many countries of the international series of quality standards is a step in the right direction.

In any event, once an organization has established and implemented its own quality system, and continually verifies its effectiveness, there is no reason why it should not meet all international standard requirements for the applicable level. There may be additional requirements 'imposed' by a customer to meet certain safety and/or environmental regulations but these requirements can be adequately taken care of when developing a quality plan for that project or contract.

A typical systems outline index would be as follows:

Contract review (planning)
Design control
Change control
Traceability control
Document control
Control of purchased items and services
Purchaser-supplied (free-issue) product

Control of special processes
Identification of items
Non-conforming items
Corrective action
Inspection, test and operating status
Control of inspection, measuring and test equipment
Handling and storing items
Preservation, packaging and shipping
Incoming inspection
In-process inspection
Final inspection
Records
Audits
Training.

Section 3   Procedures index

This section should include the procedures for all the activities and functions applicable to a company's own quality system.

While it is generally necessary to include only those procedures relevant to a given quality system level, it is worth while indexing procedures relating to all management functions. Such an index will then assist the workforce in determining the correct procedure for any given function.

The information listed in this section should include the document title with the relevant document number. The author does not recommend the inclusion of procedure revision status as this can lead only to unnecessary updating of this section.

Procedure revisions should be controlled by the responsible department. Procedures, as for any document, should carry an identification number to facilitate control. A typical numbering sequence for procedures would be the tripartite system as follows:

XYZ–MAN–001

In this example, the company's identity is represented by the first three letters (in this case the XYZ Company Limited). The department or function is represented by the second set of three (in this case MAN refers to Management) and finally the three digits refer to the procedure number.

The following is a typical, but by no means exhaustive, procedures index:

MANAGEMENT AND ADMINISTRATION
Sales and marketing	XYZ–MAN–001
Public relations	XYZ–MAN–002
Review of quality system	XYZ–MAN–003
Communications	XYZ–MAN–004
Safety policy	XYZ–MAN–005
Contract control	XYZ–MAN–006
Minutes of meetings	XYZ–MAN–007

Personnel training   XYZ–MAN–008
and others

ENGINEERING
Design criteria control   XYZ–ENG–001
Design document validation control   XYZ–ENG–002
Engineering change control   XYZ–ENG–003
Traceability control   XYZ–ENG–004
Interface control   XYZ–ENG–005
Weight control   XYZ–ENG–006
Design review   XYZ–ENG–007
Requisitions   XYZ–ENG–008
Specification preparation   XYZ–ENG–009
Computer-aided design   XYZ–ENG–010
and others

DOCUMENT CONTROL
Document numbering and identification   XYZ–DOC–001
Procedures preparation—style and format   XYZ–DOC–002
Development, approval and implementation of activity
    documents   XYZ–DOC–003
Procedures index   XYZ–DOC–004
Document storage and retrieval   XYZ–DOC–005
Operating manuals and dossiers   XYZ–DOC–006
Records/certification   XYZ–DOC–007
Document revision and distribution   XYZ–DOC–008
and others

PLANNING
Contract review meetings   XYZ–PLA–001
Progress reporting   XYZ–PLA–002
Work activity packages   XYZ–PLA–003
and others

PROCUREMENT
Vendor assessment   XYZ–PRO–001
Tender package development   XYZ–PRO–002
Bid package review and evaluation   XYZ–PRO–003
Supplier selection   XYZ–PRO–004
Purchase orders   XYZ–PRO–005
Expediting   XYZ–PRO–006
and others

QUALITY ASSURANCE
Quality manual   XYZ–QA–001
Audits—internal/external   XYZ–QA–002
Audits—extrinsic   XYZ–QA–003

| Corrective action request | XYZ–QA–004 |
| Auditor qualification and training | XYZ–QA–005 |

MANUFACTURING

Material control	XYZ–MNF–001
Special processes	XYZ–MNF–002
Identification of items	XYZ–MNF–003
Non-conforming items	XYZ–MNF–004
Handling and storage	XYZ–MNF–005
Preservation, packaging and shipping	XYZ–MNF–006
Control of inspection, measuring and test equipment	XYZ–MNF–007

and others

QUALITY CONTROL

Incoming inspection	XYZ–QC–001
Purchaser-supplied items	XYZ–QC–002
Inspection, test and operating status	XYZ–QC–003
In-process inspection	XYZ–QC–004
Final inspection	XYZ–QC–005
Hold activity notification	XYZ–QC–006
Non-destructive testing	XYZ–QC–007

and others

INSTALLATION

Mechanical installation	XYZ–INS–001
Electrical installation	XYZ–INS–002
Instrument installation	XYZ–INS–003
Pipework fabrication and erection	XYZ–INS–004
Protective coating	XYZ–INS–005
Cathodic protection	XYZ–INS–006
Pressure testing	XYZ–INS–007
Special processes	XYZ–INS–008

and others.

As can be seen from the above, when procedures are related to the function they are intended to control, very few are actually the responsibility of the quality assurance department. In many organizations, all procedures are regarded as quality assurance procedures, which can only confirm the lack of understanding of quality assurance concepts.

In summary, one should endeavour to keep the manual simple. It is, as has already been emphasized, a document of intent.

The inclusion of any information which is likely to be subject to continual amendment should be avoided. Procedures are one example of details not to be included; organization charts are another. It is recommended that titles or functions, and not the individuals names, be indicated on such charts. Titles or functions, once established, do not normally change but individuals most certainly do!

In the introduction to this book it was stated that 'quality assurance is not a massive paper generator'. It will not be if one exercises adequate controls on information and adopts the 'need to know' rather than the 'want to know' doctrine. By employing the efficiency techniques referred to earlier, the majority of individuals presently engaged in what is loosely termed 'quality engineering' could make their jobs easier and probably much more satisfying and rewarding.

9

The procedure

PROCEDURE DEVELOPMENT, ADMINISTRATION AND CONTROL

Now that the system element outlines have been developed and incorporated into the quality manual, the next step is to produce the detailed procedures. Procedures, as has been said, comprise the real evidence of quality and should be considered mandatory for any quality system.

An effective quality system can be seen to be only as good as the documentation that controls it and this documentation will, if produced in a systematic and consistent manner, formalize the system which, in turn, should:

— demonstrate a clear and concise statement to all personnel;
— encourage consistency of action and uniformity of understanding throughout the company;
— be easily distributed;
— convey the same (consistent) message or instruction simultaneously to all appropriate personnel;
— facilitate effective management of change, revision and updating (changes being easily incorporated and approval demonstrated by means of a signature, with a notification of the change being issued to all points of use concurrently);
— ensure permanence and *reduce the learning curve* when personnel changes occur;
— assist in the monitoring of the system (informal, oral instructions cannot be verified).

Quality system documentation should not, however, be excessive and should not be synonymous with 'paper generation'. It should be well planned, simple, clear, concise and well controlled. The operative word is simple; the system document must be easily understood; if it is not it can be counter-productive. Putting things simply is certainly not easy. (Try writing out instructions for erecting a folding deck chair.) Having produced a first draft of a document, pass it informally around staff to make sure it is, indeed, readily understood. Always include a note to the effect that if the reader cannot understand any part of the document he or she should ask for elucidation. Some practical guide-lines, including the concept of a 'readability index', are given at the end of the chapter.

The objectives of paperwork, believe it or not, is to make life simpler. Above all else, the documentation provides a very good checklist. If the procedures are being followed, then nothing should be overlooked or left to chance. It will eliminate the 'I did not think about it' syndrome. The simple act of having to write something down clarifies the mind wonderfully.

Also, procedures are not implemented in order to find someone to blame if things go wrong; they are designed to prevent things going wrong. Furthermore, the system, if properly developed, should not allow anyone to 'pass the buck'.

THE 'TIERS' OF DOCUMENTATION

It will be seen that associated with the quality system there are a number of types of documentation which describe what the system is intended to achieve, how it works, what deliverables are to be produced, by whom and when. This documentation is usually given the all-embracing title 'Work instructions' and is generally in four tiers, which are:

Tier 1   The quality manual
This has already been discussed and defines the policies, objectives, organizational structures and summarizes the general quality practices of the company.

Tier 2   Procedures
These describe what is to be done, by whom and how, when, where and why an activity is to be carried out.

Tier 3   Job instructions
These direct personnel in a single activity and are subordinate documents to procedures. Such instructions may be required for specific tasks; processes or operations; test and/or inspection activities.

Tier 4   Forms and records
These include files, technical, statutory and legal documents, specifications, codes of practice and all other documentation which will demonstrate the achievement of the quality system requirements.

DOCUMENTING THE ACTIVITIES

In order to document any activity, one must understand how that activity is carried out and how each step within a given activity leads into the next step. When documenting any activity the actual act of writing it down can also highlight such matters as anomalies, duplications, lack of important interfaces, and other possible deficiencies.

The understanding of how each activity is carried out must point to the fact that procedures can be considered as representing a true account of an activity only if the personnel actually carrying out that activity are involved with the procedure development. It also goes without saying that once an activity is 'proceduralized' it facilitates review by others who may have an involvement in that activity and any changes in the activity will be automatically documented. Documented changes will highlight to all concerned at the same time that such a change has been made. Documented changes will also act as an audit trail in the event of information being required at a later date to verify when and why an activity was amended.

As has been said, procedures should define the purpose and scope of an activity and specify what is to be done, by whom, and how, when, where and why an activity is to be carried out. Procedures will ensure that controls operate consistently and effectively, that people communicate and that events occur in a planned and systematic manner. They are not meant to be detailed instructions for controlling individual processes or activities; such would normally be described in job instructions which are, in turn, referenced by procedures. This would apply equally to activities which could be considered as being 'external' to the company's operations, yet which are very much the company's responsibility, such as instructions for servicing equipment at site and codes of practice.

The development of procedures is a major activity in itself and should therefore be planned and co-ordinated with the groups of people involved. The planning and subsequent development of procedures will require consideration of the following:

— who writes them (responsibilities)
— how they will be planned and developed
— how they are to be written and presented
— how they are to be identified
— who will control them and how.

In the following sections each of these aspects is dealt with in more detail.

There are several key issues in procedure development which should be determined before the preparation of procedures can begin, and all should be finalized before procedures are issued. These are:

— the definition of responsibilities
— the procedure numbering system
— methods of procedure amendment and revision
— methods of controlling distribution.

DEFINITION OF RESPONSIBILITIES

There are three primary areas of responsibility which should be defined. These are:

1. Identification, review and authorization.
2. Preparation (writing).
3. Administration and control.

Identification, review and authorization
Normally, management is responsible for identifying the need for a new procedure or set of procedures, based upon the activities of the organization concerned. Once written, procedures should be reviewed at both departmental and functional levels to ensure that:

— any conflicts within, or between, existing procedures are identified and resolved;
— procedures reflect current practice and provide adequate direction;
— interfaces are defined and agreed at both departmental and functional levels.

Ultimately, to become an official corporate document, the procedure should be approved by an authorized or nominated signatory. A procedure may require approval from any or all of the following personnel:

— departmental head or manager
— quality manager
— managing director.

Management will make this decision, which in itself, should be documented and updated as necessary.

Preparation (writing)

Utilizing the agreed structure or format, procedure writing should be undertaken by personnel who are familiar with the activities and functions to be controlled. This responsibility should not be placed upon the quality department (although this department may offer guidance on the format to be adopted). It will be necessary, therefore, to nominate an author or authors.

Administration and control

Management should determine the methods of, and the responsibilities for, the administration and control of procedures, including such issues as:

— the format in which procedures are to be written
—the numbering system to be followed
— the system for review
— the methods to be followed for approval, amendment and revision
— storage, distribution and retrieval.

PROCEDURE NUMBERING SYSTEM

A procedure numbering system should be developed. This system should allow adequate facility for expansion (i.e. the inclusion of new procedures) and should convey some meaning to the reader. A typical procedure numbering system has already been indicated earlier, but whatever method is used it should be consistent with existing corporate or divisional systems.

Forms also should be numbered so that they can be traced to the procedure that generates them. For example, a form identified as attachment 6.1 of, say, procedure XYZ–MAN–001 would be numbered MAN–0011, attachment 6.2 would be numbered MAN–0012 and so on.

PROCEDURE AMENDMENT AND REVISION

As a quality system is continually subject to review and improvement, the procedures themselves become active or dynamic documents and, from time to time, will require amendment or revision. In this respect, there are several important points to consider, namely:

— revision status
— revision identification
— revision record
— issuing revised documentation.

Revision status

Each page of the procedure should be identified with the revision status and date. Revision status indicators generally follow a numeric system commencing at 0 and proceeding through 1, 2, 3 and onwards as required. Revision 0 is generally utilized for the 'issued for comment' stage.

Revision identification

The extent of the revision made should be indicated within the text of the document. This is usually undertaken by stating the revision number in parentheses in the margin with a line extending down to the end of the text revised, thus:

$$(2)$$

Revision record

In order to determine that one is in possession of the latest revision of a procedure, it is considered good practice to include a record of revisions on the front of the document, or at the front of a manual containing a set of procedures. This record of revisions can be indicated by means of a revision record box on the front sheet of the procedure or by means of an amendment or revision record register immediately inside the cover page.

As a minimum, the revision status indicator should identify:

— the revision status (e.g. 0, 1, 2, 3)
— the date of the revision
— the pages/procedures affected by the revision
— authorization for revision.

It is important that the department which is responsible for document control maintains a master index of revisions to all procedures—an index that has itself a revision number and date for traceability.

Issuing revised documentation

There are variations in the methods by which different organizations issue procedure revisions. Some companies favour the reissue of the entire document at every revision. Others issue only the affected pages until such time as a major revision is undertaken which, in order to avoid confusion, will necessitate the complete document being reissued as a new edition. When new editions are produced, it is usual to classify them with some form of identification. As for the manual, an alphabetical sequence is generally used for this purpose.

The safest approach is to reissue the entire procedure each time it is revised. This, however, is more costly and time consuming but is generally easier to control. Holders of procedures manuals are more likely to replace complete documents than to replace individual pages.

Revisions should be issued to all holders of the procedure or procedures manual under the cover of a transmittal notice, an example of which is given as Fig. 9.1. This transmittal notice should provide for the receiver to acknowledge not only receipt of the amended document but also to signify the incorporation of the revision in their procedure manual and the disposition of the superseded document/page(s). A copy of the transmittal notice is then returned to the document control function.

DISTRIBUTION CONTROL

Document distribution should be developed on a *need to know* rather than a *want to know* basis and should be planned, formalized and controlled with clearly defined responsibilities.

Procedures may be in the form of individual documents, a bound manual, or a series of manuals. These are controlled copies, i.e. each procedure or manual is numbered and signed out to, and receipted by, a nominated individual.

Periodic audits should be undertaken to verify that copies are kept up to date, with all latest revisions incorporated and superseded versions or unofficial copies destroyed.

Unauthorized copying of documents should be discouraged by means of a document control system which clearly identifies those personnel who are responsible for document reproduction and also the method used to classify 'controlled copies'.

PROCEDURE PRESENTATION

Finally, management should determine how procedures are to be prepared, presented, printed and distributed. All personnel concerned with procedure development should be made aware of such directives. Due consideration should, therefore, be given to:

— the use of word-processing equipment and software;
— the format, font size, typeface, character facing and methods of presentation;
— the methods of reproduction such as photocopying or offset printing;
— the use of special paper.

PROCEDURE PLANNING AND DEVELOPMENT

Development of the full register of procedures is the responsibility of management and should be addressed during the planning stage of the quality system.

The development of individual procedures, however, will be the responsibility of the nominated author(s) and will require careful planning.

Procedure planning
Planning is an essential part of procedure development and if undertaken systematically will assist in the production of logical, well-structured and coherent documents.

DOCUMENT TRANSMITTAL No.....

To.............   Department...........   Date...........

From..........   Department...........   Date..........

Document No:....... Document Title...............Rev.No........

i) **This document is a first issue.**   **(*)**
ii) **This document supersedes Rev.No......Copy No(s)........(*)**
(* delete as appropriate)

Enclosed is/are controlled copy number(s)...... of the above
referenced document for your information and retention.

As required by procedure No.DOC.008, please complete section A
and, where appropriate (see ii above), section B of both the
original and duplicate of this transmittal notice. The duplicate
shall be returned to the originator within 5 days of receipt and
the original retained on file for audit purposes.

Originator................(signed)

Section A

I confirm receipt of copy number(s)..... of the captioned
document(s)

Signed.....................   Date...........

Section B (see ii above)

I confirm having destroyed my controlled copy No(s)...... of the
superseded document.

Signed.....................   Date...........

Form Doc.0083

Fig. 9.1.

Procedure planning involves, first, establishing the scope of the activity to be addressed by the procedure and, second, the objectives of the control of that activity.

Scope
The scope of an activity that is to be addressed by an individual procedure will be dependent upon a number of criteria, such as:

— the nature of the activity that is to be controlled
— the interfaces with other related activities and hence other procedures
— the amount of manageable information, or instructions, that can be covered by the document.

Objectives
The objectives for the control of an activity should be determined by management and, where possible, the achievement of specified objectives should be verifiable by measurement.

Procedure development
Experience has shown that there are ten distinct steps to be taken in developing procedures. These are:

1. Review current practice.
2. Analyse current practice.
3. Develop a draft procedure.
4. Release draft for comment.
5. Review comments.
6. Revise and issue procedure for acceptance.
7. Obtain approval.
8. Issue for use.
9. Implement.
10. Monitor and review.

Review current practice
This will involve discussions with other people concerned and will include a review of all existing applicable documentation, procedures and instructions. It will then be necessary to:

— verify and record the current routine methods of performing an activity;
— identify responsibilities, documentation and equipment used to undertake the activity;
— determine the current standards (acceptance criteria), if any, which are applied and how effectively they are being utilized;
— identify those aspects of an activity which significantly impact on quality.

Analyse current practice
An analysis of current practice should be undertaken in conjunction with all involved

personnel to verify whether such practices are indeed satisfactory and whether any changes need to be made. As a result of such an analysis it should be possible to:

— confirm that the specified objectives are currently being achieved;
— agree on the best methods of achieving the required levels of quality;
— identify any gaps, duplications or areas of weakness, especially with regard to communication problems between departments and/or functions;
— verify potential areas for improvement.

Develop a draft procedure

A draft document should be initiated which formulates the method by which an activity is (or is to be) carried out, indicating who does what, how, when, where and why. The procedure itself should be developed to an agreed format. The subject of format is discussed later in this chapter.

An effective way of logically ordering the steps of an activity is to outline them utilizing flow-chart techniques. A great deal has been written on flow charting and it is not necessary to go through these in detail here. Fig. 9.2 indicates some typical flow-charting symbols which can be used for this purpose.

In order to construct a flow chart of an activity and to develop an effective procedure, it is important to indicate how each activity is carried out, how each step is initiated and how it leads into the next. Information and instructions on how each step is conducted should be easy to follow.

The process of documenting current practice may uncover a potential for change and improvement in methods. Only instructions which are specific to the scope of the particular activity that is to be controlled should be included in the procedure. These should be clearly defined by means of 'purpose' and 'scope' statements. References, or interfaces with related documents, should be included where appropriate. In some instances, if there is too much information to be contained in a single document, more than one procedure may be required. Where possible, try to avoid wide variations in procedure length.

The degree of detail required in describing various steps/instructions will be dependent upon the personnel for whom the procedure is being written and the level of training or experience of such personnel.

One of the most important items to be determined when considering a documented instruction, or the need for such an instruction, is the effect this instruction may have on the performance of the work. The ultimate test of any procedure is in its ability to provide the control to achieve the result for which it was developed. Where relevant, the procedure should make reference to 'tier 3' or 'tier 4' documents, as appropriate. The procedure is not intended to *replace* detailed job instructions but to support them. Likewise, the development of a procedure may actually require that certain documents, e.g. 'level 4' forms and records, be designed to ensure adequate control.

Release draft for comment

Once developed, the draft procedure should be designated as revision 0 (issued for comment) and distributed to all involved personnel for their review with some indication of when the document is to be returned to the originator. Alternatively a default

Initiation of a document

An activity or operation

A decision must be made

Documents are filed

Terminator – final activity

Fig. 9.2—Some typical flow-charting symbols.

instruction could be issued which would read: 'If comments are not received by [insert date] it will be assumed that the recipient has no comment to make.' Experience has shown that reviews of this kind can extend the document development schedule if no deadline is indicated. Management must support such a ruling.

Review comments
The comments should then be reviewed to determine which are applicable and which are required to be incorporated into the document. Any amendments agreed at this stage should be recorded.

Revise and issue procedure for acceptance
Incorporate those amendments which are considered appropriate and reissue the document for approval.

Obtain approval
The procedure should then be checked by the responsible nominated person and approved by management prior to issue for use.

Issue for use
The document would then be formally issued as revision 1 (issued for use) and distributed to all relevant locations in accordance with the agreed distribution instructions. Issue does not necessarily imply that all concerned should receive an individual copy. In instances where a number of people will use the same procedure, then 'ready access' to the procedure should be sufficient. Procedures, as for the quality manual, should be issued under controlled or uncontrolled conditions.

Implement
The implementation of a procedure should include an element of instruction so that all involved personnel are familiar with the content and methods of application.

Monitor and review
After a few weeks of application, the procedure should be audited to verify implementation, effectiveness and adherence. Should the audit indicate a lack of adherence then corrective action should be undertaken to correct and prevent a recurrence of the deficiency. It may well be that the procedure itself does not truly represent actual practice, in which case it should be revised, which would entail a revision 2 (amended as indicated). On the other hand, it may well be that the person involved is not adhering to the procedure due to a variety of reasons, in which case action would be taken to rectify the problem (retraining, awareness or perhaps more drastic measures).

PROCEDURAL FLEXIBILITY

In the final analysis, a procedure is issued to direct people in executing an activity. Whereas it is possible to instruct members of one's own workforce, it is virtually impossible to involve others outside the workplace. Do not, therefore, include in a procedure any activity over which one has no direct control. For example, in a procedure issued by a company there was an instruction for all documentation issued to the client for approval to be routed through the document control section. The procedure also instructed that, after approval, the client shall route documents via the document control section to the originator. In most cases this instruction was not complied with and the documents were returned by the client direct to the originator. This meant that document control had no record of their return. The audit process could not include the client as an auditee, therefore the procedure should not have included an instruction on the client. The end result was to revise the method by which details of incoming documents were advised to document control.

Similarly, do not include in a procedure any instruction to which one cannot always be expected to adhere and, within reason, some flexibility should be permitted. For example, an instruction to undertake an activity in a given time—say within 7 days—may not be feasible during periods where there are many public holidays. The procedure should be flexible enough to accommodate such eventualities. Always ask the question: 'Can this instruction be adequately complied with at all times?'

PROCEDURE STRUCTURE AND FORMAT

To be effective procedures should be consistent in their presentation and uniform in their structure. Management should develop guidelines for their preparation, review and approval. Although procedure format is a matter of personal choice, experience has shown the following six-section format to be effective:

Section 1—Purpose
Section 2—Scope
Section 3—References
Section 4—Definitions
Section 5—Actions
Section 6—Documentation

It is strongly recommended that, when documenting an activity, the future imperative 'shall' rather than 'will' is used in the third person. This stresses the importance of the activity and that it is to be carried out without exception. 'Shall' is mandatory, 'will' signifies an intention and, as is well known: *The road to hell is paved with good intentions.*

CONSISTENCY

Consistency of presentation can be achieved by using:

— standard pre-printed forms
— uniformity of presentation.

Standard forms
It is useful for procedures to be produced on pre-printed forms which provide for the inclusion of some, or all, of the following data:

— the company's name, division or logo
— the title of the document
— the document number
— the revision status and date.

Uniformity of presentation
For ease of reference, procedures should have a standard format. For example:

— The cover page should be identified always as page 1 and carry the following information:
   —the procedure number
   —the procedure title
   —the approval authority
   —revision/edition status.
— Page 2 of a procedure should contain the contents list.

Numbering of pages and the structure and numbering of paragraphs should be consistent.

CONTENTS

Utilizing the agreed format—which in this case would be the six-section format, as
indicated above—the contents would be as follows:

Purpose

This section would outline the objectives or intention of the document. For example, if a
procedure is being written for document control, then this section would read as follows:

> The purpose of this procedure is to provide instruction and to assign responsibility
> for controlling by a systematic sequence of actions the issue, receipt and with-
> drawal of all documents and revisions thereto associated with the accomplishment
> of any work activity and the achievement of quality objectives, specified either by
> contract or company objectives.

Scope

This section would outline the function, department, or group to which the procedure
applies, i.e. it defines the limits of control for each procedure. Again using document
control as an example, the scope could read:

> This procedure is applicable to all documentation generated as a result of imple-
> menting the requirements of either the quality system of the XYZ Company Lim-
> ited or a quality plan developed by the XYZ Company Limited for a contract.

It is, however, important to remember that the wider the scope of the document the more
complicated the document could become and this would defeat the object of simplicity.

References

This section would list all other documents which have a bearing on the activities and
which are discussed or referred to within the body of the procedure itself. Such documents could include: associated procedures; job instructions; legislative directives; national standards.

Definitions

This section would include definitions of all words, acronyms, initials and abbreviations
not generally understood by the reader. It may include the definition of words which have

a specific meaning within a particular context. Where relevant, this section may make reference to associated 'quality' definitions in national standards.

Using the document control procedure, here are some examples of definitions.

Documents
Shall include procedures, specifications, drawings, job instructions, correspondence either individually or collectively.
Procedure
A document detailing the purpose and scope of an activity and specifying by whom and how it is to be properly carried out.

All other definitions are as ISO 8402, 'Quality Vocabulary'.

Actions
This section would detail the actual instructions to be followed in undertaking the activity, stating who does what, how, when, where and possibly why. A flow chart could be used for clarification purposes.

The effectiveness of a procedure can be determined by taking each clause of this section to see if it will turn easily into a question. This is an aid to auditing. For example, using the document control procedure once again, there may be a clause which reads:

All documents retained in the master file shall be filed in lockable fire-resistant filing cabinets.

This can easily be changed to a question by prefixing the statement with 'Are' and omitting 'shall be'. If this clause is being implemented then, of course, the answer would be 'yes'.

Documentation
This section would list any documentation referred to within the procedure and generated as a result of implementing the procedure. A copy or example of each such document should be attached to the procedure as an appendix. As has already been said, it facilitates control if all documents that are generated by a given procedure carry a reference number tracing that document to the procedure.

To qualify this, let us assume that a document storage and retrieval procedure carries the number XYZ–DOC–005, then any supporting forms would be numbered DOC–0051, DOC–0052 and so on. In this way it makes for extreme simplicity when identifying which procedure generates a particular document and vice versa.

General
It is important that the procedure content should always follow the same format without variation. In the event that, for example, there are no references, then under the section entitled 'References' in the procedure the word NONE should be inserted. There is nothing worse than producing similar documents each with the content in a different order.

For reference and development purposes, an example of a typical procedure for writing procedures ('Procedures—Preparation, Style and Format') is given as Appendix B to this book.

Alternative structures
Other possible variations on the above format are:

— *introduction* could replace *purpose*
— *responsibilities* could be identified in a separate section
— *appendices* could be listed and attached as a separate section.

Let us examine these alternatives:

Introduction
This would be the same as *purpose* but could also reference and quote the relevant requirement of an appropriate quality system standard.

Responsibilities
This section would define who is responsible for each activity outlined in the procedure. Experience has shown that, generally, most of the information detailed in a *responsibility* section would be repeated in the *actions* section of the procedure. A separate section covering responsibilities could therefore be considered as superfluous and paper generating.

Appendices
Appendices would include any documents (e.g. supplementary or explanatory notes, organization charts, flow charts, etc.) which are distinct from the main procedure but need to be included for reference.

PROCEDURE WRITING STYLE

Before leaving the subject of the procedure, it is worth while looking into an effective procedure writing style. The ability to put words on to paper so that the result is clear and precise is as important as the contents of the procedure.

The objective of a procedure is to give clear guidance and direction to the reader on the nature of the activity which is to be controlled; how, when, where and by whom such an activity is to be carried out; and where interfaces occur with other related activities. It is important, therefore, to use simple and direct words and to avoid the use of the passive tense and obsolete terms.

Effective writing
Effective writing should be clear, simple and direct. Always make a point of writing for the reader and not for yourself. If the reader has problems in interpreting an instruction, or has difficulty in finding a particular point, then the procedure has not achieved its objective. In such cases, both the writer and the reader have wasted time.

Punctuation

Punctuation is an important part of clear writing and, hence, understanding. Long sentences are generally difficult to comprehend and tend to confuse the reader. It is recommended that sentences and paragraphs be kept as short as possible. In general, the principle is to keep to one instruction per sentence and one theme to a paragraph.

Use of words

Precise wording is very important in procedure writing. Use words or phrases that have specific meanings rather than words or phrases which could be open to interpretation.

Initials, acronyms and abbreviations

Initials, acronyms and abbreviations have become all too commonplace in recent years and, in many instances, can convey different meanings to different industries. It is recommended, therefore, to refrain from using them where they have multiple meanings and to avoid completely their use if they are to occur only once or twice in the procedure. If it should be necessary to use initials, acronyms or abbreviations, because of the multiplicity of occurrences, then such should be listed, together with their full meaning, in the 'definitions' section of the procedure.

Clarity

Long or seldom-used words, together with long rambling sentences, cause problems when implementing procedures. They also present difficulties when auditing. It is possible to measure how clear one's writing is by means of a clarity index (sometimes referred to as a readability index). This is by no means a precise method of measurement but it is a simple aid to clarity. The index works as follows:

1. Choose a section of script containing about 200 words. Disregard titles and headings.
2. Count the major punctuation marks—full stops, question marks and exclamation marks.
3. Divide the number of such major punctuation marks into the total number of words. This will result in the average sentence length. Record this number.
4. Underline all words of three syllables or more. Exclude proper nouns or two syllable words that become three syllables by the addition of a prefix or suffix, such as unhelpful, impolite, expected appointed.
5. Determine the percentage of long words. In a 200-word sample, 40 long words would equate to 20%. Record this percentage.

To arrive at the clarity index, add the average sentence length to the percentage of long words. If the result is below 20, then the text is probably too abrupt. Over 40 indicates there could be difficulties with interpretation.

During an average conversation most people subconsciously use an index of about 30; the average index of newspaper articles on any one day is also about 30.

As a guideline, if the script is written for the reader and if one writes as one speaks, then the index should be about 30. There are limitations in the use of this index but it does provide a quick check on the clarity of one's writing.

Having reached this stage in system documentation, it is worth while recapping on events so far. All the activities from the appointment of the quality representative to the implementation of procedures are described in flow chart form as Fig. 9.3.

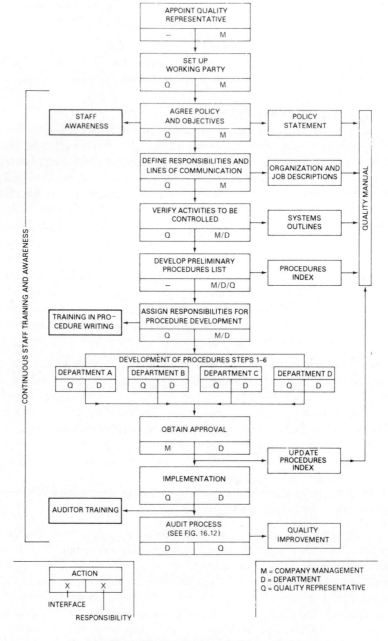

Fig. 9.3—Planning and implementation of the quality system.

10

The quality plan

As was seen in Chapter 2, the quality plan is the quality specification developed for a contract or project. It is developed from a company's quality system and should include any unique requirements applicable to a given contract or project.

The quality system, which will by now have been developed, comprises the quality manual together with the detailed procedures and instructions covering all the critical activities and functions of an organization. Imagine these on a shelf in a bookcase (Fig. 10.1). The quality manual should be a document comprising, at most, 40 pages. The

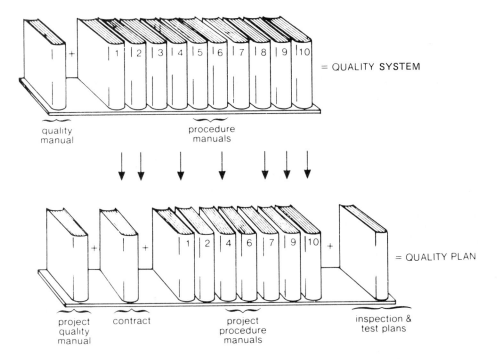

Fig. 10.1—Bookshelf.

procedures themselves, perhaps 50, 60, or more of them depending upon the size of the company and the complexity of its operations, should comprise an average of ten pages each. It is usual to keep all procedures relating to a given subject together under one cover. For example, all those relating to design would be kept together; similarly those relating to procurement, manufacture, quality control, administration, and so on, ending up with a series of what could be termed procedure manuals. The procedures index as described in Chapter 8 gives a good indication of the number of procedure manuals that may be required.

The quality manual, plus these procedure manuals, would then make up a company's quality system.

A complete quality system should be kept by very few people within a company. Generally, the only people who would need to be on a distribution list for the complete system would be those who are concerned with all aspects of the system. In the main, these would be: the senior executive, as that person and his or her management team would have been instrumental in the development and implementation of the quality system and would need to be aware of all activities and functions; the quality assurance manager, as that person and his or her department would be responsible for verifying the implementation and adequacy of the quality system; and the person or department responsible for distribution and control of such documents. Again the 'need to know' rather than the 'want to know' philosophy should prevail.

THE REQUIREMENTS FOR A QUALITY PLAN

This then is the quality system but a company can remain in business only if it has work to do. The work it does may be of a general and continuous nature and, once the quality system has been developed, it could remain continuously viable, apart from routine revisions, perhaps to update working practices or to increase efficiency.

In other circumstances, however, particularly in project-related industries such as civil engineering, power production or petrochemical, a company may be required by contract to undertake certain activities outside the normal scope of its work activities. Conversely, it may be required to undertake only some of the activities within its total scope.

For example, in the first case there could be a contractual requirement for a company to implement identification and traceablity of items which normally it does not do. This would have to be covered by the development and implementation of a procedure to cover such an activity for this contract only.

In the second case, a company could be involved in the design, manufacture and installation of certain items of equipment and would have a quality system designed to meet the requirements of a 'level 1' quality system standard but could win a contract for the manufacture of equipment designed by others. It would be necessary in this case to extract from the quality system only those procedures relating to the manufacturing activities and incorporate into them any contract requirements for additional testing, inspection and the like.

FUNDAMENTAL PROCEDURES

In all circumstances there will be activities which will be common throughout all contracts. They are fundamental to the operation of the company and cannot, and should not, be turned off and on at will. This, unfortunately, is not always the case. There have been a number of instances in the author's experience when undertaking an audit where the auditee has very proudly shown him a production line which operates a 'level 2' quality system. On questioning the auditee regarding other production lines, the answer has been: 'Commercial quality only—the customer doesn't call up any quality standard'. What a philosophy! Once a quality system is installed, it should operate automatically and become so ingrained into everyone's activities that it is a fundamental process. If a customer fails to call for a quality system, this should not be an excuse not to implement one. The type of activities which are fundamental, regardless of customer requirement, comprise such functions as:

Administration
Finance
Document control
Record storage, retention and retrieval
Planning (contract review)
Corrective action
Audits
Training
Customer liaison

This list is not exhaustive.

It surely must be totally uneconomic to switch the control of these activities on and off. What does it cost not to implement a system, notwithstanding the confusion which such a philosophy must cause?

Having said that, then, in the second case, the manufacturing controls applicable to the contract would be automatically supported by those fundamental procedures such as described above. The quality plan would, therefore, address all applicable elements and those procedures unique to the contract would be so identified and amended as necessary to suit. A case in point is the identification of documents. Many customers require a contractor to utilize a contract or project-related numbering system. This must be taken care of within the applicable procedure.

Another instance could be a requirement for a specific test on a piece of equipment. This would need to be documented but, as it relates to hardware rather than to a system, it would be documented in an inspection and test plan, which will be described later.

CONTRACT REQUIREMENTS

In order to develop the quality plan, it is apparent that one must be very familiar with the requirements of the contract work scope; therefore initially a contract review meeting is most important. All activities and functions relating to the contract should be planned. This applies to any type or level of activity—planning is of the utmost importance yet it is surprising that not all quality standards address this activity as an 'all level' requirement. It should be a fundamental activity regardless of quality system level. The scope of such a planning activity is dealt with in later chapters.

Once the contract has been reviewed, then it can be determined which procedures are necessary to control that contract and which of those already established procedures will need to be amended or modified to suit certain contract requirements.

Where required by contract, a contract quality manual should be established in the same manner and format as the corporate quality manual but, in this instance, the policy statement would be signed by the contract or project manager.

CONTRACT ORGANIZATION

The contract or project organization may well differ from that shown in the corporate quality manual and should therefore be identified. Figs 10.2 and 10.3 are typical charts showing a total project organization and the quality assurance function within a project. It should be noted that the quality assurance representative within a project, although initially reporting to the project or contract manager, also has a functional reporting route outside the project back to the corporate quality representative through to the senior executive. Notwithstanding the fact that the project or contract manager has signed the policy statement, the ultimate responsibility for quality still lies with the senior executive and the project manager must himself comply with, and implement, the quality practices of the company.

To emphasize the importance of the contract review meeting as a means of familiarizing the contract or project team with the contents of the contract, a case study is well worth considering.

There was an occasion when the author was employed as a quality assurance manager by a major contractor. This contractor had received a telex from a customer advising that a major design contract was about to be placed with him. The formal signing of the contract was to take place on a predetermined date. It was made known to this contractor that a quality plan was to be developed and implemented within six weeks of contract start date. Initially a project quality manual was to be produced and submitted to the customer for review and concurrence within 14 days of contract start-up.

Although only a telex of intent had been received, the project manager designate felt it would be worth while preparing the project quality manual beforehand and so save time once the contract was signed.

The quality assurance manager was requested to establish such a document so that it could be handed to the customer on the same day that the contract was signed. He accordingly requested the project manager designate for information on the work scope of the contract. This was not available! The quality assurance manager, therefore, said that he was unable to write a project quality manual until the full work scope was known but, because of limited authority within the contractor's organization, the quality assurance manager was virtually ordered by senior management to comply with the request.

Reluctantly the quality assurance manager set about the task of producing the manual on the work scope given orally to him—this being design, procurement and inspection. This meant developing system element outlines for such activities as:

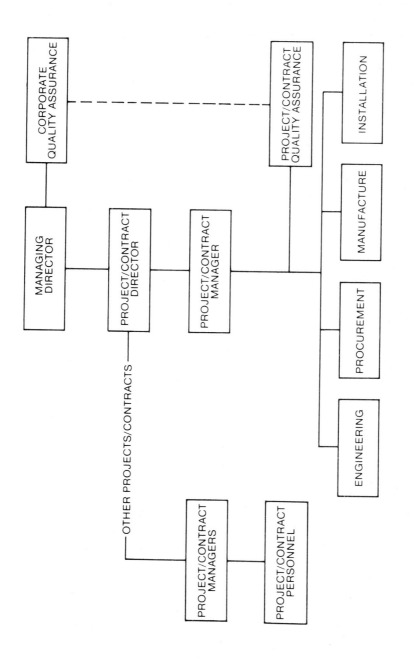

Fig. 10.2—Project/contract organization.

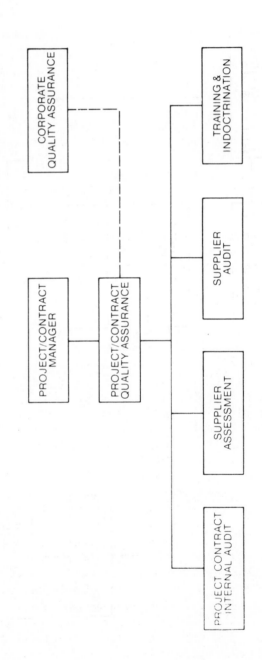

Fig. 10.3—Project/contract quality assurance organization.

Document control
Design control
Change control
Traceability
Reliability
Maintainability
Control of purchased items and services
Internal and external audits
Quality control
Corrective action
Training

The manual was duly completed and handed over to the customer well in advance of the required date.

The project manager was happy because he had beaten the first schedule milestone. The quality assurance manager was very unhappy because he had produced a document under duress, with which he was not satisfied and he had made this known to senior management who had seen fit to ignore the protest.

The worst, however, was yet to come. The contract commenced without the contract team together reviewing the work scope; each lead engineer went about his business in complete isolation, convinced that each knew exactly what his own discipline's involvement was.

The customer, having received the manual, arranged to audit the system as outlined in the manual.

Half the workforce was found not to be in possession of the detailed procedures indexed in the manual. The actual work scope was design only and did not include procurement and quality control activities. In fact, when an analysis was made with regard to percentage compliance, it was found that this contractor was only 40% in compliance with the quality plan as presented in outline form in the manual. The production of the quality manual was a contract requirement and legally the customer could have held that contractor to its contents—particularly as it had received the project manager's approval. The customer, fortunately, chose not to take such a course of action and requested the contractor to revise the manual in line with the contract work scope.

In fact, the customer confirmed that the manual did not reflect the true work scope and should not have been written until the work scope had been established by contract.

If the contractor's senior management had listened to its own quality assurance manager in the first place, then the contractor would not have been placed in such a predicament. There is a good deal of evidence in support of the view that it frequently takes an outside third party source to add credence to a decision or statement made by an employee. The very first documented evidence of such goes back almost two thousand years. The Apostle John wrote: 'For Jesus himself declared that a prophet is without honour in his own country' (John 4:44, New English Bible).

In this particular case, the quality assurance manager's standing within that organization immediately increased and from then on he reported direct to senior management and henceforth could no longer be overruled by a project manager in matters of quality assurance principles and practices. No longer did this contractor pay only lip service to quality requirements as had been the case before this event.

Two lessons emerge from this case study: first, the need to conduct a contract review meeting; second, a confirmation of the need for the independence and authority of the person responsible for quality.

THE PROJECT QUALITY MANUAL

The contents of the project quality manual should, therefore, reflect details of the contract work scope and generally follow the same format as for the corporate quality manual. There will be some differences, as follows:

(a)   The policy statement will reflect the quality policy of the project and will be signed by the project or contract manager.
(b)   Responsibilities will be defined to reflect the requirements of the project or contract.
(c)   The organization will relate to the project and may include customer representation.
(d)   The amendments and reissue will conform to contract requirements.
(e)   The system element outlines will address the applicable criteria of the quality standard specified in the contract.
(f)   The procedure index will identify only those procedures applicable to the contract.

As for the corporate quality system, once the system element outlines have been developed, the supporting procedures can be identified and then taken from the corporate system and used as they stand or amended to suit contract requirements and, where necessary, new procedures written to cover activities not normally undertaken.

The manual, plus the supporting procedures, then become the contract or project quality plan.

11

The inspection and test plan

The quality plan, as described in Chapter 10, could be summed up as a series of documents which serve to direct the activities of personnel assigned to a contract or project.

As has been seen, corporate procedures which are used on contracts or projects may require modification to suit certain contractual requirements, although almost certainly many procedures will require no modification as they are fundamental to everyday activities.

Similarly, in a manufacturing environment there are standard methods of controlling production activities and these activities are formalized in a document known *generally* as an inspection and test plan. The word generally is italicized as the document described in this chapter may unfortunately be given many other titles, such as—'quality control plan', 'quality assurance plan', 'quality plan'—thus adding to the confusion in terminology and to the misunderstanding of quality assurance which presently obtains.

In instances where production of an item is standardized and unvarying, the inspection and test plan should be a standard document indicating the inspection and test requirements relating to the item. In many instances, however, the customer may specify additional inspection and test requirements over and above those stated in the standard documents so as to satisfy certain safety or regulatory requirements or, perhaps, to satisfy some special requirements of the design engineer.

EVIDENCE OF SPECIFIED REQUIREMENTS

At all times it will be necessary to specify in-process and final inspection and/or test requirements. These requirements should be planned in order to provide objective evidence that the manufacture of an item is proceeding, or has been completed, in accordance with the specified requirements. In all cases, so as to reduce subsequent rectification work, the responsibility for the 'correctness' of a manufacturing activity must lie with the person who does the work. This person should not rely on the activities of others subsequently to verify such 'correctness'. The 'self-check' is the first link in the 'assurance chain'.

In all too many instances in the manufacturing environment, 'inspectors' physically remove an item from a machine (lathe, milling, planing, or the like), take it to an inspection bench to check dimensions and surface finish—reject it and return it to the operator who realigns the item on the machine and rectifies the fault. The inspection process is then repeated to verify corrective action. This is a waste of time and effort! Surely it would have been more effective and productive for the operator to have first checked his or her own work; then, if an independent inspection was required, to have the inspection carried out 'in situ'. This approach is by no means uncommon. It also occurs in areas other than manufacturing.

In project management the author has often been presented with a pile of engineering documents and has been asked: 'Have these been quality assured?' The question is best left unanswered.

It should now become apparent that the inspection and test plan bears a certain relationship to the quality plan, as does the quality control activity to the quality system.

The quality system and the quality plan are both total presentations related to the company and the contract or project quality specification respectively. The quality control activity and the inspection and test plan are both related to 'hardware'.

THE NEED FOR AN INSPECTION AND TEST PLAN

The inspection and test plan describes, therefore, the inspections and tests specified for a given item.

The contractor may well be manufacturing many different items for a given contract, or market-place, in which case inspection and test plans for each of the items could be required. These plans will form only part of the quality plan, as many activities over and above actual manufacturing should be controlled, such as design (where necessary), procurement of items and services, document control, records, auditing, training, and so on.

It is not unusual for a customer to request the submission of an inspection and test plan for approval or concurrence before commencement of manufacture. Such submission gives the customer the necessary confidence, or otherwise, that due consideration has been given by the contractor to any special inspection and/or test requirements specified.

There are also many instances where the customer may well formulate his or her own inspection and test plan for a contracted item and impose the requirements upon the contractor. In either event, it should be clearly indicated in the tender documents what is required. It should not be left until the contract has been placed, as this leaves the way open for the contractor to start claiming 'extras'.

FORMAT AND CONTENTS

The inspection and test plan, as with any series of documents, should be of uniform presentation. As with quality manuals and procedures there is no defined format. The presentation is again a matter of personal choice, but it should contain certain basic information, which, as a minimum, should include:

1. Inspection and test points.
2. Inspection requirements.

3.   Mandatory hold points (customer and regulatory).
4.   Sampling schemes (where required).
5.   Applicable standards.

Let us take each in turn:

Inspection and test points
Each inspection and test point should be determined together with its relative location in the production, shipping, installation and commissioning cycle. In the case of small consumer items, there may not be an installation and commissioning activity, but where there is, then there should be a facility for inspection and/or testing during such activities.

Unfortunately, inspection and testing during the installation and commissioning activity is something very often neglected by so called 'quality conscious' companies—particularly those in the building industry. Double glazing, home extensions, central heating, are some which spring readily to mind.

Once the item has been manufactured, the installation and commissioning work is often subcontracted and the prime contractor absolves himself of any further responsibility. If the contract is to supply (manufacture), deliver, install and commission then, regardless of any activities which may be subcontracted to third parties, the prime contractor is responsible all the way down the line and should 'build in' to his own inspection and test plan the necessary controls to assure confidence that each activity in the production, delivery, installation and commissioning cycle is not only right but also right first time, every time.

Inspection requirements
At each specified inspection and/or test point the requirements of such inspection and/or test should be detailed, either in whole or by reference to a particular inspection and/or test procedure. Details of any special equipment required for the inspection and/or test should also be indicated, together with any related qualification/experience criteria of inspection personnel.

Acceptance and rejection criteria should be indicated.

Details of any customer inspection points should also be indicated and a procedure established for liaison with the customer when such inspection points are scheduled.

Mandatory hold points
In many safety-related industries there are mandatory requirements that certain items or processes must be verified, by an approved third party source, as meeting minimum legal requirements. In order that the certifying or regulatory body can determine that such requirements have been met, in certain instances it is necessary to inspect and/or test at predetermined critical 'milestones' during production or installation.

In such instances there will be a requirement imposed on the contractor by the customer that once these defined 'milestones' have been reached no further work should be carried out until the certifying or regulatory body has verified acceptability and has issued a formal instruction to proceed.

Such 'milestones' are given the title *mandatory hold points*. These hold points should be suitably documented or 'flagged' in the inspection and test plan in an 'eye-catching' form. To fail to notify the certifying or regulatory body that such a 'milestone' has been reached could result in, at worst, the item being refused its certificate or, at best, undoing all the work carried out after the mandatory hold points—reverting to bare metal, so to speak.

These hold points should be established in agreement with the certifying body and all responsible personnel made aware of the problems which could arise when failing to notify the appropriate regulatory authority. It is essential, in such instances, that the appropriate interfacing personnel should be identified in project records.

Sampling schemes
Where used, or where specifically required by contract, sampling schemes should be indicated and the location in the manufacturing cycle where they are used should be specified. Reference to published sampling plans should also be indicated. Where applicable, batch or lot sizes should be defined. The acceptance and rejection criteria related to sampling schemes should be also laid down.

Applicable standards
All applicable related standards and procedures should be indicated within the inspection and test plan, together with the latest applicable revision status.

The inspection and test plan is an official document and should be identified and controlled. Amendments to such plans should be procedurally controlled, with the responsibilities for updating and revising being clearly defined.

In some situations it could be a contract requirement that, in the event of amendments, these should be submitted to the customer for approval or concurrence.

Fig. 11.1 is an example of an inspection and test plan document.

The contents of a quality system and a quality plan have now been defined. It is hoped by now the reader will have a firm understanding of what the total presentation of a quality system covers. It is now time to look at the various elements within this total presentation. The first element to be dealt with is design control.

CUSTOMER:	CONTRACT NO.	EQUIPMENT DESCRIPTION:		IDENTIFICATION/ROUTE CARD NO.									REGULATORY BODY	
				QUALITY CONTROL			CUSTOMER			REGULATORY BODY			AUTHORIZATION 1 — QC 2 — CUSTOMER 3 — REG. BODY	
INSPECTION POINT NO.	INSPECTION/TEST DESCRIPTION	INSPECTION/TEST CHARACTERISTICS TO BE VERIFIED	APPLICABLE DOCUMENTATION	ACCEPTANCE CRITERIA	H	W	R	H	W	R	H	W	R	
														1
														2
														3
														1
														2
														3
														1
														2
														3
														1
														2
														3
														1
														2
														3
														1
														2
														3

Legend and Instructions:-
H = Mandatory hold point. Customer/Regulatory Body to be advised 7 days prior to the inspection and test point being reached. No further operations to be carried out until Customer's authorization to proceed is received.
W = Witness point. Quality Control and Customer/Regulatory Body to be advised.
R = Review of documents required.

PLAN NO.

REVISION

APPROVAL

XYZ-QC-008.1

Fig. 11.1—Inspection and test plan.

12

Design control

It is regrettable that most expertise in what is termed quality engineering currently lies in controlling the quality of manufacture, and a great deal of time and effort is spent in assessing manufacturers' abilities to control their own quality. Manufacturers can be assessed and audited regularly and, indeed, they often are. In fact, it is not unknown for a single manufacturer to be audited or assessed a dozen times in as many months.

But what do such activities tell the customer? Only how good this manufacturer's procedures and controls are. Yet, if the design is in error, this manufacturer, even though his procedures and controls are more than adequate, will present the customer with hardware which is unsuitable for the service requirements.

At the risk of stating the obvious, it is therefore essential for the design to be right before placing the specification with a manufacturer. This means that not only should the design be correct but it should be correct first time. In order for this to be achieved it is necessary to put design controls on a formal basis and to develop a quality plan which meets the needs of the contract scope of work. It is worth while considering how an engineering department or design contractor can use quality assurance as a means of controlling design.

The first problem facing an engineering department or a design contractor is that, in the main, industry has not as yet agreed the need for, let alone a uniform approach to, quality assurance. Existing quality system standards are not completely comprehensive as far as engineering design is concerned. While such standards as BS 5882 and ANSI/ASME NQA.1 go a long way towards meeting design control requirements, they would be generally unacceptable to most of industry because of their nuclear connotations. ISO 9001 does bridge the gap to a certain extent but, in the author's opinion, does not go far enough. Therefore some of the controls discussed here will not be found in all of the quality system standards, yet they do reflect what is perhaps becoming the general custom and practice.

DESIGN PROCEDURES AND INSTRUCTIONS

The procedures, methods and instructions to be utilized on a project or contract will probably comprise corporate documents, amended where necessary to suit specific contract requirements. In all cases, these contract procedures should be reviewed and approved by the appropriate contract manager in conjunction with the quality assurance manager and the relevant discipline or department manager. The customer will very probably wish to see and review them also and give his agreement before they are released.

Each manager of an engineering department or design contractor should be responsible for maintaining up-to-date procedure manuals for his area of management, including procedures for:

(1) the checking of such documents as drawings, data sheets, calculations and specifications;

(2) the control of design or construction work by the use of philosophies, procedures and standards;

(3) standard preparation methods for specifications, data sheets, drawings and work packages.

Each lead discipline engineer or supervisor should ensure that all significant activities are properly conducted and documented throughout a contract or project, verifying that:

(a) all necessary data, specifications, standards and other documents are available before the start of any activity;

(b) all the required work, drawings, reports and calculations are in fact produced during each activity;

(c) all the required checks, reviews and audits are carried out on completion of each activity;

(d) any deviation from the above requirements is properly documented;

(e) all documents are systematically numbered or otherwise identified, filed, updated as required, and held securely in a system which ensures that they are readily available upon request to assist reviews or audits by the contract or project team, the relevant corporate discipline manager, quality assurance staff or the customer's representative.

THE MAJOR ACTIVITIES

The controls considered to be the most important in a design activity have been compiled for ease of reference into a tabulated form (Fig. 12.1).

It will be seen that this table is divided vertically under four headings, as follows:

Design control activity—which is self-explanatory.

Scope—which identifies the scope of work within that activity.

Performed by—which identifies those involved in, and who are responsible for, that activity.

Action by QA—which summarizes the responsibilities of the quality assurance department to verify that the activity is being, or has been, effectively implemented and controlled.

DESIGN CONTROL			
DESIGN CONTROL ACTIVITY	SCOPE	PERFORMED BY	ACTION BY QA
1 Contract review	Review: Work scope Specifications and standards Philosophies Design criteria Regularity requirements Organization	Project management Discipline engineers Quality assurance	Verify that missing or ambiguous informa- tion has been fol- lowed up and satisfactorily closed out by the responsi- ble person
2 Document preparation, control and retention	Ensure correct and uniform presentation of docu- ments Ensure formal preparation, identification, checking, approval and distribution, including amendments Verify retention, retrieval, storage and hand over re- quirements	Project management Discipline engineers (Customer)	Audit adherence to pro- cedure
3 Discipline check	Verify content and accuracy of documents originating from own discipline	Relevant discipline	Audit adherence to pro- cedure
4 Interdiscipline check	Assure compatibility of de- sign between design dis- ciplines. Accuracy of content	Project management Discipline engineers	Audit distribution and approval. Verify as necessary that comments have been closed out by the originating engineer
5 Internal design review	Review of design activities in progress or completed	Project management Discipline engineers Quality assurance	Verify that comments have been closed out
6 Design interface control (see also 4)	Check physical interfaces between systems/contrac- tors, authorities	Project management Discipline engineers (Other contractors) (Customer)	Audit distribution and approval. Verify that comments have been closed out
7 Change control	Check changes in design criteria	Project management Discipline engineers	Monitor changes as re- quired to close out and approval
8 External design reviews	Detailed audit of design —Adequacy of design —Adherence to contract —Account taken of studies	Independent teams of dis- cipline engineers (In-house or customer)	Project management also involved. Audit to verify that any non-conformances have been closed out
9 Audit and corrective action	Ensure non-conformances promptly identified and corrective action taken to prevent recurrence	Project management Discipline engineers Quality assurance	Co-ordinate and verify that corrective action completed and that action has been taken to prevent re- currence

Fig. 12.1—Design control matrix.

Contract review

This is a most important activity but unfortunately insufficient emphasis is given to it in most quality assurance standards. Before any work starts, it is important that all concerned are aware of their responsibilities within the design contract and that they have the right tools with which to perform their job. A review team must therefore be assembled, comprising contract or project management, discipline lead engineers and quality assurance representative.

Work scope
The review team should consider in detail the scope of work and should establish that this is fully understood by all concerned and that the quality plan identifies all the required procedural controls to cover the true scope.

Specifications and standards
It should be ensured that all applicable specifications and standards, of correct issue, are readily available at all activity locations.

Philosophies
These can cover studies, design philosophies—even quality assurance philosophies (where these could be interpreted in different ways). Are these philosophies agreed upon and understood?

Design criteria
Are they all available and understood?

Regulatory requirements
If any regulatory authority is involved regarding safety and/or environmental requirements, then the contract or project team should be aware of all parties involved and the exact nature of the statutory requirements in their current form.

Organization
Who does what in the contract or project task-force? Who reports to whom and what are each individual's terms of reference? If the organization is defined and made generally known immediately, then there can be no misconception about reporting responsibilities. A considerable amount of time and misunderstanding can be avoided when the right person to approach concerning any given issue is known.

The same must also be said for the customer's organization. The customer's representatives who interviewed the project team prior to contract placement need not necessarily be the same people who will be representing the customer on the actual project. In many instances they are not and they may have different ideas and philosophies.

To emphasize the requirements that personnel should be aware of customer's current philosophies, it is worth while considering a not uncommon example.

In one such instance, prior to contract placement, discussions duly took place between the quality assurance managers representing the supplier and customer who 'spoke the same language' with regard to quality assurance philosophies.

When the contract was eventually placed, the customer appointed his own project quality assurance manager who had a different approach from that discussed and agreed before contract placement. The philosophies presented by the customer's project quality assurance manager proved to be a 'super-checking' activity, which caused the contractor having either to protest vehemently to the customer and stand his ground or to accept the situation and 'staff-up' the quality assurance group to fulfil the additional responsibilities placed upon him.

As this situation occurred during the halcyon days when most major projects were reimbursed on a basis of time-cost or cost plus rather than lump sum payment, it suited the contractor to take on the additional staff required and to submit a change order to cover the additional costs incurred.

In the long run, neither the customer nor the contractor really benefited from this. The contractor would have made an additional, but unexpected, profit—for which the customer duly paid but it did not increase the contractor's efficiency. In fact, it would have had the opposite effect.

Additionally, the customer suffered because when the time came to let future contracts that same contractor, remembering the previous experience, would build into the bid the cost of the necessary resources to cover a 'super-checking' activity. Other possible bidders, having heard about the experience, would no doubt include a similar contingency cost.

This philosophy can do nothing other than increase what could, in the final analysis, be termed quality costs. The checking activities performed by the project quality assurance department in such a situation should have been carried out by the departments or disciplines actually responsible for undertaking that work.

In this and similar instances, of which there have been many, such costs were not associated with putting things right but with duplicating activities carried out by others. One could ask the question: 'Who eventually benefits from such a philosophy?' In all probability—no one!

Action by quality assurance

The contract review meeting, as for any formal meeting, should be minuted. Minutes of meetings, as for any series of documents, should be produced in a formalized manner. Actions identified during this meeting should be placed on individuals and not departments. These individuals will be named under an action column in the minutes (see Fig. 12.2 for a typical minutes format).

The quality assurance representative should utilize these minutes as a form of checklist and would verify that actions placed on individuals had been dealt with satisfactorily. Where the action remains unresolved, then steps are taken by the quality assurance representative to expedite resolution.

This type of activity is known as auditing and will be dealt with in much greater detail later.

Document preparation, control and retention

Document preparation is another important activity not given sufficient attention. Documents in this context cover drawings, specifications, data sheets and so on. These should be presented in a correct and uniform manner. Personnel quite often have different ideas on how documents should be formulated. Sometimes ideas developed for previous contracts or projects are used and may not be compatible with current requirements and the

XYZ COMPANY	MINUTES OF MEETING NO.	
Client/Contractor	Contract/ Project No.	
Place & Date of Meeting	Date typed	
Subject:	Typed by:	
	Page of	
PRESENT	DISTRIBUTION	
ITEM	DESCRIPTION OF DISCUSSION	ACTION BY

XYZ-MAN-007.1

Fig. 12.2—Minutes.

rules need to be overhauled. A uniform approach should be agreed, defined and communicated to all concerned before work commences. The customer should be brought into these discussions, since there may be specific contract requirements. For example, the customer may require standard drawings based on A1 sizes and he would be very concerned to find that at the end of a contract the design for which he has paid is presented as a large number of A0 sized drawings, which are too large for existing files and which cause the additional expense of purchasing new filing equipment for which there is no suitable accommodation.

Uniform document presentation helps to avoid errors and facilitates checking, allowing more use of standard checking routines. It is far easier to handle documents when, for example, the contract or project number can always be found in the same corner. It is difficult and time-consuming to check documents whose contents are distributed in different patterns or sequences.

Document identification should be standardized and controlled using logical procedures. Complex numbering systems should be avoided, as these tend to confuse rather than assist in identification and retrieval of documents. The simpler the system the easier it is to operate and control. Numbering systems should, as a minimum, contain the following:

— Contract or project number.
— Document type (denoting whether it is a specification, purchase requisition, design brief, data sheet or drawing).
— Document serial number.
— Document revision status.

The following is a typical arrangement for document identification:

```
                                               8742—S—345—1
Contract or project number ———————————————————┘   │   │   │
Document type ————————————————————————————————————┘   │   │
Serial number ————————————————————————————————————————┘   │
Revision status ——————————————————————————————————————————┘
```

Whatever the identification system to be used, the customer will probably require some input and should be consulted before the system is put to use on the contract.

Document approval procedures should be formalized and all those carrying the authority to give approval at each stage (including the customer's representatives) should be named. Specimen sets of initials or signatures should be registered in the appropriate records.

Document checking, including amendments
Checking routines should be formulated. These routines should include as a minimum the types of documents to be checked, the methods of checking and the personnel responsible for checking.

It is important to establish the types of documents to be checked and not make it mandatory for all. In all too many cases has a senior engineer been seen to be furiously appending his signature to a great pile of drawings. All this process involved was for him to lift the bottom right-hand corner of each of the drawings in the pile and sign it off as checked. No attention was paid to the content of the drawings and so this 'checking' routine became a meaningless and mechanical exercise.

Why was it done? Because instructions were given that all drawings should be checked regardless of content. A waste of valuable time.

The same principle should apply in the approval of documents. Those which require approval, and by whom the approval is to be given, should be clearly stated. It is as well, also, to specify those which do not require such approval so as to avoid misunderstanding.

The checking and approval of amendments to documents should be similarly formalized.

Document distribution
In these days of readily available (if expensive) photocopying, the sending of copies of all documents to everyone who might conceivably be interested in seeing them is all too common. Such instances are counter-productive and self-defeating. Procedures should, therefore, be established to identify which documents are really needed by selected recipients. Many people may wish to be included on the distribution list whether they need to be or not. Involvement by those who have no need to get involved creates confusion. A matrix chart which lists document types along the left-hand vertical column and has the remaining columns headed with all potential recipients is a useful and concise method for denoting the standard distribution arrangements for documents. In the matrix, each box will link a document type with a possible addressee, and the matrix will automatically cover all possible permutations. It is simply necessary to leave blank boxes where there is to be no distribution. In each case where documents need to be sent to an addressee, the number of sets to be sent is written in the relevant box. It is stressed again that this should be arranged strictly on a 'need to know' rather than a 'want to know' basis.

A formalized procedure for distribution is also essential to ensure not only that each person who requires documents appears on the list, so that he or she gets them in the first place, but also to ensure that they are in the right quantities (number of sets), of the correct form (e.g. full-sized drawings or microfilms), and that the initial issues are backed up by all revisions.

Retention, retrieval, storage and handover
Details should be documented covering the procedures to be implemented to control document retention, retrieval, storage and handover.

In all probability there will be specific contractual requirements for retention of documents and records generated during the execution of the contract. For example, many sector-based quality assurance specifications demand a limited period for retention of documents. The safety-related industries may be required to retain documents for 25 years or more. Provision should be made to fulfil these requirements.

The longer the retention period the more susceptible the documents will become to damage and/or loss, therefore provision should be made for proper storage and for the method of storage to be adopted. If hard copies are to be retained, then space becomes a major factor, as does the size and type of the containers to be used. The storage problem can be minimized by the use, if approved, of computerized data storage or microfilm.

Whatever the retention period and storage methods, there should be a system installed to facilitate ease of retrieval should the need arise—as is very often the case.

Where computerized data storage is utilized, it is worth while remembering that the means to read the information should be retained. There have been instances, in the author's experience, where computerized records were found to be irretrievable because the current hardware had replaced outmoded equipment but little thought had been given to archived data.

On contract completion, if there is a requirement that documents must be handed over to the customer, then the method of handover should be documented.

All these requirements should be considered in the planning stage of a contract or project and not left until documents start to be generated.

Regardless of company size, there is always the need properly to control documentation.

The action by quality assurance would be to verify, initially, the formulation of all necessary procedures to control the document control activity, and to confirm that such procedures have received the required approvals, and subsequently audit to verify the implementation and adherence to the document control system.

Discipline check

A discipline check is carried out to verify the content and accuracy of a document originating from a single engineering discipline. Such checks should be performed by engineers of the appropriate discipline but the checking engineer must not be the same person who carried out the original work. The checker should be of at least the same grade of seniority as the originating engineer. In the case of a one-man discipline (which often occurs on small contracts), it will be necessary to appoint the checker from outside the contract from a corporate department, from another project team or, in the case of extremely critical design, from some qualified third party source.

This type of check not only checks engineering calculations but also the integrity and application of the design. Hence the requirement for the experience qualifications of the engineer carrying out this check to be of, at least, the same level as the originating engineer. Where an independent check of a calculation is required the check should also be done by independent means.

The discipline check procedure should identify the documents which require to be checked and the methods for undertaking the check. One method, for example, would be the issuance of a check print and the checker would identify each satisfactory item in a denoting colour (say green) with queries and/or comments on unsatisfactory or ambiguous conditions in a contrasting colour (say red). The check print would be returned to the originating engineer for action as necessary. This check print should be retained for control purposes. The document, when completed satisfactorily, would be signed by the checker and, when required, by the approval authority.

Before any document is put forward for checking it is in the originating engineer's own interest to verify the quality of his or her own work by means of a self-check. This should be a fundamental requirement practised by all personnel regardless of discipline.

The action by quality assurance would be again to verify initially the formulation and approval of the required procedure to cover this activity and, subsequently, to audit, as required, to confirm compliance.

Interdiscipline check

Interdiscipline checking assesses not only the content and accuracy of a document but assures compatibility between all the design disciplines involved.

This is an important activity and, if carried out correctly, will minimize manufacturing and installation problems. To give an example, there are many instances in the installation phase of a contract where proper consideration proves not to have been given to the routing of pipework, ducting, cabling and the like, resulting in a great deal of rectification work on site. Liaison between the involved disciplines at the design stage would reduce costs in such instances. It seems obvious that the routing of heating, ventilation and air-condition ducting should be known before concreting takes place on site. Liaison between the HVAC discipline, the architectural and structural disciplines at the design stage is imperative, otherwise it may well become necessary to drill through concrete and steel to accommodate the ducting. Unfortunately, this tends to happen all too often. Such rectification work could have an effect on the integrity of the structural design and may affect safety standards, particularly so if such work is carried out without consulting or liaising with the originating design engineer, as again happens all too frequently.

In the case of an interdiscipline check, a procedure should be developed that would identify which documents would be subjected to such a check, the distribution of the documents and the methods to be adopted when commenting on such documents. The procedure would also identify those responsible for commenting.

Here a document distribution list would be important and it should list all those required to comment on a document. Figs 12.3, 12.4 and 12.5 are typical examples of such lists. There is also the need to log all documents on an interdiscipline check and Fig. 12.6 shows a typical register. There are various ways of distributing documents for interdiscipline checks.

Parallel issue

This issue, although expeditious, entails considerable copying of documents and requires a strict control. The document to be reviewed is issued simultaneously to all interfacing disciplines for their review and comment. The latest date for the return of comments should be indicated and every involved discipline should make comment, even where this means writing 'no comment'. The department responsible for document control should issue the review copies on behalf of the originating discipline, and control and expedite progress to ensure the return of all copies within the latest completion date. Parallel issue is obviously the method best suited where a fast turn-round of documents is required.

Circular issue

As its name implies, this depends upon the circulation of a single issue of the document which is circulated to all interfacing disciplines on a 'round robin' basis. This type of distribution is used where urgency is not the first priority. Care should be taken in arranging the list to include the disciplines required to make comment in order of priority.

DOCUMENTS PRODUCED BY **Mechanical** DISCIPLINE	ARCHITECTURAL	ELECTRICAL	FIRE & SAFETY	HVAC	INSTRUMENTATION	MECHANICAL	PROCESS	STRUCTURAL	QUALITY ASSURANCE	PROJECT MANAGER	
GENERAL SPECIFICATIONS		√	A			O					
UNIQUE SPECIFICATIONS		√	A			O					
PHILOSOPHIES		√				O				√	
REPORTS		√	A			O				√	
STUDIES		√	A			O				√	
CALCULATIONS	NOT GIVEN AN IDC										
DRAWINGS	√	√	A					√	√		
DATA SHEETS	√	√	A					√			
REQUISITIONS	NOT GIVEN AN IDC										
MECHANICAL EQUIPMENT		√	√			O	A				

IDC   MATRIX MINIMUM DISTRIBUTION
O=   ORIGINATOR
√=   REVIEW
A=   REVIEW AS APPLICABLE

XYZ-ENG-002.1

Fig. 12.3—IDC matrix.

IDC REVIEW TRANSMITTAL FORM				IDC NO:	
DOCUMENT TITLE: DOCUMENT NO: DISCIPLINE: IDC REQUESTED BY:				REVISION NO: DATE:	
CONTROL DATES					
TO ACTUAL	FROM REQUIRED	FROM ACTUAL	CIRC. ORDER	DISCIPLINE	REVIEWER'S SIGNATURE
				ARCHITECTURAL	
				ELECTRICAL	
				FIRE & SAFETY	
				HVAC	
				INSTRUMENTATION	
				MECHANICAL	
				PROCESS	
				STRUCTURAL	
				QUALITY	
				PROJECT MANAGER	
RETURN 'IDC' COPY TO: REMARKS:					

Fig. 12.4—IDC matrix.

Here again the department responsible for document control, after issuing the document on behalf of the originating engineer, should expedite and control its progress around the circuit. As for parallel issues, all involved disciplines should make comment.

IDC REVIEW		
REVISION		
DISCIPLINE	SIGNATURE	DATE
ARCHITECTURAL		
ELECTRICAL		
FIRE & SAFETY		
HVAC		
INSTRUMENTATION		
MECHANICAL		
PROCESS		
STRUCTURAL		
QUALITY		
PROJECT MANAGER		

Fig. 12.5—IDC matrix.

Flood issue, in conjunction with a review meeting
This is similar to a parallel issue but, instead of inviting comments through the distribution circuit, a meeting is called to review and co-ordinate any such comments. As for any meeting, minutes will be tabled and these will list the comments made for the subsequent attention of the originating discipline. Minutes of meetings are objective evidence of quality and can be used by quality assurance personnel as checklists for audit purpose.

   The action by quality assurance would be as for the previous activities.

Internal design review
At important stages throughout design activities, internal design review meetings should be called to review progress. These meetings will consider all aspects of activities to date. There may be areas of concern, perhaps even updated information from the customer or new legislation concerning such items as safety and certification.

   Internal design reviews should be undertaken on a regular basis and should be scheduled at contract commencement. The scheduling of such reviews will be determined by management based upon the duration and complexity of the contract work scope. Regardless of duration of contract, even if only a few weeks, at least one review should be scheduled.

   The methods of scheduling reviews, the people involved, the location and details of such reviews should be subject to procedural controls as with any other activity.

INTERDISCIPLINE CHECK (IDC) REGISTER

IDC No.	DOCUMENT DETAILS			ORIGINATING DISCIPLINE	DATE IDC COMMENCED	ESTIMATED DATE IDC COMPLETED	DATE IDC COMPLETED	REMARKS
	No.	REV.	TITLE					

XYZ-ENG-002.2

Fig. 12.6—IDC register.

All meetings of this kind should be minuted and any action required assigned to individuals.

The action by quality assurance would be to confirm by audit that any such assigned actions have been satisfactorily dealt with by the person or persons concerned.

Design interface control

Although the design interface control could be linked to the interdiscipline check, it goes far deeper. Design interface control sets out to control the interfaces between systems, contractors, and even regulatory bodies. There are many instances in large projects where more than one design contractor is used, creating not only interfaces between disciplines within one organization but complex interfaces between the different contractors. The problems encountered in persuading all parties to liaise with one another are enormous, but not insurmountable. Providing that each of the participating organizations has a compatible design control system, the interface control can work smoothly. A strong customer is needed to set the rules and to get all concerned to keep to them. If different philosophies are allowed to prevail, then interface control can be a great problem.

Methods of interfacing, together with the interface areas, should be clearly defined. The distribution chain for documentation should be directed through a single channel so that definite control is established. In such instances, it is usual to appoint an interface engineer to define the methods and procedures. The customer should be responsible for this activity.

The overall control of this activity, and the responsibility for auditing the interface system, must lie with the customer if this activity is to be effective.

Change control

The control of engineering changes is another very important activity which some quality assurance standards treat much too lightly. It usually receives only a passing mention under the subject of 'document control'. It is generally accepted that many of the major problems arise through the lack of engineering change control, with changes being made to a design without reference to the original design source.

Design changes can emanate from many areas: changes in client requirements, updated information from external sources, new legislation from government bodies relating to safety, environmental matters and the like, and internally from departments within the contracting organization. All must be documented and they must be subjected to consideration and review in the same systematic manner as the original documents. In addition to aspects of quality, these reviews have to take into account the likely effect of each proposed change on the costs and schedule. Formal procedures for controlling engineering changes will ensure that the customer is always consulted where this is relevant, and a suitably qualified group of people will be selected to give approval to, or reject, each change considered (typically known as a change committee).

Engineering changes could be, in the final analysis, termed document changes, as any change in design will ultimately result in an amendment to design documents. In the author's experience, however, engineering changes should be procedurally controlled separately from ordinary document changes.

The system for control of engineering changes should ensure that such changes, from wherever they originate, are channelled or directed through one recording area, both in and out.

The system should also ensure that all engineering changes are properly documented and receive approval from the responsible person. Responsibilities for authorization of changes should be identified in the same manner as for the authorization of the original design.

The level of engineering changes should also be documented. There may be some small changes which could well be authorized by the site manager. Other, more important changes, which could affect the integrity of the design, should be referred back to the original design source for authorization and approval.

The following are examples of engineering changes which could require alternative procedural controls:

1. Additions to the contracted scope of work which result in changes to specifications.
2. Changes to specifications that become necessary to maintain the design integrity.
3. Changes to specifications that are proposed as desirable to meet new or additional requirements relating to safety, efficiency, cost and schedule, and also those which become necessary to meet customer requirements resulting from market research.
4. Changes to the original scope of work due to the activities of third party sources which result in excess variations to cost, time and resources.

Whatever the change, it should be controlled and authorized at the appropriate level.

Where changes could affect the activities of others, then engineering change control should ensure that, in such cases, the interfacing disciplines are given the opportunity to comment on them. In other words, they are distributed on an interdiscipline check.

In the case of a change in design to meet customer attitudes—consumer items for example—there should be the means to review the impact of such changes. The department concerned with market research should interface not only with the design department but with sales, finance and production. A change in design to accommodate customer requirements may well prove to be totally uneconomic and difficult to achieve. It is therefore important that the procedures should clearly expose this.

Fig. 12.7 is an example of a typical design modification proposals, which shows the source of the required change and the description of the change (part 1).

At this stage, the decision to proceed or not to proceed further with the change is taken by the responsible person, in this case the project manager (part 2).

If the decision is to proceed, then all involved disciplines estimate the effect of the proposed change on their individual disciplines (part 3).

The effect of the cost in time and resources should be documented and Fig. 12.8 is an example of a typical form which identifies such costs.

Once the impact of the change is calculated, it is then documented in part 4 of the design modification proposal, which is then accepted or rejected by the designated person (part 5).

Should the proposal receive approval by the contractor's management, then it should go forward to the customer for authorization to proceed. A change in the contract will be

XYZ COMPANY	DESIGN MODIFICATION PROPOSAL	PROJECT TITLE PROJECT No. DMP No.

PART 1.
ACTIVITY
ORIGINATOR   DISCIPLINE   DATE

SOURCE OF MODIFICATION PROPOSAL — INDICATE
☐ CLIENT   ☐ XYZ COMPANY   ☐ OTHER

DESCRIPTION OF MODIFICATION (SKETCH, DESCRIPTION
GENERAL INFORMATION, e.g. AFFECTED DOCUMENTS)

PART 2.
THIS MODIFICATION PROPOSAL IS REJECTED/ACCEPTED
FOR FURTHER PROCESSING REASON/AFFECTED
DISCIPLINE

SIGNED.................
PROJECT MANAGER

PART 3.
.........DISCIPLINE. PLEASE ESTIMATE THE EFFECT OF THE ABOVE
PROPOSED MODIFICATION ON YOUR DISCIPLINE

DOCUMENT AFFECTED

☐ FLOW DIAGRAMS	☐ FIRE PROTECTION	☐ CERTIFICATION
☐ P & I.D.	☐ TELECOMS	☐ COMMISSIONING
☐ GA/LAYOUT	☐ OPERATIONS	☐ MAINTENANCE
☐ STRUCT. DRG	☐ STUDIES	☐ FABRICATION
☐ PIPING DRG	☐ REQUISITION	☐ INSTALLATION
☐ INSTR. DRG	☐ SPECIFICATION	☐ HOOK-UP
☐ ELECT. DRG	☐ INTERFACE	☐ HISTOGRAMS
☐ OTHER DRG	☐ WEIGHT	☐ SCHEDULE
☐ VENDOR DRG	☐	☐

PART 4.
SUMMARY OF MODIFICATION IMPACT.

SIGNED.................
PROJECT PLANNING ENGINEER

PART 5.
THIS MODIFICATION PROPOSAL IS ACCEPTED/REJECTED.
PREPARE DMR   YES/NO

SIGNED.................
PROJECT MANAGER

XYZ-ENG-003.1

Fig. 12.7—Design modification proposal.

XYZ COMPANY	SUMMARY OF ADDITIONAL HOURS AND COSTS	PROJECT TITLE
		DMR No.

ENGINEERING & DRAUGHTING HOURS

POSITION / DISCIPLINE	DIRECTOR/ PROJECT MANAGER	SENIOR ENGINEER	ENGINEER	INTERFACE ENGINEER	WEIGHT CONTROL ENGINEER	SENIOR DESIGNER/ CHECKER	DRAUGHTS PERSON	PLANNING ENGINEER	DOCUMENT CONTROLLER	QUALITY ASSURANCE
ARCHITECTURAL										
ELECTRICAL										
FIRE & SAFETY										
INSTRUMENTATION										
INTERFACE CONTROL										
LOSS CONTROL										
MECHANICAL/HVAC										
PROCESS/PIPING										
STRUCTURAL										
QUALITY ASSURANCE										
WEIGHT CONTROL										
ESTIMATED TOTALS										
PROJECT CONTROL										
PURCHASING										
EXPEDITING										
ESTIMATED TOTALS										
ESTIMATED OVERALL MANPOWER COSTS										

SUMMARY OF MODIFICATION COSTS

MANPOWER COSTS		
COMMUNICATIONS		
PRINTING & COMPUTER		
TRAVEL & SUBSISTENCE		
OTHER		
OVERALL TOTAL COSTS		

XYZ-ENG-003.2

Fig. 12.8—Summary of additional hours and costs.

required and this should be documented. Fig. 12.9 is a typical example of a design modification request form.

The action by quality assurance would be to verify the formulation and approval of the necessary procedures to control engineering changes and to monitor, as necessary, such changes through to the designated design source for action, approval and close out.

XYZ COMPANY	DESIGN MODIFICATION REQUEST	PROJECT TITLE PROJECT NO:
TO:	DATE:	INITIATOR ☐ CLIENT ☐ CONTRACTOR

TITLE:	PAYMENT ☐ LUMP SUM ☐ REIMBURSABLE ☐ UNIT RATE

CONTRACTOR IS HEREBY INSTRUCTED TO PROCEED
WITH THE WORK DESCRIBED HEREUNDER:

APPLICABLE CORRESPONDENCE

ADJUSTMENT TO CONTRACT: TOTAL ESTIMATED HOURS	TOTAL ESTIMATED COST

DOCUMENTS AFFECTED

ESTIMATED IMPACT ON PROGRAMME

WORK TO COMMENCE BY:	EFFECT ON CONTRACT SCHEDULE:
PLANNED COMPLETION DATE:	EFFECT ON MANNING

ACCEPTED BY CONTRACTOR	APPROVED BY CLIENT
NAME:	NAME:
SIGNATURE:	SIGNATURE:
DATE:	DATE:

XYZ-ENG-003.3

Fig. 12.9—Design modification request.

External design reviews

External design reviews can be carried out either by the contracting company itself, using its own corporate disciplines, or by the customer. The reviews amount to a detailed audit of the design, verifying such items as design adequacy, adherence to contract and the account taken of studies. The timing of these reviews is usually stated in the contract or project schedule, so they should come as a surprise to no one. It is pertinent to pose a number of key questions:

Adequacy of design

Does this accord with the scope of work? This corresponds with the first listed design control, 'contract review'.

Adherence to contract

Has due consideration been given to all contract clauses?

Studies

Has due considerations been given to the results of all field studies which may have been carried out by others?

Engineering management also should be involved in monitoring the results of such a review. All comments and non-conformances should be documented and monitored through to close out and approval.

In addition to the design controls so far described, the terms of the contract, or even the nature of the industry, may call for requirements relating to:

Traceability
Weight and centre of gravity control
Reliability
Criticality
Maintainability
and others

All these should be taken into consideration at the contract review stage and the necessary controls established and implemented.

Traceability

In cases where traceability of certain materials, components and equipment is required, it will be necessary to implement and operate a system which will trace such materials, components and equipment to their specific source and identify them with their respective material and test certificates.

Traceability, in such instances, should operate throughout the design, manufacture, installation and operational life of the unit.

It should be the responsibility of the relevant design engineer to determine which items require traceability. It is not the quality assurance department's responsibility. A system for traceability should provide for:

(a)   the traceability of materials, components and equipment which may contribute to an accident resulting in loss of life, injury or loss of production;

(b)   the establishment, with certainty, of the number and location of all materials, components and equipment items, which, if found to be defective, should be replaced;

(c)   the data and information necessary for the preparation of the most efficient maintenance procedures;

(d)   the data and information necessary for generating future design modification and improvements.

The extent of traceability to be applied to materials, components and equipment should be specified in the contract documents and should be governed by its application and potential contribution to a safety or loss of production related incident.

The above statement on traceability control would serve as a typical system outline for a quality manual.

The contract review meeting should establish traceability when required and this should be identified in the minutes of the review meeting.

The action by quality assurance should be to verify that traceability requirements have been identified and that the necessary action has been taken to implement such requirements.

To illustrate how traceability could operate, it is worth while considering an actual example. A particular contract called up a requirement for a quantity of a special type of relief valve, to be inserted in different locations in the high-pressure system of a major plant.

The relief valve bodies were to be constructed from a very sophisticated material and traceability was required both 'in and out'.

In this case, the requirement would be not only to trace the material in to the supplier through the material certification but to trace the material out again via its heat and cast numbers to other valves which had bodies made from the same batch of material.

This 'in and out' traceability is particularly important in high safety-related projects where a number of identical components have been manufactured from the same heat or cast of material.

In the event of failure of one of the components, it would then be necessary to trace the location of all other components which have been manufactured from the same batch in order to take remedial action.

Traceability in such cases demands strict control. Computerization of the information can ease the burden substantially.

The material certification documentation should identify each valve body with a unique number, together with its specific location in the plant.

Location details should identify the material certification and where it is filed. This, of course, highlights the necessity for the strict control of documentation discussed earlier.

Weight and centre of gravity control

This is a requirement relating particularly to two industries: offshore oil and gas structures; and to certain civil engineering installations. In such cases there are requirements to establish weight limits and to control the weight of equipment and material so as to keep below such limits.

For example, an offshore oil drilling and production platform will operate in a known depth of water. The jacket structure (i.e. the supporting framework for the platform and superstructure) will be designed to support a predetermined topside weight. The total topside weight will be calculated using information obtained from material and equipment suppliers, and others.

Once determined, the weight of the material and equipment should be monitored. This will mean that each specification should include a requirement for each supplier to submit final weights for their item of supply. A continuous monitoring and evaluation system will be required to control this activity effectively.

Any substantial additions to, or reductions in, the total topside weight could have an adverse effect on the integrity of the jacket structure and possibly affect the centre of gravity loadings.

Similarly, the civil engineering industry could have weight control requirements when designing bridges, high-rise developments, multi-storey car parks, and the like.

Reliability
Here again, design controls should be implemented to take into consideration the reliability not only of individual items of material and equipment but also complete plants. If, for example, a power generation unit is required to operate at a given level for 90% of its working life, then a detailed review of all components should be undertaken to evaluate their capability to meet such reliability requirements. The criticality of each item would therefore need to be defined.

Criticality
Many customers are now looking at the criticality of plant and materials, in order to establish the level of inspection or tests required to 'prove' the item.

Criticality can be related to safety or loss of production and it determines, in effect, the weakest link in a chain.

Many attempts have been made to establish a formula to determine criticality levels but none has been completely effective as there are so many variables to be considered, such as:

The complexity of design
The complexity of production
The complexity of maintenance
Safety requirements
Ecological and environmental hazards
Monetary investment.

All of these must be equated against the reliability requirement of the total plant.

In many instances the criticality of plant and materials has been left to the judgement of the individual design engineer but this has resulted in 'overkill', as most engineers consider their own equipment to be the most important and demand all sorts of inspection and tests to prove it. Not enough consideration has been given to the use of tried and tested components and the avoidance of tight tolerances which are difficult, if not impossible to achieve, during production. Lack of discipline checking aggravates the problem. The end result has been to inspect everything regardless of its end use.

The use of criticality determination is, therefore, a logical step in the reduction of unnecessary inspection. Whatever the methods used, the end result can only be effective and economical.

As an example, consider a pump. A customer orders two identical pumps to a known specification. One of these pumps is to be used in a fire-fighting situation; the other in a waste water disposal situation. It stands to reason that the fire pump is therefore more 'critical' in its application than the other pump. The customer may, therefore, feel that he needs to attend the testing of the fire pump and should possibly highlight this in the contract.

Maintainability
This goes hand in hand with reliability. The maintenance requirements of a unit should be determined. For example, a power generation unit may be required to operate continuously, in which case, in order to achieve what is in effect 100% reliability, it will probably be necessary to include a back-up unit, and the installation of two units side by side. The location of these units, if placed too close together, could hamper the activities of maintenance crews. The location of vital components, if badly located, could result in unnecessary dismantling work to carry out a simple maintenance task.

It is a matter of common experience that many major maintenance problems have occurred due to lack of attention in this area. Indeed this matter of maintainability is of very wide application. Motor vehicles, for example, are usually better in this respect than they used to be, although still leaving much to be desired. In the case of a home appliance, such as a vacuum cleaner, there are instances where, on some models, it is necessary virtually to dismantle the complete machine to change the brush drive band. Lack of consideration to such maintenance details is all too common.

The action by quality assurance in all these instances would be to verify, initially, the establishment of procedures to control these activities and then to monitor, by audit, their implementation, effectiveness and adherence.

It is unfortunate that, in many industries, the responsibilities for undertaking the actual activities for traceability, weight control, reliability and maintainability are placed upon the quality assurance department.

These activities are 'safety' related and, as safety and quality are regarded as synonymous, the philosophy in such cases is that the quality department must therefore be responsible. This is rather a short-sighted policy, as the result can be neither productive nor cost-effective. Traceability, reliability and maintainability are engineering matters and should be dealt with by engineers. The quality assurance department would verify that all such activities have been carried out in accordance with requirements.

Audit and corrective action
It is most unlikely that the design activities will be completed without some corrective action becoming necessary. This is where the quality assurance department requires the support of senior management. Without it, they would not have the authority to carry through their job. All non-conformances identified during the checks and audits already

described, whether discovered by the quality assurance staff or by the engineers themselves, should be dealt with immediately and steps taken to prevent their recurrence.

Where a non-conformance is identified, but the corrective action taken by the department responsible is considered to be insufficient to prevent repetition, then the quality assurance representative must be able to call upon support from management in order that the problem can be resolved effectively. The intention of design control is to ensure that the eventual design meets all customer and regulatory requirements. At the completion of this activity, the design will result in the commitment of expensive resources to produce the hardware. It is therefore essential that the audits carried out by the quality assurance representative are taken seriously and their results acted upon.

SYSTEM ELEMENT OUTLINE

The details of design control discussed in this chapter can be summarized into a system element outline for incorporation into a quality manual. See Appendix A, section 2.2.

The next element in the total presentation is to ensure that the purchasing of the hardware and associated services is controlled in the same systematic manner as the design.

13

Procurement control

Regardless of the industry with which an organization is concerned, there will always be the need to purchase items and/or services of some sort or another. The control over these activities therefore is most important if one is to obtain value for money plus on-time delivery. All the quality system standards, at all levels, stress the requirement for adequate controls in this area.

Referring back to Fig. 4.3, 'Quality assurance in making a cake', it is to be noticed that even the person concerned with cake-making goes through a verification of purchasing sources. Not only does the cook know the type and make or brand of the ingredients which enhance the finished cake, but he or she invariably knows the cheapest source of supply. Although this information is not actually documented as it would be in a formalized quality system, nevertheless an assessment of procurement sources has been effectively carried out.

Similarly in industry, be it a hardware-related or a service industry, there should be some system for evaluating procurement sources.

THE MAJOR ACTIVITIES

As for design control, those activities considered to be the most important in the procurement activity have been compiled for ease of reference into a tabulated form, Fig. 13.1. The table carries the same headings:

— Activity
— Scope
— Performed by
— Action by QA

Each activity will be dealt with in a similar manner.

Master inspection and test checklist
As mentioned during the formulation of the inspection and test plan, there may be instances where the customer (in this case the purchaser) imposes certain inspection and test requirements upon the supplier to 'prove' that an item meets certain additional safety

PROCUREMENT CONTROL

ACTIVITY	SCOPE	PERFORMED BY	ACTION BY QA

1
Master inspection and test check-list (MITCL)
	Establish and document:
	  Equipment criticality
	  Inspection check-points
	  NDT requirements
	  Acceptance tests
	  Certification
	  Weight control
	  Traceability
		Design engineers
		Quality control department
			Verify issue and approval of MITCL

2
Approve suppliers for bid list (if not previously approved)
	Assess suppliers for acceptability in:
	  Engineering
	  Quality
	  Economics/schedule
	  Financial stability
		Discipline engineers
		Purchasing department
		Quality assurance
			Assess the implementation and effectiveness of suppliers quality system and compare MITCL with supplier's in-house controls

3 Tender package development and issue	Collate all documents/specifications/drawings/MITCL etc. and submit to approved bidders	Purchasing department Discipline engineers Quality assurance	Review, as required, tender packages for completeness

4
Bid package review
	Review bid packages for:
	  Engineering
	  Schedule
	  Economics
	  Quality
		Contract management
		Discipline engineers
		Purchasing department
		Quality assurance
			Monitor, as required, bid reviews to the acceptance of one supplier

5 Pre-award meeting	Review with approved supplier(s) the contract requirements including inspection and test	Contract management Discipline engineers Purchasing department Quality control department Quality assurance	Verify supplier's intended compliance with contract requirements Establish audit schedule and confirm inspection and test plan
6 Contract award	Collate all documents/specifications/drawings/final inspection and test plan and issue to approved supplier(s)	Purchasing department Quality assurance	Review, as required, contract documents for completeness

7
Post-award meeting
	Review and confirm with supplier(s):
	  Inspection requirements
	  Certification requirements
	  Hold points
	  Test programme
		Quality control personnel
		Quality assurance
			Verify supplier's compliance with requirements
			Finalize QA audit schedule

8
Supplier surveillance
	Issue relevant sections of contract to quality control personnel and:
	  Review inspection details
	  Confirm certification/documentation requirements
	  Reporting requirements
		Quality control personnel	Monitor supplier's performance with own quality plan
			Verify QC personnel compliance with inspection and test plan

9 Audit and corrective action	Ensure non-conformances promptly identified and corrective action taken to prevent recurrence	Contract management Supplier's management Quality assurance	Co-ordinate and verify that corrective action completed and that action has been taken to prevent recurrence

Fig. 13.1—Procurement matrix.

or critical conditions. In such cases, it is recommended that the customer or purchaser develops his or her own inspection and test plan for inclusion in the tender documents. In such instances, this document could be termed a master inspection and test checklist to differentiate it from the supplier's own document.

This master checklist should identify all the inspection check points relevant to the criticality of the materials and equipment; it should also list requirements for non-destructive testing, acceptance testing, certification and documentation.

This master inspection and test checklist is, as has already been established, basically a schedule of inspection and test points which the customer would expect the potential supplier to include within his or her own quality control system for the contracted material. It becomes a guideline which sets out the minimum requirements for control and surveillance.

Where weight control is a requirement, then methods of reporting weights should be included. Similarly, traceability of items or batches should also be included, if required.

The master inspection and test checklist is not considered to be a mandatory exercise but its development is recommended if only as a check to place the criticality of materials and equipment at the right level. The customer's own quality control department should have an input into this document as that department would be concerned with its administration after contract award. The quality control department should also review the requirements for 'inspectability and testability'. For example, some configurations of a fabricated item may not lend themselves to certain methods of non-destructive testing. Only those continuously involved in non-destructive testing would be aware of the associated problems.

In other words, the supplier should not be expected to perform tests which are difficult to achieve and the results of which might be worthless. The supplier will, no doubt, be happy to produce test pieces, at a price!

Unfortunately, it is all too common in practice to seek to impose unnecessary tolerances and test requirements on suppliers which may, indeed, be impossible to meet. The supplier is not always blameless, and very often will accept a contract knowing full well that he or she will be unable to comply with all requirements.

The action by quality assurance should be to verify that the master inspection and test checklist has been developed where required and that all interfacing disciplines, including the quality control department, have reviewed and commented on it and that all comments have been satisfactorily closed out. Approval of the document by the correct approval authority should be also verified.

The master inspection and test checklist will form part of the tender package, together with specifications, drawings, data sheets, contract conditions, quality assurance requirements, and so on.

Approve suppliers for bid list

Before a tender package can be issued, it will be necessary to establish who is to tender for the items or services. In all probability, there will be a number of potential suppliers but, if there is no previous history of a supplier on record, then it would be prudent to assess that potential supplier's capability.

The assessment of a supplier can take many forms. A history of a supplier's capability can be established purely on a quality/delivery record. Where such a supplier makes frequent and regular deliveries to a customer, then confidence is established and maintained on a continuing basis. This method of assessment should be documented and updated by delivery analyses.

In other instances, one could verify a supplier's capability either by inspecting the items at the supplier's premises before delivery or by incoming inspection on receipt. Although effective this may not be very economical when items are rejected. This method of assessment should also be documented and updated by inspection results.

The responsibility for quality should lie with the supplier and it should not be necessary for the customer to 'inspect' quality into supplied items.

There are a number of countries—UK, Canada, Australia and others—which operate assessment programmes. Assessments are carried out by accredited bodies to the appropriate national quality system standard and successful companies are registered accordingly and are entered in a buyers' guide.

If an organization uses such a buyers' guide as an assessment source, then this method should be similarly documented.

In the cases of very complex plant or equipment, such methods of assessment would not be very meaningful, particularly if additional quality requirements are to be stipulated. It will be necessary, therefore, particularly when the firm is unknown, to carry out an assessment to verify whether or not the potential supplier is capable of meeting not only quality requirements but engineering, delivery and economic requirements.

An assessment, therefore, falls into four distinct parts:

— Engineering
— Quality
— Economics/schedule
— Financial stability.

Engineering

An evaluation should be made of the potential supplier's manufacturing facilities to verify whether he has the capability to manufacture or supply the materials/equipment to the specification.

A study of his fulfilment of recent contracts of comparable size and complexity should also be undertaken, as this would assist in substantiating his capabilities.

As this part of the assessment relates to the manufacturing capabilities, it should be carried out by personnel who are familiar with production activities, i.e. qualified engineers.

Quality

An evaluation should be made of the potential supplier's own quality system. This should be documented in the form of a quality manual and the evaluation would verify whether his or her quality system is being effectively implemented and receives the full support of senior management.

At this stage, with no contract made, there is nothing binding upon a potential supplier to conform to any given requirement. It is possible only to review the quality system and to make observations on any apparent deficiency; perhaps advising the supplier that the deficiency, if not rectified, could have an adverse effect on contract award.

The customer's own quality assurance personnel would be responsible for this activity.

Economics/schedule
An evaluation should be made of the potential supplier's prices and delivery record. Have prices for similar contracts been competitive and is there a proven ability to deliver on time?

Financial stability
An evaluation should be made of the potential supplier's financial stability, particularly where high-cost, long-delivery contracts are concerned. In times of recession, it is not uncommon for companies to go into receivership. If this should happen, then there is no knowing what effect this could have on contracts already half-completed (possibly after considerable advance progress payments have been committed—and perhaps lost irrevocably). It is often prudent therefore to examine the supplier's published accounts or seek a report from an accredited agency.

The last two items would be evaluated probably by the customer's contracts department.

During the assessment, a comparison could be made between the supplier's own inspection and test plans for recent orders of comparable size and complexity and the master inspection and test checklist. This comparison should verify whether the supplier does take into consideration, during the planning stage, any unique customer requirements for inspection and testing, and whether mandatory hold points are documented and adhered to.

The results of the assessment should be evaluated by all parties involved, resulting in an agreement to approve or disapprove the supplier. In the case of approval, the supplier would then be entered on the bidders' list.

Methods of carrying out assessments and methods used in evaluating results should be procedurally controlled.

Tender package development and issue
During the assessment period, possibly even earlier, tender packages will have been assembled. These will comprise the specifications, drawings, data sheets, delivery requirements, inspection and test plans, and so on, which together define the commitment which the supplier is being invited to undertake. Although the purchasing department should compile and issue the tender package, both the engineering and quality assurance departments should be involved. The tender package is, in effect, subjected to an interdiscipline check as in design control. Thus the tender package should receive a review for completeness and accuracy. It should then be issued to approved potential suppliers.

Again, as for any series of documents, tender packages should follow a uniform presentation with a standard index. This means, of course, that there will be a requirement for a procedure, which should establish the methods for development and issue of such packages.

The action by quality assurance should be to verify, as required to establish confidence, that tender packages have been developed, approved and issued in accordance with procedure and that all appropriate documents, specifications, drawings and quality requirements are included and that the packages were issued to the agreed and approved bidders.

Bid package review

When all tenders from suppliers have been received, they should be reviewed for engineering content, quality, price and delivery.

Engineering department should review the tenderers' proposals for supply. There may be cases where a supplier proposes alternative methods, materials or equipment from those listed in the specification, and the engineering department should comment on this, stating whether or not the changes represent improvements or otherwise, and whether or not they are acceptable. The purchasing department should consider the price and delivery proposals. When the potential sources of supply are remote from the sites where goods are to be delivered, especially where overseas transport and international boundaries are involved, it is necessary to consider not just the ex-works price quoted but the total cost of purchase, transport, insurance, duties and taxes payable to obtain an on-site cost. The quality assurance department should review the package for compliance with the quality system level, quality acceptance criteria, inspection and test plan and certification.

Bid summary

When a choice has to be made between a number of suppliers, it is of benefit to tabulate the main points arising from the review on a bid summary sheet. This is arranged to display the various price and delivery promises, all translated to a common set of units for easy and meaningful comparison. For example, all the costs converted to one monetary system: US dollars, pounds sterling.

Tabulations are less useful for technical and quality comments, being too limited in space, but they can be used for brief comments, especially where such comments give a definitive preference or rejection. Final choice of supplier is often a complex affair, involving the company's quality, technical and commercial departments.

All too often, unfortunately, the 'bottom line' is the deciding factor and the contract is awarded to the lowest bidder. The fact that the lowest bidder may have a poor quality system is not given sufficient weighting, with the end result that the customer may well be in the position of having to decide between quality and delivery. There is much truth in that well-known saying:

The bitterness of poor quality remains long after the sweetness of low price is forgotten.

It is necessary, therefore, for the views of the quality assurance department to be taken into account in the selection of the actual supply source, together with those of the engineering and purchasing departments. This again serves to emphasize the importance of the quality assurance department within the organization.

Having reviewed the bid packages in their own right, the *action by quality assurance* will be to verify that all comments made by others have been considered and actioned, thus leading to the acceptance of one supplier (or more as the case may be, depending on the scope of supply).

Having identified this supplier, in the case of large or highly critical items and prior to the issue of a formal contract or purchase order, it is prudent to call in that supplier to attend what is usually termed a pre-award meeting.

Pre-award meeting

Pre-award meetings with the selected suppliers are held to review jointly the contract requirements and to obtain the suppliers' understanding and agreement. Such meetings correspond to the contract review meetings discussed in design control.

A quality assurance representative must be present at this meeting—this is most important! Experience has shown that this is one meeting where the quality assurance department involvement is often overlooked and any quality problems encountered at this meeting tend to be swept aside in the desire to place the order and commence production. This is where the 'we didn't have time' syndrome first manifests itself, resulting in much greater problems further down the line with the subsequent high cost of rectification.

A procedure should be developed which indicates where and how such a meeting is to be arranged, who is to organize and chair it and who is to attend. Quality assurance should, in all circumstances, be invited to attend such meetings. It is at the discretion of the quality assurance representative, and not others, to determine whether or not it is necessary to attend.

Each pre-award meeting will verify the supplier's intended compliance with the contract and will also take into account quality systems deficiencies observed when the supplier was assessed before the issue of the bid package. Items identified on the master inspection and test checklist should be reviewed against the supplier's own inspection and test plan, and this comparison will confirm whether or not the customer will need to exercise any quality control activities his or herself. Any contentious issues should be resolved at this meeting, or at least very shortly afterwards. Ambiguities and unresolved problems could result in delays or additional costs later on.

The quality assurance representative may at this time establish an interim audit schedule, although this is a little difficult to do until the supplier has produced a project quality plan for approval, which, as for the design control element, should be established in accordance with tender document requirements.

The pre-award meeting should be minuted and any actions required assigned to individuals. It should be recognized that an interface problem may arise as two organizations are involved—the customer and the supplier.

It should be the responsibility of the customer's quality assurance department to verify by audit that any assigned customer actions have been closed out. The verification of close-out of supplier-assigned actions should be the responsibility of the supplier's own quality assurance department. Both the customer's and the supplier's quality assurance departments should liaise to establish total conformance.

All verification activities should be documented.

Contract award

The purchase order or contract package issue, apart from being issued only to the chosen supplier(s), should be treated in the same way as the invitation to tender documents. Again, it involves the interdiscipline check and review to verify completeness, accuracy and compliance with any agreements arising from the pre-award meeting.

The action by quality assurance should be to verify—as required to establish confidence—that contract documents have been developed, approved and issued in accordance with procedure and that all comments resulting from the pre-award meeting have been taken into consideration.

Post-award meeting

Among the scheduled dates proposed in the tender documents and firmed up in the issued contract should be the date by which the supplier is expected to present the customer with a quality plan. About seven days after receipt of the quality plan, it should be reviewed between customer and supplier in a post-award meeting. An audit schedule can be agreed at the same time, together with inspection hold points, certification and other documentation requirements, and the test programme. The audit schedule should make provision for an initial system audit to confirm quality plan awareness, with subsequent compliance audits arranged to cover weak or possible non-conforming areas exposed during the original supplier assessment. In addition to any audits undertaken by the customer, the supplier should verify, also by audit, that his or her own quality plan is being effectively implemented.

Attendance at this meeting is usually limited to quality assurance and quality control personnel of both customer and supplier.

Supplier surveillance

Once manufacture is under way, the supplier's own quality control department should be verifying by inspection and/or surveillance that each activity in the production cycle is correct to specification and objective evidence evaluated to confirm this.

Additionally, the supplier's own quality assurance department should be verifying, by internal audit, that all activities related to the quality plan, including production and quality control, are effective.

The customer's own quality control department should limit their involvement to verifying that specific inspections and tests required by contract are carried out correctly and at the right time, and that there is objective evidence to substantiate this, i.e. test reports, certificates.

Audit and corrective action

The customer's quality assurance activities are threefold:

(1)   to verify, initially, the establishment of procedures to control the customer's own procurement activities and then to monitor, by audit, their implementation, adherence and effectiveness;

(2)   to verify the establishment by the supplier of a quality plan and then to monitor by audit the implementation and effectiveness of, and adherence to, the plan;

(3)   to verify the establishment of both the master inspection and test checklist and the supplier's inspection and test plan, and to monitor, by audit, the activities of quality control personnel in the implementation of the inspection and test plan.

All non-conformances exposed during these three activities would be addressed by corrective action requests upon the appropriate party, with follow-up action to verify that corrective action has been taken and steps taken to prevent a recurrence of the deficiency.

SERVICE CONTRACTS

Most of the activities described in this chapter have been centred around the procurement of hardware. It should be borne in mind that the procurement of services (people-related industries) should also follow the same pattern.

Companies offering services should also be evaluated in the same manner as those manufacturing and supplying materials and equipment.

The companies would be assessed to confirm acceptability of the services they offer, that the personnel carrying out the services are suitably qualified and experienced and that the service can be completed on time and within budget.

Tender package development would apply, as would bid package review.

A pre-award meeting would be also a requirement where applicable.

A service contract award would be controlled in the same manner as a contract award for a manufactured item.

The post-award meeting could also be applicable.

The monitoring, by the customer, of personnel fulfilling a service contract would, in all probability, be part of the contract requirements. Particularly so in the case of personnel 'bought-in' to perform a given task: draughting, office cleaning, security, and the like.

Audit and corrective action would be equally applicable.

The requirement, therefore, of all quality assurance standards is that control of procurement should cover both items and services.

SYSTEM ELEMENT OUTLINE

The activities thus detailed in procurement control can now be condensed into a system element outline. An example of such an outline is given in Appendix A, section 2.4.

The contract has now been placed and the manufacture is about to commence. The next element is manufacturing control.

14

Manufacturing and services control

Manufacturing control is a function which is given a great deal of prominence in all quality system standards. It is a function which relates directly to the hardware and it is the hardware which customers use as the yardstick to measure quality.

FITNESS FOR PURPOSE

The production of hardware in a fit for purpose condition is, therefore, considered to be in the majority of instances the sole criterion of a quality system. While such a philosophy is admirable, it does not, unfortunately, take into consideration the efficiency and effectiveness of all the other functions which are directly or indirectly connected with the manufactured item and lead subsequently to customer satisfaction. The control of manufacture should be considered, therefore, as only a part of the total presentation and should not overpower, or be subservient to, any other controls.

Manufacturers, in the main, do supply items fit for purpose, but, in some instances, because of the high cost involved in achieving the fit for purpose condition due to ineffective control, many manufacturers become uncompetitive and gradually lose their share of the market. This loss of market share leads to a massive reappraisal of a company's position, usually resulting in a reduction of the workforce. If the company concerned has no real means of locating the problem area, due to lack of a documented quality system, there is no means of 'measuring' the effectiveness of the manufacturing process, or any other process for that matter. The end result, in such a situation, may well be to reduce the 'overhead' staff as they are considered not to be contributing to the fit for purpose condition of the hardware.

It is important, therefore, that all activities and functions of an organization should be controlled, including manufacture, but not to the detriment of other functions such as administration, sales, marketing, maintenance, installation and after-sales service.

There are many companies that do not manufacture a hardware product: they offer a service, such as insurance, banking, security, office cleaning, and so on. These companies must also consider the control of the service(s) which they offer. The services rendered must totally satisfy the customer just as a manufactured item must also totally satisfy the customer.

It has been stated by many service organizations that quality assurance standards are related to design and manufacturing only and cannot be used in a service environment. This is most certainly not the case, as has been partially shown in procurement control. The majority of 'manufacturing' controls apply equally as well to services.

THE MAJOR ACTIVITIES

As for both design and procurement control, the activities considered to be the most important in manufacturing have been compiled into a tabulated form (Fig. 14.1). In this instance, however, additional columns have been added to show a service scope and performance which will identify how the controls used in manufacturing relate equally to service organizations.

As previously, each activity is dealt with in detail.

Contract review (planning)

As has been discussed, a system to review customer requirements and to plan for the contract or project execution is most important. It should be carried out regardless of the size or nature of the contract. Even a very small company, when receiving an order from a customer, usually carries out a contract review activity, without perhaps recognizing it as such, by reading the order and then determining what actions, equipment, materials, and so on, are required to fulfil the order. In many instances, however, this activity is not documented but it occurs just the same. The larger organization, where numbers of staff are involved, should document the contract review activity, in order that the necessary co-ordination, liaison and understanding of contract requirements can be achieved and can be seen to have been achieved.

The manufacture of an item, or the execution of a service, as for design, should include such an activity and this should be undertaken before any work commences. All concerned should be aware of their responsibilities and a review team should be assembled to review the contract and to plan its execution.

Work scope

The review should entail a detailed consideration of the scope of work and a verification that the scope is fully understood by all concerned.

A manufacturing organization should then consider:

Specifications and standards

It should be established that all applicable specifications and standards of correct issue are readily available at all activity locations.

Material requirements

It should be ensured that the correct materials, in the right sizes and quantities, are available. Where materials have to be ordered, then the sources of such materials should be assessed together with delivery, price and quality. The actual mechanics of this activity would be covered by the control of purchased items and services.

MANUFACTURING & SERVICES CONTROL

ACTIVITY	SCOPE-MANUFACTURING	PERFORMED BY	SCOPE-SERVICES	PERFORMED BY	ACTION BY QA
1 Contract review	Review work scope Specifications and standards Material requirements Inspection and test requirements Manufacturing processes Organization	Management Production Quality control Quality assurance	Review work scope Customer requirements Staffing levels and experience Organization	Management Service departments Quality assurance	Verify that missing or ambiguous information has been followed up and satisfactorily closed out by the responsible person
2 Document preparation control and retention	Ensure correct and uniform presentation of documents Ensure formal preparation, identification, checking, approval and distribution, including amendments Verify retention, retrieval, storage and handover requirements	Management Production Quality control	Ensure correct and uniform presentation of documents. Ensure formal preparation, identification, checking, approval and distribution, including amendments. Verify retention, retrieval, storage and handover requirements	Management Service department	Audit adherence to procedure
3 Control of inspection Measuring and test equipment	Verify: Equipment to be controlled Standards for control Calibration method Calibration interval Identification of calibration status	Management Production	Verify: Equipment to be controlled Standards for control Equipment status Servicing interval	Management Appropriate department	Audit adherence to procedure
4 Control of purchased items and services	Assure methods of adequately assessing supplier's ability to meet contract requirements	Purchasing department Production Quality control Quality assurance	Assure methods of adequately assessing supplier's ability to meet contract requirements	Purchasing department User department Quality assurance	Audit adherence to procedure as required
5 Incoming inspection	Verify: Conformity to requirements	Quality control	Verify that purchased items conform to requirements	Purchasing department	Audit adherence to inspection and test plan (work routines)

Fig. 14.1—Manufacturing and services matrix.

MANUFACTURING & SERVICES CONTROL

ACTIVITY	SCOPE-MANUFACTURING	PERFORMED BY	SCOPE-SERVICES	PERFORMED BY	ACTION BY QA
6 Purchaser-supplied items (where applicable)	Verify: Type, condition and quantity on receipt Identify and separate from own items	Quality control	Verify type, condition and quantity on receipt. Identify	Contract department	Audit adherence to inspection and test plan (work routines)
7 In-process inspection	Verify adherence to specification during manufacture by inspection and/or test. Identification Documentation	Quality control	Verify adherence to requirements during the service activity	Supervisory staff	Audit adherence to inspection and test plan (work routines)
8 Final inspection	Verify adherence to specification on completion by inspection and/or test. Identification Documentation	Quality control	Verify adherence to requirements on service completion. Identification Documentation	Supervisory staff	Audit adherence to inspection and test plan (work routines)
9 Sampling (where applicable)	Verify use of sampling schemes Methods Standards	Quality control	Verify use of sampling schemes	Supervisory staff	Audit adherence to inspection and test plan (work routines)
10 Inspection and test status	Verify methods of indicating inspection status for: Awaiting inspection Inspected and accepted Inspected and rejected	Quality control	Verify methods of indicating action status for: Awaiting action Actioned and accepted Actioned and rejected	Supervisory staff	Audit adherence to procedure
11 Identification and traceability (where applicable)	Verify requirements for traceability of materials Identification Documentation	Production Quality control	Not applicable	Not applicable	Audit adherence to inspection and test plan
12 Handling and storage	Verify handling and storage methods	Production Quality control	Verify handling and storage methods	Supervisory staff	Audit adherence to inspection and test plan (work routines)

Fig. 14.1—Manufacturing and services matrix.

MANUFACTURING & SERVICES CONTROL

ACTIVITY	SCOPE-MANUFACTURING	PERFORMED BY	SCOPE-SERVICES	PERFORMED BY	ACTION BY QA
13 Special processes	Verify which manufacturing processes fall into the special category. Determine methods of control, maintenance and calibration of special process equipment. Suitability of personnel performing special processes	Production Quality control	Verify which processes fall into the special category. Determine methods of control. Maintenance of special process equipment. Suitability of personnel performing special processes	Supervisory staff	Audit adherence to procedure
14 Preservation, packaging and shipping	Verify requirements and availability of materials, processes and equipment	Production Purchasing Quality control	Verify requirements and availability of material and resources	Supervisory staff	Audit adherence to inspection and test plan (work routines)
15 Non-conforming items	Verify methods of identifying and dispositioning non-conforming items	Production Quality control	Verify methods of identifying and correcting non-conforming or unacceptable services	Management Appropriate department	Audit adherence to procedure
16 Records	Verify: Requirements Format Contents Storage Retrieval Retention period	Library Document control centre	Verify: Requirements Format Contents Storage Retrieval Retention period	Library Document control centre	Audit adherence to procedure
17 Training	Verify and document training needs Methods Records	Management Department heads	Verify and document training needs Methods Records	Management Department heads	Audit adherence to procedure
18 Audit and corrective action	Ensure non-conformances promptly identified and corrective action taken to prevent recurrence	Management Quality assurance	Ensure non-conformances promptly identified and corrective action taken to prevent recurrence	Management Department heads	Audit adherence to procedure

Fig. 14.1—Manufacturing and services matrix.

Inspection and test requirements

If any special inspections or tests are required by contract, or if any regulatory body is involved, then the review team should be aware of these and should schedule the requirements into their own inspection and test plan. Specialized testing equipment may have to be contracted-in and arrangements should be considered. The team should also consider any requirement for the development and submission to the customer of a quality plan or an inspection and test plan.

Manufacturing processes

The review team should consider any special processes which may be required and which may have to be supported by special process procedures. The subject of special processes will be dealt with later.

Considerations

A service organization should consider:

Customer requirements

Are there any special requirements which are out of the ordinary?

Staffing levels and experience

Consideration should be given to the number of staff required to complete the contract on time, together with the experience and qualifications of such staff.

Organization

In both a manufacturing and service situation the organization for contract execution should be determined.

Action by quality assurance

The contract review meeting should be minuted, as in design control.

The quality assurance representative should then utilize the minutes to verify that any missing or ambiguous information in the contract has been followed up and satisfactorily closed out by the responsible person(s).

General

In the small organization, both manufacturing and service, where such a formalized review is impracticable, then contract understanding could be confirmed by utilizing a checklist to mark off the requirements. This is a method to confirm that all requirements have been actioned—a type of 'shopping list' so to speak. Very few people have photographic memories, and therefore an *aide mémoire* should not be thought of as unprofessional. Any form of document, however simple, is worth considering as it can be useful during the latter stages of a contract as objective evidence that an activity was actually carried out.

The author's organization utilizes such checklists to verify that all the necessary course work, delegate name tags, video equipment, visual aids, and so on, are assembled and correct when presenting a training course.

Documentation preparation, control and retention
This activity is identical to that described for design control. The documents themselves, however, will be generally of a different nature and will relate to the manufacturing or service requirements and could cover such things as:

Inspection and test plans
Testing procedures (mechanical and non-destructive testing)
Special process procedures (manufacturing and service related)
Work instruction (manufacturing and service related)
Mill certification
Manufacturing processes
Inspection procedures (manufacturing and service related).

In all cases, the methods of preparing, identifying and approving documents, methods of changing and approving the changes to documents and methods of removing and recalling obsolete documents should be formalized and controlled.

The action by quality assurance would be to verify, initially, the formulation of all necessary procedures to control this activity and to confirm the implementation and adequacy of, and adherence to, the document control system.

Control of inspection, measuring and test equipment
Both manufacturing and service industries utilize equipment which requires some form of regular servicing and/or calibration to confirm its accuracy and its continued fitness for use.

In the first instance, it is necessary to establish the equipment which falls into this category. In general terms, this is equipment which can affect quality.

In a manufacturing environment such equipment would include micrometers, Vernier gauges, go and no-go gauges, pressure gauges, mechanical testing machines, jigs, fixtures, templates, and so on.

In a service industry quality can be affected by poor copying machines, word-processing equipment, typewriters, and so on.

A system should, therefore, be established which will identify the equipment that is to be calibrated and/or serviced and a calibration and maintenance schedule should be drawn up. This schedule would include such information as:

— Equipment location
— Number or type
— Frequency of calibration or service checks
— Methods of calibration or servicing
— Action that is to be taken in the event of unsatisfactory conditions.

Where inspection, measuring and test equipment is to be verified or calibrated against primary master standards, then such master standards should be certified by approved facilities which, in turn, have standards which are verified or calibrated to national standards.

Records should be maintained which detail the frequency and results of calibration and/or servicing and these records should be evaluated on a regular basis to determine the adequacy of the calibration or servicing intervals. It could well be that the calibration intervals of some equipment may have to be reduced due to an increased frequency of use. The reverse may be equally applicable. All such conditions should be documented and the results analysed and actioned.

Where equipment is subject to regular calibration and/or servicing, then the equipment should carry some form of identification label, either adhesive or tie-on. This label should indicate the calibration status, for example the date of last calibration or service plus next calibration date. Where it is not possible to affix a label, due to the configuration or the size of the equipment, then calibration and/or servicing details should be traceable through to the master indexing and scheduling system.

Privately owned equipment, where used to determine finite measurement, should also be included in the calibration system. This is important, as experience has shown that the employees of many manufacturing organizations who purchase and use their own personal measuring equipment quite often feel that, because only they themselves use the equipment and take great care of it, it can never go out of calibration. This is far from the case. In many instances of dimensional error the cause has been traced back to uncalibrated, privately owned equipment. Where such equipment is used as a guide to measurement only and is not used for finite measurement, then it should be marked and carry a statement, such as:

Not to be used for finite measurement—not subject to calibration.

Preferably, however, it should not be used at all.

Equipment which has been checked and found out of calibration, or equipment which has gone over its calibration date and is awaiting calibration, should be labelled to indicate that it is not to be used.

All newly purchased equipment should undergo an initial calibration check to prove its accuracy before being released for use. Again, experience has shown that this is not always the case. Many manufacturing organizations rely on measuring and testing equipment to be accurate just because it is new. How long does it remain new? The author has been shown 'new' equipment which, when traced back to the delivery order, was found to have been in use for well over a year and out of calibration.

Copying machines, computers, and the like, are normally installed by the manufacturers or their agents and undergo a calibration or fitness for use check before handing over to the customer. This can be regarded as a calibration check prior to use but the owner should be satisfied before acceptance.

Many large organizations have a great deal of equipment to calibrate or service. Such cases could utilize a computer program to update and control this activity.

The smaller organization would normally utilize a card indexing system or a record book. Whatever the system used it should be the responsibility of one person or department.

It is recommended that the production department should take the responsibility as it is this department that is responsible for the quality of the hardware it produces. It should not rely on others, such as a quality control department, to do this work for them.

The action by quality assurance would be initially to verify the establishment of the calibration and/or servicing system and to monitor its implementation, effectiveness and adherence.

Control of purchased items and services
This activity is applicable to all industries and levels of a quality system.

The customer should verify the adequacy of the prime purchasing sources. Similarly the contractor will verify the adequacy of subcontracted sources and so on down the line. The customer should not have to evaluate the adequacy of any supply source other than the first party source.

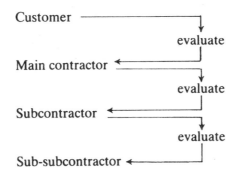

Unfortunately this is far from general practice, as many customers are still experiencing a great reluctance on the part of the main contractors to evaluate subcontracting sources. This surely must place an unnecessary burden on the customer's time and resources and take the responsibility away from the organization to whom it should belong. Augustus de Morgan (1806–1871) has been quoted as saying: 'Great fleas have little fleas upon their backs to bite'em, and little fleas have lesser fleas and so ad infinitum.' This is how it should be in the case of customer, contractor and subcontractor procurement sources.

The methods of controlling purchased items and services have already been dealt with in detail in Chapter 13.

Incoming inspection
This activity is carried out to verify the acceptability and condition of bought-out materials and equipment. It is one method of assessing a supplier's capability but it is a method not to be relied upon where tight schedules are concerned. An incoming inspection will serve only to verify whether an item is acceptable or not. If it is not acceptable then, of course, a decision has to be made whether to scrap and reorder, return to the supplier for rework or repair in-house. Whichever decision is made, there will inevitably be a delay in attaining fitness for use.

Other methods of assessing capability have already been discussed.

The methods to be used during an incoming inspection activity will depend upon the nature and quantity of the items. Such information should be incorporated into an inspection and test plan and would include:

Inspection and test requirements
Sampling methods (if required)
Documentation requirements
Acceptance/rejection criteria

as has been described previously in Chapter 11.

Any item which is received without the required supporting documentation should preferably be withheld from production pending the receipt and acceptance of such documentation, or if such items are released for production, then there should be a means of recalling the items if problems subsequently arise.

Items rejected upon receipt should be identified as rejected and placed in a quarantined area pending a decision on the action to be taken.

Incoming inspection is normally carried out by a company's quality control or inspection department, although other qualified personnel could do it provided such responsibility is clearly defined. The results of all such inspections should be documented. Inspection results can be utilized to evaluate supplier performance and, as for any type of information, the results should be made available to the people who need to know. There is no point in the quality control or inspection department keeping detailed analyses of incoming inspection results if these are not made known to the engineering or purchasing departments.

Engineering should be aware of problems as they may reflect upon a specification. For example, it may be found that the specification is too tight and requires amendment.

Purchasing should be aware of supplier performance in order to update their records.

Again—communication is important.

In the case of service organizations most, if not all, bought-out items should be checked upon receipt. Normally the person responsible for the purchase would carry out this activity. Office or service routines (job instructions) should indicate responsibilities and action to be taken in the event of unacceptable items.

The action by quality assurance would be to verify the establishment of the appropriate inspection and test plans, procedures or routines and confirm implementation, effectiveness and adherence.

Purchaser-supplied items

These could be termed 'free-issue'. They are items supplied free of charge by a customer for use on a given contract. Items may be supplied free of charge to both manufacturing and service organizations.

Although the majority of quality assurance standards include the control of purchaser (customer) supplied items in the list of criteria, it is necessary only to implement such a system if an organization is regularly in receipt of such. Do not implement a system for control just because it is listed in a quality assurance standard! Unfortunately many organizations, and many quality assurance consultants for that matter, are of the opinion that to comply with a given quality assurance standard one must implement every control listed in that standard. This is certainly not the case and this is one control that falls into that category.

To explain more fully the exact nature of purchaser-supplied items, it is worth while looking at some examples.

In a service industry there may be many areas of free-issue material:

— A house decorator may be supplied by the customer with paint and paper which he is to apply.
— A printer may be supplied by the customer with special paper.
— A public service worker may be supplied with a free uniform.
— A laundry is supplied with soiled linen to clean
and so on.

In a manufacturing industry it is not uncommon, especially in offshore oil and gas, for the customer to purchase the materials and equipment for a jacket structure and supply it, free of charge, to a fabrication yard where it will be 'made up' into the jacket.

Whenever a product is supplied 'free issue', it should be under strict control from initial receipt until despatch as, or part of, a finished product. Or, in the case of free-issue clothing, from receipt until the end of its requirement or useful life. A system for this control should be documented.

Initially, all items supplied by the customer should be inspected on receipt for damage, completeness and for compliance with contract requirements. Any special storage and handling instructions should be complied with.

During storage inspection should be carried out on a regular basis, either by the production department or by a quality control inspector, to verify condition. Adequacy of the storage facilities should be reviewed at the same time and shelf-life conditions may also be evaluated where necessary.

If, during storage, any damage or unsatisfactory conditions are observed then, of course, the customer should be advised and action taken to determine the cause and prevent a recurrence of the condition.

The system should also ensure that all documentation received with the items is correct and that any deficiencies, or abnormalities, are reported to the customer for verification and action.

All deficient or defective customer-supplied items should be marked, segregated and placed in a quarantined area where they will be protected and prohibited from use.

Any testing which may be required by the customer should be conducted on receipt and prior to use, and the results documented.

A separate storage area should be set aside for customer-supplied items and the necessary records should be maintained to identify to the customer where and when such items were used.

In the case of a steel jacket fabrication for example, there will, in all probability, be a requirement for the fabricator to control and store, for the customer's eventual disposal, all the steel off-cuts. The customer will have supplied a known quantity of steel. A given number of tonnes will be used in building the jacket and the remainder, either in whole plate or off-cuts, will need to be accounted for to the customer for disposal. Hence the requirement for the maintenance of records.

The development of a system to control purchaser (customer) supplied items can be developed only with customer participation. Any non-conforming items cannot be handled in the same way as one's own non-conforming items. The customer must always be involved, as it is the customer who will determine the action to be taken for the disposition of the items.

The action by quality assurance should be to determine that customer requirements relating to the control of free-issue products have been incorporated into an appropriate procedure and then to verify, by audit, that such requirements are being implemented and that the system is effective and being adhered to.

In-process inspection

All requirements for in-process inspection should be included in the inspection and test plan. The requirements would include the points during manufacture where inspection is required and whether manufacture should cease until the inspection has been carried out (mandatory hold point). The type of inspection (visual, dimensional or non-destructive test) should be indicated and also whether any sampling schemes are to be used.

As each inspection and/or test is completed, it should be recorded on an appropriate document, usually the relevant manufacturing route card (Fig. 14.2 is a typical routing card for machine-shop activities).

Non-conforming items should be dealt with in accordance with a written procedure established for such an activity.

Initially, the machine operator should be responsible for checking his or her own work (the self-check). Wherever possible this should be the only check necessary. By making operators responsible for their own quality, there should be a reduction in the inspection workforce leading to a reduction in subsequent rectification work.

Conversations with management and engineering personnel often suggest that a requirement for increased 'QA/QC' to overcome quality problems in manufacturing is necessary, whereas what is really required is an increase in 'QA' (prevention) with a decrease in 'QC' (cure).

Whoever is responsible for in-process inspection should document the results and all data maintained for subsequent evaluation.

Service organizations carry out a form of in-process inspection, although in many instances it is not recognized as such. Normally supervisory staff evaluate work as it progresses.

The responsibility of quality assurance would be to verify, as for all other activities, the establishment, implementation, and effectiveness of and the adherence to the documented system for in-process inspection.

Final inspection

As for in-process inspection, all requirements for final inspection should be included in the inspection and test plan. The requirements would include the type and nature of the inspection to be carried out, together with any testing which is to be undertaken and which the customer and/or regulatory body may wish to witness. In the case of large batches of identical items, sampling methods should also be indicated.

The inspection and test plan should also include documentation which will be required to verify the acceptability of the item, such as:

	JOB No.	DRAWING	PATTERN	PAGE	ITEM	MAT	QUANTITY

DESCRIPTION: DO NOT WORK TO THIS SKETCH:

DATE:

ROUTED BY:		DATE REQUIRED:		INSPECTED BY:	
OPERATION:				SET UP	EACH
				ADD FOR FIRST PIECES %	
		MACH No.		ADD FOR NEXT PIECES %	
OPERATION:				SET UP	EACH
				ADD FOR FIRST PIECES %	
		MACH No.		ADD FOR NEXT PIECES %	
OPERATION:				SET UP	EACH
				ADD FOR FIRST PIECES %	
		MACH No.		ADD FOR NEXT PIECES %	
OPERATION:				SET UP	EACH
				ADD FOR FIRST PIECES %	
		MACH No.		ADD FOR NEXT PIECES %	
OPERATION:				SET UP	EACH
				ADD FOR FIRST PIECES %	
		MACH No.		ADD FOR NEXT PIECES %	
OPERATION:				SET UP	EACH
				ADD FOR FIRST PIECES %	
		MACH No.		ADD FOR NEXT PIECES %	

AFTER INSPECTION DELIVER TO:

MAT'L. REQ'D.

XYZ-MNF-009.3

Fig. 14.2—Route card.

Material certificates
Functional test results
Non-destructive test results
Sampling results
Dimensional results
and so on.

In the case of non-compliant items, they should be identified and quarantined pending arrangements for dispositioning, which would be carried out in accordance with a procedure for non-conforming items.

The acceptability of an item should be indicated on the appropriate documentation.

The procedure adopted for in-house final inspection would apply also to purchased items where final inspection is to be carried out by the purchaser at a subcontractor's premises.

Service organizations also carry out forms of final inspection.

For example, the work of hotel room cleaning staff is generally checked by a supervisor against a checklist to verify that not only is the room clean but to confirm that clean towels, soap, shoe-cleaning cloths, tea-making facilities, and so on, have been taken care of.

The responsibility of quality assurance would be to verify, as for all other activities, the establishment and effectiveness of, and the adherence to, the documented system for final inspection.

Sampling

As for purchaser-supplied (free-issue) items, the majority of quality assurance standards include sampling schemes as one of the criteria. There are many organizations who do not manufacture identical items in sufficient quantities to warrant the use of sampling schemes and, in such cases, it would not be necessary to establish such a procedure.

Where considerable numbers of identical items are produced, then it is beneficial to introduce a sampling scheme which will, in all probability, be based upon an applicable standard.

Sampling schemes are established to give the manufacturer and the purchaser the confidence that an acceptable quality level (not to be confused with system level) has been achieved.

It has been proved that a well-designed sampling scheme can achieve the same level of confidence as a 100% inspection.

Experience has shown that given 100 items to inspect for dimension and finish there will be as many different acceptance levels as there are inspectors taking part. Or, to make the point another way, give a number of people the same page from a book and ask them to count the number of R's on the page, then the probability is that there will be as many different answers as there are people taking part in the exercise.

In such cases where sampling schemes are utilized, such schemes should be indicated on the inspection and test plan.

So much has been written on sampling techniques that the author has no intention of adding to the myriad of publications on the subject. Suffice to say that a number of standards and publications dealing with sampling and statistical quality control are included in the bibliography.

Service organizations can also utilize sampling schemes where considerable numbers of identical functions are carried out. One area which lends itself to sampling is the reproduction of identical documents which are to be distributed to many individuals—the 'mail shot'. Word processors are utilized to make this operation much more effective but even then there is no guarantee of 100% accuracy.

The action by quality assurance should be to verify that the requirements for sampling have been established and that such are being effectively implemented.

Inspection and test status

There should be some means of identifying the status of an item during production. By this is meant an identification system which would indicate at a glance whether an item (or items) is (or are) awaiting inspection and/or test, has (or have) been inspected and/or tested and accepted or rejected.

Inspection and test status is invariably overlooked by many organizations and a lack of an identification system has caused many problems due to rejected items being processed further only to be re-rejected later on.

Many times during the auditing of manufacturing organizations it has been found necessary to request the status of manufactured items because no positive identification methods were used. The time involved in obtaining the answers to such requests was quite considerable.

On one such occasion it meant tracing the whereabouts of the chief inspector, as he was the only person who had the information. The manufacturing facility concerned covered a wide area and the chief inspector could have been in any one of a dozen places. By the time a positive indication of his location was found, he had gone to lunch! In all, it took three hours to obtain the required information. This is far from an isolated incident.

A simple identification system, known to all shop-floor personnel, would have saved the time of all the people involved, not to mention the frustration experienced by all concerned.

Some form of positive identification of status should be used. The methods are, as for most other systems, a matter of company choice. For example, a typical system would be:

— Items or batches awaiting inspection and/or test are unmarked.
— Items of batches inspected and accepted are tagged with green adhesive labels.
— Items or batches inspected and rejected are tagged with red adhesive labels or 'rejected' tags.

Whatever system is used, it should be documented and implemented without variation.

The authority for the application or removal of any identification labels or stickers should be documented; such authority is usually given to the quality control department.

Service organizations can utilize an inspection and test status system to identify the acceptability, or otherwise, of a process or function during an activity.

The action by quality assurance would be to verify the establishment of a suitable identification system and confirm its implementation and effectiveness.

Identification and traceability

Traceability is generally a requirement only by contract and is, therefore, another of the criteria of the quality assurance standards which is not applicable to all organizations. It would not normally apply to any service-related organization.

The subject of traceability was introduced in design control, when it was established that it should be the responsibility of the relevant design engineer to determine which items require traceability.

Having established the requirement in the design stage, this requirement would be written into the specification.

The manufacturing organization should then inject such traceability requirements into its own production planning system and inspection and test plan.

A method of identifying the items or batches which require traceability should be established. This identification method should be unique to the contract and will be carried through all stages of manufacture and on to installation and thence throughout the operational life of the unit.

This unique identification should be recorded on all applicable documentation.

The action by quality assurance would be to verify the requirement for identification and traceability, and to audit the implementation of the system.

Handling and storage

All items received into either a manufacturing or service organization should be stored and protected against misuse, damage and deterioration, and also controlled against unauthorized use.

Once cleared through incoming inspection, items generally go into store pending use.

Similarly, items which are being processed through a manufacturing cycle can go into store pending further processing. For example, material which has to undergo planing and drilling could complete the planing process and then go into store pending the drilling operation. In such cases, there would be a requirement for protection of the surface finish against corrosion and damage.

Storage should be controlled so that any items subject to deterioration due to limited 'shelf-life' are released in strict rotation.

Items subject to corrosion should be stored in the appropriate environmental conditions where humidity and temperature can be regulated to minimize corrosion.

It is strongly recommended that entry to all storage areas should be limited to authorized personnel only, so as to prevent unauthorized use of items.

Experience has shown that such limited access to storage areas is not generally practised and shop-floor personnel are able to obtain items from stores without control. Apart from the security aspect (which is probably such that items could not leave the premises), such a free-for-all attitude does nothing to eliminate damage, use of expired shelf-life components, and the like, not to mention disturbance of records.

Not only should storage areas be of limited access but regular monitoring of the storage of items during processing should be carried out.

Any unsatisfactory conditions brought to light during monitoring should be dealt with in accordance with an appropriate system.

The normal practice is for the monitoring of storage facilities to be carried out by quality control personnel, but this is surely a function that should be undertaken by responsible production personnel. Production should be made responsible for the quality of the work they produce and not rely on others to do it for them.

The action by quality assurance would be to verify the establishment of the appropriate handling and storage system, and to audit implementation.

Special processes

Special processes are processes which cannot be verified as having been properly carried out by final inspection or testing. In other words, processes which require continuous or intermittent monitoring throughout.

Special processes fall into two distinct categories: those relating to manufacture and those relating to inspection and testing.

The manufacturing special processes include such things as:

Welding
Casting
Concrete mixing
Protective coatings
Heat treatment.

The inspection and testing special processes include such things as:

Radiography
Magnetic particle inspection
Dye penetrant inspection
Ultrasonic inspection
Pressure testing.

It should be noted that some everyday activities are listed among these special processes: welding, heat treatment and non-destructive testing. Problems arise because such activities are not regarded as 'special'! If they are treated as special, and the necessary control procedures developed and implemented, then many of these problems can be prevented. To quote some examples:

In the case of protective coating (painting), all that one is able to establish at final inspection is that the coating thickness and colour are correct. Final inspection will not confirm that the surface finish of the base material was in accordance with specification, neither will it confirm the thickness of the ground coat, undercoats and finish coat. It will also not confirm whether the curing (time, temperature and humidity) process was carried out to specification.

In the case of welding, it is not possible to verify at final inspection whether the consumables were temperature and time controlled, whether the correct pre-heat temperature was attained, and so on.

All that a heat-treatment graph will convey is that the temperature rise, hold and reduce were carried out according to specification. What the graph will not disclose is whether other items were placed in the oven at the same time, whether the item itself was placed in the correct location in the oven and whether the thermocouples were correctly situated.

The quality of a special process cannot usually be verified by subsequent inspection and testing of the processed material. It will, therefore, be necessary to establish full conformance by evidence obtained during the process. This is achievable by:

(1)   establishing documented procedures which will ensure that all special processes are carried out under controlled conditions by qualified personnel using calibrated equipment in accordance with applicable contract codes, specifications, standards and regulatory requirements;

(2)   maintaining current records of qualified personnel, equipment and processes, in accordance with the requirements of the applicable codes and standards;

(3)   defining the necessary qualifications of personnel, equipment and processes not covered by existing codes or standards, or when contractual clauses define stricter requirements than those already established.

Service organizations also have a requirement to establish special process procedures and there are some manufacturing processes which are equally applicable to service organizations. These processes include:

X-ray
ultrasonics
heat treatment

which are used mainly in hospital services.

The action by quality assurance would be to verify that the processes which are classified as special are procedurally controlled. Such controls would include: maintenance and calibration of special process equipment and the suitability of personnel performing special processes; auditing the implementation and effectiveness of, and adherence to, the system and verifying the utilization of qualified personnel.

Preservation, packaging and shipping

Where preservation, packaging and shipping requirements are not defined by contract, then a system should be developed to assure the effectiveness of this function.

The system should define the methods of preserving and packaging items to assure cleanliness, prevention of damage and preservation during shipment and possible storage at final destination. Such details should be included in the inspection and test plan.

Prior to shipment the acceptability of the item should be verified. Verification should include the adequacy of preservation and packaging, together with the inclusion of correct documentation.

The methods of transportation, where not defined in the contract, should be such as to ensure safe arrival at destination.

Inadequate packing and inappropriate transport facilities are the causes of much customer dissatisfaction. Regardless of the care taken to assure the quality of an item, all this can be negated by the item being lost in transit, arriving late or arriving in a damaged condition.

Fitness for purpose is the condition required for use.

Service organizations also have a responsibility to respond to requirements for preservation, packaging and shipping.

For example, documents (legal, banking and so on) should be packed and shipped (posted) to be received by a customer on time and in a fit for purpose condition.

The action by quality assurance should be to verify the inclusion of preservation, packaging and shipping details in the inspection and test plan, and to audit the implementation and effectiveness of the system.

Non-conforming items

Any inspection process can result in an item being found unsuitable. This can occur upon receipt, during manufacture or at final inspection. Whenever it does occur, there should be a system to direct personnel in the actions to be taken.

Initially, a non-conforming item should be identified as being non-conforming with a suitable tag, adhesive label or paint mark. It should then, wherever possible, be segregated from all other items to prevent unauthorized use, shipment or inclusion with conforming items.

The applicable documentation should then be completed, which should identify the item, the nature of the defect or discrepancy. The documentation should then be forwarded to the appropriate department for review.

It will be the responsibility of the appropriate person to determine the action to be taken. In some instances, particularly in cases of high-value or safety-related equipment, it could be necessary to set up a review board to discuss the implications of the discrepancy. In any event, the outcome will be one of the following:

Scrap
Repair or rework
Use as is.

The level of authority at which dispositioning of non-conforming items can be made should be clearly established. For example, deviations of a minor nature could well be handled by inspection personnel, provided the necessary rework or repair procedures have been agreed previously.

All other deviations should be dealt with by reference back to the original design source, which may well include customer participation. Whatever the outcome, the system should ensure that the appropriate action is taken and documented.

Service organizations will also have a requirement to comply where a service has been unacceptable to the customer.

The action by quality assurance should be to verify that the system for dealing with non-conforming items is established and to monitor, as required, its implementation and effectiveness.

Records

All quality assurance standards call for a system to control records, which could be defined in three words: filing and finding.

The filing of the records and the ability to find such records with the minimum time and effort is the hallmark of a well-organized document control system.

In the main, the records that are to be developed and maintained relate to what are described as quality-related activities. These records provide the objective evidence that an item, or service, meets contract or specification requirements, and it is this objective evidence which the quality assurance auditor will seek to confirm compliance with the system. (Auditing is dealt with in Chapter 16.)

Records would comprise such items as:

1. System and compliance audit reports.
2. Results of inspections performed in accordance with the inspection and test plan.
3. Data covering the reliability of purchasing sources.
4. Material certification.
5. Data covering the calibration of inspection, measuring and test equipment.
6. Details of non-conforming items.
7. Details of corrective actions.
8. Results of inspection of stores areas.
9. Results of tests, approvals and audits by customers, regulatory bodies and other third party sources.
10. Certification for approval of personnel.
11. Functional test reports and data.
12. Installation and commissioning test reports.

All records should be reviewed and evaluated regularly by responsible personnel. The results of such reviews should be used for the purpose of improving and updating the quality systems.

Records should be retained for the period set by legislation or by the contract (whichever is the maximum).

Records should be stored in a suitable environment which will minimize deterioration or damage, and prevent loss. In normal circumstances, this should be in steel cabinets which are water-resistant and fire-retardant.

Other methods of record retention may be used, such as computerized data storage, microfilm or microfiche, but such should be agreed with the customer where necessary.

Service organizations will also have a requirement to maintain and retain records.

The action by quality assurance should be to verify the establishment of the record system and to monitor, by audit, the implementation and effectiveness of, and the adherence to, the system.

Training

Not all quality assurance standards identify the requirement for training of personnel, yet it is a most important activity.

Training can be required in many areas in both manufacturing and service environments. The introduction of new machinery and equipment, the upgrading of personnel to meet new employment criteria, the retraining of operatives to take on additional responsibilities and to meet the demands of new technology, are just some of the areas which should be covered by a corporate training policy.

In determining training requirements, consideration should be given to those functions which require acquired skills and those functions which could be adversely affected by lack of skill. Such functions should be identified, categorized and documented.

The following is a non-exhaustive list of functions which could be considered as requiring skills which should be covered by training:

Manufacturing	*Services*
Quality assurance management	Quality assurance management
Auditing (internal and external)	Auditing (internal)
Welding	Word processing
Ultrasonic examination	Telephone answering
Magnetic particle examination	Computing
Radiography	Radiography
Penetrant examination	

Management should establish, by review, examination, or other means, whether personnel carrying out such functions require training or additional experience to make good any shortfall. Management should also establish how competence in a given function is determined, by examination, testing, certification, and so on.

The methods to be used in making good such shortfall in experience or training should also be documented and would include training or indoctrination by in-house training schemes or by third party training organizations.

Records of training involvement, together with examination or test results (where applicable), should be documented and made available to the customer or regulatory body as required.

Training in certain functions requires regular updating and the necessary evidence that such retraining or maintenance of qualifications has been carried out should be documented. For example, welders and weld inspectors require retesting at regular intervals to retain qualification; quality assurance assessors require re-evaluation on a regular basis to retain registration, and so on.

The action by quality assurance should be: to verify the establishment of a training policy and to monitor, by audit, that the requirements of such a policy are being implemented; to verify that personnel are receiving, or have received, the training as required and that qualification and requalification records are maintained and updated.

Audit and corrective action

The quality assurance department would verify, initially, the establishment of procedures to control all the foregoing activities and then to monitor, by audit, their implementation, adherence and effectiveness.

All non-conformances exposed during audits would be addressed by corrective action requests upon the appropriate party, with follow-up action to verify that corrective action had been taken and steps taken to prevent a recurrence of the deficiency.

Once manufacture is complete, the item is either delivered to the customer for use or it is to be installed and commissioned. The next element in the total presentation is installation control.

15

Installation control

The control of installation processes is a very neglected area. There are a number of quality assurance standards that refer to installation in the title yet very little guidance is given on the subject in the standard itself.

In the main, the control of installation covers the same criteria as manufacture and it is to manufacturing control that one should look to determine the procedural requirements.

THE MAJOR ACTIVITIES

Again, as for previous elements in the total presentation, the most important activities have been tabulated (Fig. 15.1). As previously, each activity is dealt with in detail.

Contract review (planning)

Should a contract cover installation activities only then, of course, a complete formal contract review meeting should take place to review the customer requirements and to plan for the installation. If, however, as is most likely to be the case, installation forms only part of a total package, then the contract review meeting should have taken place previously. Nevertheless, before the installation activity, a review of requirements should be carried out and all functions planned in a systematic manner.

All concerned should be aware of their responsibilities and, if necessary, a review team assembled to review the requirements and plan for the installation of the equipment or plant.

Installation requirements

The planing for installation will entail a detailed consideration of the installation requirements and a verification that the requirements are fully understood by all involved personnel.

Specifications and standards

It should be confirmed that all applicable specifications and standards are available to the installation team and of the correct issue. If there should be any shortfalls or ambiguities, these should be resolved before the installation activity commences.

INSTALLATION CONTROL

ACTIVITY	SCOPE	PERFORMED BY	ACTION BY QA
1 Contract review (planning)	Review: Installation requirements Specifications and standards Materials Tools Installation processes Inspection, test and commissioning requirements Organization	Site management Installation Quality control (site) Quality assurance	Verify that missing or ambiguous information has been followed up and satisfactorily closed out by the responsible person
2 Document preparation control and retention	Ensure correct and uniform presentation of documents Ensure formal preparation identification, checking, approval and distribution, including amendments Verify retention, retrieval, storage and handover requirements	Site management Installation Quality control (site)	Audit adherence to procedure
3 Control of inspection, measuring and test equipment	Verify: Equipment to be controlled Standards for control Calibration method Calibration interval Identification of calibration status	Site management Production	Audit adherence to procedure
4 Control of locally purchased items and services	Assure methods of adequately assessing supplier's ability to meet contract requirements	Site purchasing Installation Quality control (site)	Audit adherence to procedure
5 Incoming inspection at site	Verify product conformity to requirements	Quality control (site)	Audit adherence to inspection, test and commissioning plan
6 Purchaser-supplied items (manufacturer-supplied)	Verify: Unpacking methods Type, condition and quantity on receipt Storage requirements	Quality control (site)	Audit adherence to inspection, testing and commissioning plan
7 Inspection during installation (in-process inspection)	Verify adherence to specification during installation by inspection and/or test Identification Documentation	Quality control (site)	Audit adherence to inspection, test and commissioning plan
8 Final inspection	Verify adherence to specification on completion by inspection and/or test Identification Documentation	Quality control (site)	Audit adherence to inspection, test and commissioning plan

Fig. 15.1—Installation matrix.

INSTALLATION CONTROL

ACTIVITY	SCOPE	PERFORMED BY	ACTION BY QA
9 Sampling (where applicable)	Verify use of sampling schemes Methods Standards	Quality control (site)	Audit adherence to inspection, test and commissioning plan
10 Inspection and commissioning status	Verify methods of indicating inspection and/or commissioning status	Commissioning personnel Quality control (site)	Audit adherence to procedure
11 Identification and traceability (where applicable)	Verify requirements for traceability of items Identification Documentation	Installation Quality control (site)	Audit adherence to inspection, test and commissioning plan
12 Handling and storage	Verify handling and storage methods	Installation Quality control (site)	Audit adherence to inspection, test and commissioning plan
13 Special processes	Verify which installation processes fall into the special category Determine methods of control, maintenance and calibration of special process equipment Suitability of personnel performing special processes	Installation Quality control (site)	Audit adherence to procedure
14 Non-conforming items or processes	Verify methods of identifying and dispositioning non-conforming items or processes	Installation Commissioning Quality control (site)	Audit adherence to procedure
15 Records	Verify: Requirements Format Contents Storage Retrieval Retention period	Library Site document control centre	Audit adherence to procedure
16 Training	Verify and document training needs Methods Records	Management Installation	Audit adherence to procedure
17 Audit and corrective action	Ensure non-conformances promptly identified and corrective action taken to prevent recurrence	Site management Installation Quality assurance	Audit adherence to procedure

Fig. 15.1—Installation matrix.

Materials

It should be ensured that the correct materials and equipment are available and that such are properly identified. In the case of unassembled units, each section of the unit should be match-marked to facilitate installation. This latter requirement is most important, as experience has shown that a great deal of time can be expended by installation teams trying to verify which piece goes where. Mistakes can also be made by installing almost identical parts in the wrong location, only to discover the error much later on and thus have to redo all the work to rectify the fault.

Tools
The need for special installation tools should also be considered. It may be necessary to purchase or hire specialized equipment.

Installation processes
Consideration should be given to the use of any special installation processes, which may have to be supported by special process procedures.

Inspection, test and commissioning requirements
An inspection, test and commissioning plan should be developed which should take into consideration any special requirements imposed by contract. Specialized testing and/or commissioning equipment may have to be contracted-in and arrangements for either purchase or hire should be considered.

Organization
The organization structure of the installation and commissioning team should be established, together with any customer interfaces. Consideration should also be given to the staffing requirements, together with experience and qualification levels.

General
In the case of consumer products such as washing machines, central heating units, double glazing and so on, the planning for installation and commissioning would take place but on a much smaller scale. In many instances, installation is a one-person operation but, nevertheless, that person should make sure before undertaking an installation process that all the materials, equipment tools, testing procedures and the like are available, in order that the installation and commissioning activities are carried out correctly and efficiently.

Action by quality assurance
In the case of an installation only contract, the contract review meeting should be minuted. The quality assurance representative should verify that any missing or ambiguous information in the contract has been followed up and closed out by the responsible person(s).

In the case where the installation process is part of a total package, then in all probability the planning activity for installation would be established in the form of an installation and commissioning plan, which the quality assurance representative would verify as having been established.

Document preparation, control and retention
This activity is identical to that described for design control but the documents themselves will be generally of a different nature and will relate to the installation and commissioning requirements and could cover such things as:

Installation procedures
Inspection, test and commissioning plans
Testing and commissioning procedures
Special process procedures for installation and commissioning
Job instructions
Inspection procedures.

In all cases, the methods of preparing, identifying and approving documents, methods of changing and approving changes to documents and methods of removing and recalling obsolete documents should be formalized and controlled.

The action by quality assurance should be to verify, initially, the formulation of all relevant procedures to control this activity and to confirm the implementation and adequacy of, and adherence to, the document control system.

Control of inspection, measuring and test equipment
The installation and commissioning activities will, in all probability, utilize equipment which requires some form of regular servicing and/or calibration to confirm its accuracy and its continued fitness for use.

The methods for such control are identical to those detailed in Chapter 14 but, depending on the size and nature of the equipment or plant to be installed, the calibration centre could well be located at the installation site with its own master standards and its own gauge room.

A petrochemical or power production plant are cases in point. The actual installation process is at the site itself and, when commissioned, the plant will continue to be operated and maintained for many years, thus inspection and test equipment will be in regular use at the site location.

With small items of equipment, however, where installation and commissioning are part of a total contract, then of course measuring, test and inspection equipment would be drawn from stores by the installation crew (which may comprise one or more personnel). The stores would be located in the manufacturing facility and, therefore, the calibration of such equipment would be controlled, for example, by the production department.

The action by quality assurance should be to verify the calibration status of equipment used by installation personnel.

Control of locally purchased items and services
In the main, personnel will be installing items supplied by others (i.e. their own manufactured items or items supplied by the customer) and there should be no requirement to purchase additional items or services.

In the case of large projects such as petrochemical or power production plants mentioned earlier there will, in all probability, be a project management team established on-site. A good deal of material/equipment and services will have to be purchased locally and could comprise:

Material	*Services*
Consumables	Welders
Structural steel	Inspection and
Plate material	non-destructive testing personnel
Fasteners	

In this case site management should evaluate procurement sources in the same manner as for procurement control (Chapter 13).

The action by quality assurance will be exactly as before.

Incoming inspection at site

As for manufacturing control, this activity is carried out to verify the acceptability and condition of bought-out items.

This activity should be formalized both in the case of the large projects already mentioned, and also in very small installation tasks where it may be done without the installer actually recognizing the fact. As an example, a technician who installs a washing machine may require a pipe fitting not supplied with the machine. The installer goes through two functions:

1.   He identifies the procurement source (possibly a local hardware store).
2.   He inspects the item for conformance.

If he actually goes to the store himself, inspection will be carried out at source. If the item is sent by the store or is collected by the installer's helper, then inspection is carried out on arrival (incoming inspection at site).

In all probability, the method for dealing with this case will have been established by the washing machine manufacturer and should be recognized as being the most effective method of dealing with such a circumstance. Is it, however, as effective or efficient as one might suppose? How much simpler to have included in the installation kit a set of pipe fittings to cover all possibilities! The cost of the time taken in first identifying the procurement source and then collecting the part (at most wholesale outlets there is usually a long wait to be served) will be, in all probability, far in excess of the cost of the part!

Many organizations fail to realize the time involved in rectifying a problem. In times of high labour costs this can be very significant.

The action by quality assurance is twofold. In the case of the large project situation it should be to verify, as in manufacturing control, the establishment of the appropriate inspection and test plan which will call up incoming inspection as required.

In the case of our washing machine installer, quality assurance should be aware of such circumstances and should draw management's attention to the inefficiency of such practices. It will mean, of course, that the installer should have the means of communicating back to base and that such communications are distributed on the 'need to know' basis and not kept just for reference in the shipping or such other department. Management can act only if it is aware of the problem.

It should not be assumed that only washing machine manufacturers adopt such procedures. Most organizations who supply and install their own products do leave their installers to purchase locally whatever has been forgotten. The author has experienced similar situations with respect to double glazing, central heating, home extensions, and others. There is nothing worse than looking at a gaping hole where a window should be because some part or other was not included in the shipment and the local supply source was temporarily out of stock of that part.

Purchaser-supplied items (manufacturer-supplied)

This activity could be said to be more applicable to the construction and installation site than to the manufacturing process. Most items to be installed will have been supplied to the installer by someone else. In the case of our washing machine installer, the machine would have been supplied to him by the company who employs him. In the case of the large construction and installation site, the items would have been supplied by the central purchasing body.

In either case, it should be regarded as 'free issue' and the necessary controls implemented to verify its completeness and freedom from damage.

British Standard 5750, Part 4:1990 states that:

When materials, commonly described as 'free issue' are provided by the customer to the supplier the onus for their conformity to specified requirements is that of the customer. However, the supplier should not knowingly incorporate non-conforming parts into the production or service supplied to the customer.

The supplier's system should include the provision for verification, proper storage and maintenance of such materials supplied.

There should also be a formalized method for dealing with losses, damage or other problems discovered with such material.

The installer or, in the case of large projects, site management, should therefore ensure that there are satisfactory arrangements for the following:

1. Examination of the material upon receipt to check quantities, identities, and to detect any damage caused during transit.
2. Periodic inspection during storage to detect any sign of deterioration; to check on any outdating risk where storage time exceeds recommended shelf-life; to ensure the maintenance of storage conditions which will not cause deterioration and to check generally the condition of stored material.
3. Compliance with any contractual requirement for reinspection, appropriate identification and safeguarding of material to prevent unauthorized use or improper disposal.

Procedures should exist which define the manner in which any shortages, damage or other factors rendering the material unfit for use are reported to the customer.

The action by quality assurance should be to determine that the installer or site management are aware of, and have access to, procedures as described above and to verify their implementation and effectiveness.

Inspection during installation (in-process inspection)

The requirements for inspection during installation should be documented. The inspection and test plan described in Chapter 11 would be the ideal vehicle for this activity.

The requirements would include the points during installation where the installer (or installation crew) would cease pending an intermediate check to verify acceptance at a given point. The type of acceptance check or test should be indicated.

As each acceptance check or test is completed, it should be reported on an appropriate document—the installation checklist, for example, could include the facility for this.

As for any activity, the installation personnel should be responsible for checking their own work before calling on the appropriate inspection personnel to verify acceptability. In the case of the domestic appliance installer, he will, in all probability, be working alone and will undertake the verification activity himself. The use of a checklist in such situations is, therefore, most important.

The action by quality assurance would be to verify, as for all other activities, the establishment, implementation and effectiveness of, and the adherence to, the documented system for inspection during installation.

Final inspection

As for inspection during installation, all requirements for final inspection on completion of the installation process should be included in the appropriate document, such as the inspection and test plan.

As for the manufacturing control, the requirement would include the type and nature of the inspection to be carried out, together with any testing which is to be undertaken and which the customer and/or regulatory body may wish to witness.

The requirements for regulatory body involvement are not unique to large projects in this respect. The installation of domestic gas and electrical appliances has in some instances, in many countries, to be checked for safety aspects by an accredited agency prior to 'switch-on' and release, for use, to the customer.

All such requirements should be established before installation and taken into consideration. This serves, once again, to confirm the importance of the planning or contract review activity, which should be carried out regardless of the quality system level or the size and nature of the contract.

The action by quality assurance would be to verify that the necessary planning had been carried out and that final inspection requirements are understood and are effectively implemented.

Sampling

In all probability sampling would not be applicable during installation but should it be so then such requirements would be dealt with in the same manner as for manufacturing control.

Inspection and commissioning status

As for manufacturing, there should be some means of identifying the status of an item or system (mechanical, electrical, instrumentation, and so on) during installation and eventual commissioning.

Again, as for manufacturing, the identification system should indicate, at a glance, and at any point during the installation and commissioning process, whether an item or system is awaiting inspection (or commissioning), has been inspected and accepted (commissioned) or inspected and rejected (failed commissioning test).

The methods and procedures for such identification are, as for most other systems, a matter of company choice and the example given for manufacturing control could be adapted to suit the installation and commissioning process.

The action by quality assurance would be to verify the establishment of a suitable identification system and confirm its implementation and effectiveness.

Identification and traceability

As has already been said, traceability is generally a requirement only by contract and, in such instances, should operate throughout the design, manufacture, installation and operational life of the unit.

Traceability requirements were established and discussed during design control, carried through manufacturing control and should now be implemented during installation.

The traceability requirements should be detailed in the installation planning system and the inspection, test and commissioning plan.

The items requiring traceability should have already been identified during manufacture. During installation, the location of such items in the plant layout should be documented, together with the unique identification number, or symbol, of the unit. This information should, of course, be relayed back to 'central records' to complete the traceability cycle.

Once central records have this information, it should be possible, assuming the 'filing and finding' system is working satisfactorily, to trace such items 'in and out' as described for design control.

The action by quality assurance would be to verify the requirement for identification and traceability, and to audit the implementation of the system.

Handling and storage

All items received at the installation site should be stored and protected against misuse, damage and deterioration, and also controlled against unauthorized use.

Installation sites are generally very lax in this area and one particular industry which springs readily to mind is the building industry. A considerable amount of loss, damage and misuse occurs on building sites due, primarily, to the lack of control over handling and storage.

In cases where expensive and sophisticated equipment is concerned, time, effort and cost are expended to minimize loss, damage and misuse, yet the lesser valued items are generally left lying around. There is a saying that 'if one looks after the pennies, the pounds will take care of themselves'. This could apply to the construction site. The attitude in general is that as the items have been supplied by others, 'the others' should be responsible for it. Not so! The requirement to control purchaser-supplied items is quite specific.

The systems to control handling and storage are generally as described for manufacturing control.

The action by quality assurance should be to verify the establishment of the appropriate handling and storage system, and to audit implementation.

Special processes

The installation site, having received the purchaser-supplied items and any locally purchased items, will now have to translate all this into a finished and fit for purpose product. Special processes are paramount in this operation.

If one looks at the special processes listed for manufacturing control it should be apparent that these, and others, can be applicable to all manner of installation and construction site situations. Commissioning activities also utilize special processes. The purging of piping and vessel installations and the sealing to prevent ingress of moisture before actual 'switch-on' is one example.

In addition to those already mentioned, certain applications of forming, plastics and wood fabrication also can fall under the special process category.

Company or site management should verify, therefore, which installation processes fall into the special category and determine methods of control, maintenance and calibration of special process equipment.

The suitability of personnel performing these special processes should also be established and should include the methods of evaluation. Instructions should be available to determine training and qualification requirements, and the updating and maintenance of qualifications by either periodic examination or continuous satisfactory performance.

The action by quality assurance would be: to verify the establishment of special process procedures; to audit the implementation and effectiveness of, and adherence to, such procedures and to verify the utilization of appropriately trained and qualified personnel.

Non-conforming items or processes

In the installation and commissioning phases an inspection activity can uncover an unsatisfactory condition. Whenever such an unsatisfactory condition is found, there should be a system to direct personnel in the action to be taken. A method of identification should be utilized, such as that described in 'Identification of inspection and test status' in Chapter 14.

During installation, it may not be possible to segregate the non-conforming item (if it is an item), and therefore a clear identification of the non-conformance should be clearly visible. The action to be taken in such circumstances will follow the same pattern as for manufacturing control.

The action by quality assurance should be to verify that a system for identifying and dispositioning non-conforming items, or processes, is established and to monitor, as required, its implementation and effectiveness.

Records

As for manufacturing, a system should be established to control the records generated during the installation and commissioning activities.

In the case of large projects, these records will, in all probability, be maintained at the construction site and handed over to the customer or back to the central document control area on completion of activities.

In all other cases, the installer would return the records to his employer for filing.

The action by quality assurance should be to verify the establishment where required, of a site-controlled record system and to monitor, by audit, the implementation and effectiveness of the system.

Where records are returned to a central document control area by the installer, then quality assurance should monitor, as required, to verify that such records are returned and filed as the system dictates.

Training

The subject of training in the installation phase has been touched upon already in special processes. There are other areas of activity which should require training of personnel and these are detailed in manufacturing control.

Site management should determine those activities which are to be covered by training needs. These training needs should be documented, together with the methods for training, and the documentation required to verify satisfactory completion of training. The frequency for updating training qualifications should be also established, as well as requirements for retraining in the event of poor performance or non-participation in an activity.

The action by quality assurance should be: to verify the establishment of a training policy and to monitor, by audit, that the requirements of such a policy are being implemented throughout; to verify that installation and commissioning personnel are receiving, or have received, the training as required and that the records of such training, or retraining, are maintained and updated.

Audit and corrective action

The quality assurance department would verify, initially, the establishment of procedures to control all installation and commissioning activities, and then monitor, by audit, their implementation, adherence and effectiveness.

As before, all non-conformances exposed during audits should be addressed by corrective action requests upon the appropriate party, with follow-up action to verify that corrective action had been taken and steps taken to prevent a recurrence of the deficiency.

Installation and commissioning are complete and the entire plant, facility or whatever is handed over to the customer in a fit for purpose condition.

MAINTENANCE (SERVICING)

Maintenance of the unit will be periodically necessary if the unit is to continue to perform satisfactorily during its anticipated service life.

The requirements for maintenance should have been established during the design stage.

A programme for maintenance should be documented and here again most, if not all, of the activities described in this chapter from planning to audit and corrective action will be just as applicable to maintenance (particularly of major capital equipment and plant).

Audit and corrective action has been mentioned many times as being the means of verifying the implementation and effectiveness of, and adherence to, the documented quality system.

The next element in the total presentation is to establish exactly what an audit is, and what it entails.

16

Audit and corrective action

Once a quality system has been established and implemented the only possible way an organization can verify the effectiveness of the system is to carry out regular audits. It will be necessary, therefore, to develop a capability to manage the entire process. This audit function should be independent from and have no direct responsibility for the implementation of the quality system elements.

AUDIT/ASSESSMENT OBJECTIVES

The term 'audit' is used generally to indicate an internal or post-award contract activity, and the term 'assessment' a pre-contract activity. The objectives of an internal audit would therefore be:

— to determine the implementation and effectiveness of one's own quality system
— to determine conformance or non-conformance of quality system elements to specified contractual requirements
— to provide a basis for improvement of a quality system
— to meet regulatory requirements
— to achieve second or third party registration.

The objectives of an assessment or external audit, as discussed in Chapter 13, would therefore be:

— to evaluate a potential supplier with a view to establishing a contractual relationship (assessment)
— to verify that a supplier's quality system continues to meet specified requirements and is being effectively implemented (post-contract audit).

THE RESPONSIBILITY FOR AUDITING

As has been said, one of the responsibilities of the quality assurance department or function is to undertake internal or external audits. Any such audits should not result in transferring the responsibility for the achievement of quality from operating staff to the auditing function.

In the very small organization, the responsibility for auditing may rest with the senior executive. After all, the senior executive has the ultimate responsibility for quality and the quality system has been developed by him or her in conjunction with the company's senior management and, therefore, he or she should be aware of the efficiency of the organization.

There is a requirement for a company to be aware of its financial status and an audit is carried out to verify that a company's accounting system is in order and that the results are accurate. With a financial audit, however, this is undertaken as a legal requirement under the Companies Act. The results do identify a company's profit and loss position and a company's board of directors will act on the results. The 'bottom line' is the spur.

WHY AUDIT?

A company's quality system is not generally seen in the same light as the financial accounting system, yet, because of inefficient control over all its activities, a company could well be losing a great deal of money. The inefficiencies due to duplication of activities, high repair and scrap rates, malpractices and so on, may result in the quality costs (the cost of putting things right) being higher than the overall profit margin.

A quality audit, if effectively undertaken, should uncover such problems, providing the audit is carried out against documented requirements and by trained and qualified personnel.

WHAT IS AN AUDIT

All quality system standards call up a requirement for the auditing or the review of the quality system and, in general, such an activity could be defined as:

A planned and documented independent activity performed in accordance with written procedures and checklists to verify by investigation, and the examination and evaluation of objective evidence, that applicable elements of a quality system have been developed, documented and effectively implemented in accordance with specified requirements.

The ISO 8402 definition is as follows:

A systematic and independent examination to determine whether quality activities and related results comply with planned arrangements and whether these arrangements are implemented effectively and are suitable to achieve objectives.

AUDIT DEPTH, SCOPE AND TYPE

As has already been stated, there is a requirement to seek objective evidence to determine that an activity has been carried out in accordance with specified requirements. These specified requirements are the procedures and job instructions. Initially, however, immediately after establishing a quality system, an audit should be carried out to confirm that all the relevant procedures and instructions are available at the activity locations and that personnel are aware of their responsibilities within the system. In project-related industries this would be undertaken at the commencement of each project. The objectives of such an audit are to confirm the existence and validity of the necessary quality system. Such an audit is known generally as a system audit.

In order to appreciate this more fully, a case study is worth considering. A contractor was awarded a contract for the design of a major piece of equipment. The controls to be implemented for this contract were outlined in the project quality manual and comprised the following:

Contract review
Document preparation, control and retention
Discipline check
Interdiscipline check
Internal design review
Design interface control
Change control
External design review
Audit.

The contract included the requirement for a system audit to be carried out within three weeks of contract start-up to confirm the existence of the necessary controls. The system audit determined whether or not the quality plan was adequate to meet the needs of the project. It also served to verify that the project personnel were aware of the requirements of the quality plan and that the procedures were available at the activity locations, but the system audit did not verify whether the procedures were actually being complied with.

Depth of audit
The system audit is, therefore, a superficial or 'shallow' audit and can be utilized very effectively to get the 'feel' of a quality system.

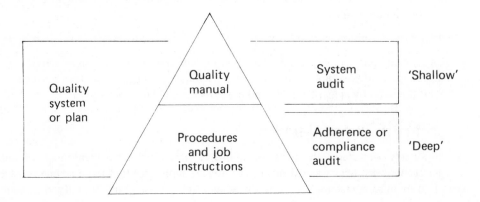

In order to confirm whether or not a procedure or job instruction is actually being implemented and is effective, an 'adherence' or 'compliance' audit is carried out. This 'adherence' or 'compliance' audit is a 'deep' audit. It gets down to the nitty-gritty so to speak.

Scope of audit

The 'scope' of an audit relates to the amount of the quality system or plan that should be reviewed to confirm that the activities are in compliance with requirements.

In the case of an internal activity, management, together with the quality function, will determine which quality system elements, procedures and instructions are to be audited within a given period.

Externally, the customer will make this decision. In any event, the auditee should be consulted when determining the scope of the audit.

Type of audit

It will have been noted in previous chapters that the quality assurance function covers not only the auditing of a company's own quality system but, in the case of purchased items and services, the assessment and auditing of a supplier's quality system. There are, therefore, two types of audit: *internal* and *external*. This chapter will deal in a general way with internal auditing only.

The scope and depth of an audit are variable factors which have to be considered in detail during the preparation and planning of audits. The type of audit is determined by who is performing the audit and the location of the auditee, and can be an internal, external or extrinsic audit.

An *internal audit* is an audit carried out by a company to evaluate its own performance. The notification procedure and the conduct of the audit are not quite as formal as for an external audit.

An *external audit* is an audit carried out by a company to evaluate the activities of its contractors, suppliers, agents, licensees, etc. The notification procedure and procedure for the conduct of the audit are more formal and necessitate more planning and preparation than for the internal audit.

An *extrinsic audit* is an audit carried out by a customer, third party organization, regulatory authority, etc., on a company to assess its activities against specific requirements. It is an audit carried out by external sources on your own organization. An extrinsic audit would normally not be addressed by an audit procedure but by a job instruction, which should describe how the company will deal with such an audit. Such a job instruction could well include:

— the requirement to advise relevant employees of the objectives and scope of the audit
— the appointment of suitable members of staff to accompany members of the audit team (generally known as escorts)
— the provision of resources for the audit team (office accommodation, telephone, copy facilities and others)
— the requirement to provide access to facilities and objective evidence as requested by the audit team members

— the requirement to co-operate with the audit team members to permit the audit objectives to be achieved
— the necessity to determine and implement corrective action based on the audit results.

AUDIT SCHEDULE

The need to perform an audit should be determined taking into account the maturity of the system, specified or regulatory requirements and any other pertinent factors.

In the case of external audits, significant changes in management, organization, policies, techniques or technologies could well affect the system and would need to be verified. Changes to the system itself and the results of previous audits are other circumstances which should be considered when deciding audit frequency.

Internally, audits are organized on a regular basis to verify the implementation and effectiveness of one's own system and to review the results of any significant changes as described above.

In both the external and internal situations it is important to establish an audit schedule.

The audit schedule

This should be established as soon as possible after a quality system is implemented. It is recommended that a system audit be undertaken within four to six weeks of implementation and then compliance audits scheduled to commence immediately thereafter. The system audit could identify areas of concern, which should be used to establish priorities for future audits.

A typical schedule is given as Fig. 16.1. This schedule can be utilized for both internal and external activities.

The assessment schedule

This would be established when a major purchasing activity is to be undertaken and a number of potential suppliers are to be assessed. The schedule would indicate the companies to be assessed and when.

THE AUDIT PROCESS

Audits, like most other activities, require considerable preparation and planning, which should take into consideration the following:

— the scope and objectives of the audit
— the identification of the auditee's personnel who have significant responsibilities regarding the scope and objectives
— the identification of reference documents such as the applicable quality system standard, quality manual, procedures, job instructions, contract work scope and others
— the identification of audit team members
— the language of the audit
— the place, date and time where the audit is to be conducted

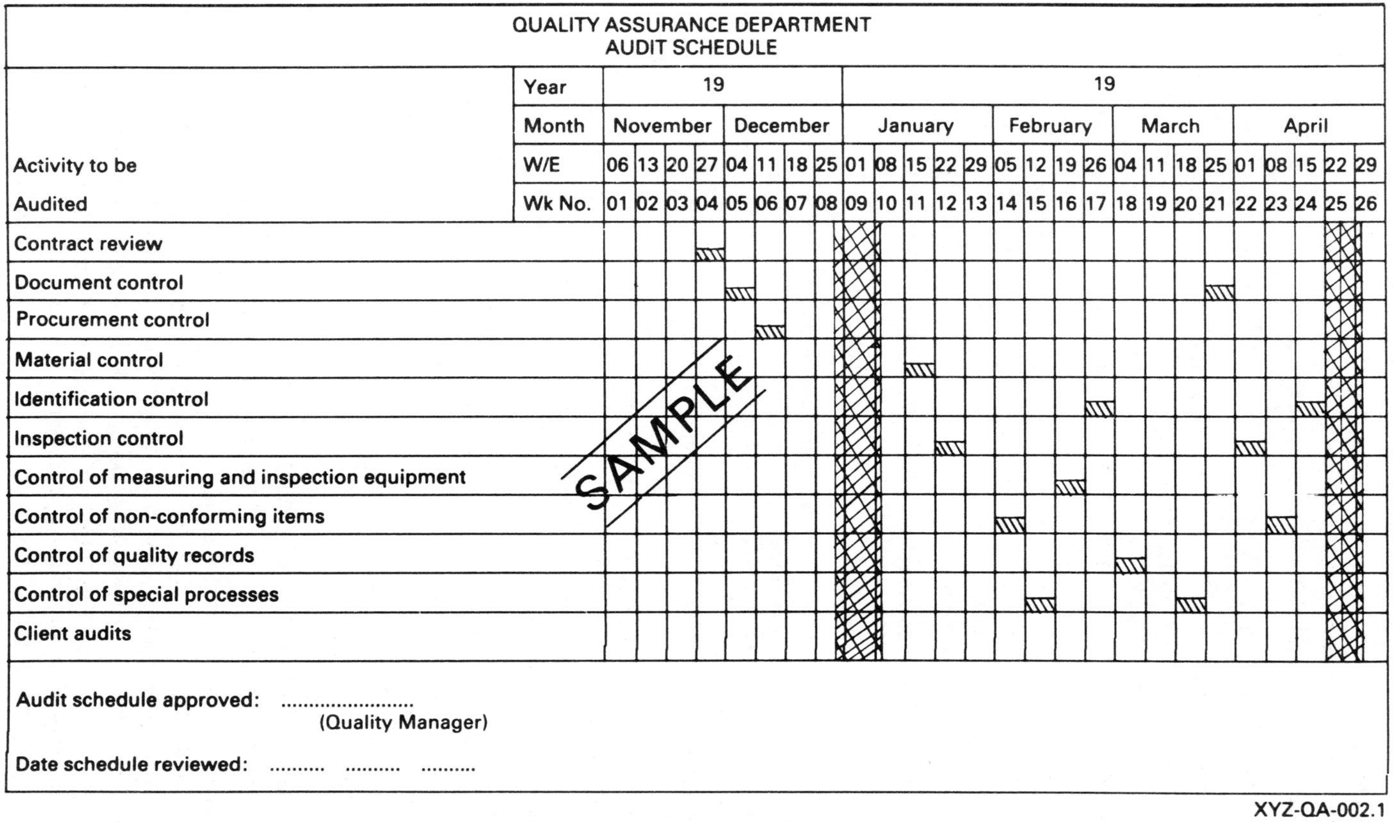

Fig. 16.1—Audit schedule.

— the identification of the organizational functions, or system elements, to be audited
— the anticipated time and duration for each activity
— the development of checklists
— the format and distribution of the audit report.

The total audit process could, therefore, be considered as having four distinct phases, which are:

Preparation and planning
Performance of the audit
The audit report
The follow-up.

Preparation and planning
This phase of the audit process is itself divided into six subsidiary activities as follows:

1.   Appoint a person or persons to be responsible for the audit.
2.   Notify the auditee.
3.   Agree the audit timetable.
4.   Identify, obtain and review all relevant documentation.
5.   Brief the audit team members.
6.   Develop the audit checklists.

A review of each of these activities is too be considered in detail.

Appoint a person or persons to be responsible for the audit
About two weeks prior to a scheduled audit, the quality manager should formally assign a person to be responsible for the audit process. This person is normally a member of the quality assurance function and may even be the quality manager. The auditor would be advised of the date scheduled for the audit, the organization, department or discipline to be audited, the names of the persons to contact and the scope and objectives of the audit.

Once nominated, the auditor becomes responsible for planning, preparing, performing and reporting the audit. Should the scope of the audit necessitate the use of more than one person, i.e. an audit team, then the auditor becomes the team leader and will be responsible for briefing the team and controlling the audit. The individuals selected as audit team members need not be from the quality assurance function. They should, however, have undergone training and indoctrination in auditing techniques and should not have direct responsibility for any of the work in the areas to be audited.

Notify the auditee
This should be done in writing with at least seven days' notice of the intention to conduct an audit. Initially, the auditor (or team leader in the case of major audits) should informally contact the auditee to confirm the scheduled date and to discuss the audit scope. Confirmation of all such discussions should be made formally.

In the case of internal audits, the notification would normally be in the form of an internal memo and should include, as a minimum, the following information:

— date and time of audit
— audit scope and objectives
— name(s) of auditor(s)
— request to advise if date and time should not be convenient.

An example of a typical notification memo is given as Fig. 16.2.

```
                    INTER-OFFICE MEMORANDUM

    TO:        S.J. BRYAN - PURCHASING

    FROM:      N. DOE - QUALITY MANAGEMENT

    SUBJECT: DEPARTMENT AUDIT            DATE:  20 October 1992

    ------------------------------------------------------------


    This is to confirm the arrangements for the forthcoming scheduled
    audit of your department's quality system.

                Date of audit: 27 October 1992
                Time of audit: commencing 1000 hours

    The audit scope and objectives are to verify the implementation
    and effectiveness of the following procedural documents:

        - procedure XYZ-PR-001 rev. 2 Vendor assessment
        - procedure XYZ-PR-004 rev. 1 Supplier selection
        - procedure XYZ-PR-006 rev. 1 Incoming inspection.

    The audit team will consist of N. Doe (team leader) and N. Dixon.

    Please contact the undersigned should these arrangements not be
    convenient.

    Regards,



    N. Doe
    Audit team leader
```

Fig. 16.2—Typical notification memo.

Externally the formal notification would be much more detailed and should include, as a minimum, the following information:

— date and time of audit
— audit scope and objectives
— name(s) of auditor(s)
— audit timetable or itinerary
— invitation to senior management to attend both entry and exit meetings

— request for escorts to be available to accompany each member of the audit team
— request for office and other facilities to be made available
— request to confirm the arrangements (RSVP).

An example of a typical external notification letter is given as Fig. 16.3.

Mr. A.N. Other   6 October 1992
Quality Manager
The XYZ Engineering Company Limited
Alphabet House
Sigma Street
Beta Town, Fernshire

Dear Mr Other,

Quality Assurance Audit Notification

This letter is to confirm our intention to undertake a quality
audit of The XYZ Engineering Company Limited on Monday and
Tuesday the 16 and 17 October 1992. The purpose of the audit
is to verify compliance with the requirements of your quality
manual and, in particular, your procedures for the control of:
documentation; purchasing; internal audit and corrective action.

Our audit team will comprise Mr. L. Stewart (team leader),
Mr. B. Western and Ms. J.L. Jones.

The audit will commence with the entry meeting at 0930 on
16 October 1992 and will be followed by the audit review, which
is scheduled to commence at 1000 and to continue through until
1630 with a break for lunch and will recommence at 0930 on the
17 November, continuing through until 12 noon. The exit meeting
is provisionally scheduled to commence at 1430 on 17 October.

It would be appreciated if you could arrange for representatives
of your senior management to be available to attend both the
entry and exit meetings.

It is our intention that the audit should be conducted with the
minimum of disruption to your normal work programme. It would
be appreciated, therefore, if you could arrange also for the
provision of office facilities for our audit team and for the
necessary cognizant personnel to be available to accompany each
member of the team during the audit.

Would you please confirm that these arrangements are acceptable.
Should you have any queries with regard to this forthcoming audit
please do not hesitate to contact the undersigned.

Yours sincerely,

N.DOE, Quality Manager

Fig. 16.3—Sample audit notification letter.

Having made the formal notification, then all relevant information relating to the activities or functions to be audited should be obtained.

Agree the audit timetable

This should be done in conjunction with the auditee. The timetable should be planned to be most effective and to avoid involving too many people. It is considered good practice to plan to commence audit proceedings at least half an hour after the auditee's commencement of work. This gives time for the auditee to prepare for the day's work and to allocate responsibilities to those not involved in the audit.

A late finish should be avoided where possible as the auditee could have other pressing matters to attend to, the concern for which may make the auditee less attentive to the audit.

Identify, obtain and review all relevant documentation

This refers to documents such as procedures, job instructions, inspection and test plans, specifications, and so on. If a previous audit has already been carried out, then the report of that audit should form part of this documentation. There may be corrective actions still outstanding, which should be followed up. Once all relevant information has been reviewed the next step should be to:

Brief the audit team members

The audit team leader would be accountable for briefing the team members as to their responsibilities within the audit. The team leader assumes total charge of the audit and must ensure that all team members are aware of the part they must play. At this juncture he or she would allocate audit tasks to the team members based upon their areas of expertise and would assign to them the appropriate documentation. Team members should then review the documentation and develop their own checklists.

Develop the audit checklist

A checklist is not a mandatory exercise but it is strongly recommended. In developing a checklist, the auditor would be required to read all the relevant documents in depth. This should then make the auditor familiar with the auditee's activities, which would lead to a greater understanding between the two parties. A checklist also acts as an *aide-mémoire* and governs the continuity and depth of the audit.

Many organizations utilize standard pre-prepared checklists but the use of these generally results in the audit becoming a mechanical exercise on the part of the auditor, with the auditee becoming little more than an answering machine.

Checklists should be developed utilizing the system or procedural criteria. The procedural documents, if established to an agreed format, should be auditable documents and would readily lend themselves to checklist development.

An example of a typical checklist is given as Fig. 16.4. Continuing with the case history given on page 59 relating to the design contract, the checklist developed for that system audit is given in Figs 16.5a to 16.5e.

When developing checklists for the audit of procedural activities (the adherence or compliance audit) care should be taken not to include items which would not produce

ITEM NO.	REQUIREMENT	ACTIVITY COMPLIANCE	COMMENTS/REMARKS

CHECKLIST FOR AUDIT REPORT NO.   Page   of

XYZ-QA-002.2

Fig. 16.4—Audit checklist.

ITEM NO.	REQUIREMENT	ACTIVITY COMPLIANCE	COMMENTS/REMARKS
1.	DESIGN CONTROL Is A QA Manual available and approved? 1.1 Are copies controlled? 1.2 Are copies latest revision? 1.3 Are all disciplines aware of their responsibilities within the Manual?		
2.	Does the organizational structure define quality responsibilities and authority? 2.1 Does this authority operate in practice?		
3.	Was contract review carried out? 3.1 Was action log maintained for missing/ambiguous information? 3.2 Have queries been actioned and closed out?		

XYZ-QA-002.2

Fig. 16.5a—Audit checklist—completed.

ITEM NO.	REQUIREMENT	ACTIVITY COMPLIANCE	COMMENTS/REMARKS
4.	Has contact been made with Certifying Authority to establish certification requirements? 4.1 Is the procedure approved and in operation?		
5.	Is an adequate documentation control procedure in operation? 5.1 Is the procedure approved? 5.2 Does the procedure: 　5.2.1 Ensure uniform presentation? 　5.2.2 Detail identification requirements 　5.2.3 Detail distribution requirements?		
6.	Is a discipline check procedure approved and in operation? 6.1 Are all disciplines aware of their responsibilities within the procedure? 6.2 Is the procedure auditable? 6.3 When was the last audit carried out?		

XYZ-QA-002.2

Fig. 16.5b—Audit checklist—completed.

CHECKLIST FOR AUDIT REPORT NO.		
ITEM NO.	REQUIREMENT	ACTIVITY COMPLIANCE	COMMENTS/REMARKS
7.	Is an interdiscipline check procedure available and approved? 7.1 Are all disciplines aware of their responsibilities within the procedure? 7.2 Is the procedure auditable? 7.3 When was the last audit carried out?		
8.	Is there facility within the project schedule for internal design reviews? 8.1 Is the procedure approved and in operation? 8.2 Is the responsibility defined for initiating reviews? 8.3 Is there facility for follow-up of comments? 8.4 Has a review yet been carried out? 8.4.1 Comments closed out?		
9.	Is there evidence of design interface control in operation? 9.1 Is the procedure available? 9.2 Is the procedure approved?		

XYZ-QA-002.2

Fig. 16.5c—Audit checklist—completed.

ITEM NO.	REQUIREMENT	ACTIVITY COMPLIANCE	COMMENTS/REMARKS
10.	Is a change control procedure available? 10.1 Is the procedure approved? 10.2 Are all disciplines aware of their responsibilities? 10.3 Is the procedure auditable? 10.4 When was the last audit carried out?		
11.	Is there facility within the project schedules for external design reviews? 11.1 Procedure? 11.2 Is the responsibility defined for initiating reviews? 11.3 Is there facility for follow up of comments? 11.4 Has a review yet been carried out? 11.4.1 Comments closed out?		

XYZ-QA-002.2

Fig. 16.5d—Audit checklist—completed.

ITEM NO.	REQUIREMENT	ACTIVITY COMPLIANCE	COMMENTS/REMARKS
12.	Is there corrective action procedure? 12.1 Is the procedure approved? 12.2 Are corrective measures taken when a non-conformance is observed? 12.3 Is the QA Manager advised of all non-conformances? 12.4 Is corrective action documented? 12.5 Does management review the status of the system?		

XYZ-QA-002.2

Fig. 16.5e—Audit checklist—completed.

objective evidence. The procedure for auditing should give the auditor the flexibility to determine whether an activity is acceptable or not rather than a strict 'Yes' or 'No'. There are some instances where an activity may not be strictly in accordance with procedure but may otherwise be perfectly acceptable. It is, therefore, prudent to denote acceptability and qualify the result.

Performance of the audit

As for preparation and planning (phase 1), the performance phase is subdivided into a number of distinct activities. There are four in all, but these should not be confused with the four phases of the total audit process. They are:

1. The entry meeting
2. The audit itself
3. Evaluation of results
4. The exit meeting.

The entry meeting

Upon arrival at the audit venue, the auditor (or audit team leader) should convene a brief meeting between the auditor and the auditee. This meeting is given many titles such as entry meeting, entry interview, pre-audit meeting, opening meeting and others. The purpose of an entry meeting is to:

— introduce the auditor (or audit team) to the representatives of the auditee, if they are not already known to each other;
— confirm briefly the purpose and scope of the audit;
— review the audit scope, timetable and agenda;
— provide a short summary of the methods and procedures to be used to conduct the audit;
— clarify any ambiguities of the audit process;
— introduce the method by which any non-conformances will be addressed (i.e. the corrective action request);
— agree a tentative time for the closing meeting and invite senior management of the auditee to attend;
— arrange for escorts to accompany the audit team;
— in the case of external audits, confirm that suitable office facilities and resources will be made available to the audit team and also arrange to undertake a familiarization tour of the facility, if time permits.

The names of those present should be recorded. An attendance register (Fig. 16.6) is a suitable document for this. It should be stressed, however, that names and positions should be printed to retain legibility.

The audit itself

This should be conducted using the prepared checklists as a guide. These checklists could be expanded, if necessary, to determine compliance with specified requirements and/or determine the effectiveness of the implementation of a system's element.

ATTENDANCE REGISTER

NAME (Please print)	POSITION	Entry (Please initial)	Exit

COMPANY ADDRESS: DATE:

Fig. 16.6—The attendance register.

Objective evidence should be collected and examined and details recorded on the checklist. All essential information, for example, identification of the evidence examined, specific details of non-conforming or adverse conditions, together with any applicable references, should be also recorded. If they appear significant, any clues suggesting a non-conformance should be noted and investigated, though they may not have been covered by the checklist. Information gained by interviews should be corroborated by acquiring the same information from other independent sources.

It is important that the auditor should:

— explain clearly what is required
— listen carefully to responses
— avoid making personal judgements
— remember the auditee may be defensive.

In completing the audit checklist under the heading *Activity compliance* the auditor should state 'acceptable', 'not acceptable', 'not applicable' (N/A) or 'see comment'. The *Comments/remarks* column should be used to expand on the activity or to reference objective evidence and non-conformances. When a non-conformance is identified, it is good practice to request the auditee to acknowledge the finding by appending his or her signature, or initials, to the objective evidence documented in the checklist. It should be explained that such an acknowledgement does not mean that a request for corrective action will be issued. This will be decided when the results of the total audit are subsequently evaluated.

During the audit, in order to ensure the optimal achievement of audit objectives, it may become necessary to make changes to the auditors' work assignments and perhaps to the audit itinerary or timetable. In the case of a team exercise this is the responsibility of the team leader and any such changes should be made in agreement with the auditee.

Should the audit objectives appear to become unattainable, then the auditor (team leader) should make the decision to terminate the audit and should report the reasons to the auditee and to his or her own management.

Evaluation of results

Upon completion of the audit, and before the closing meeting, the audit team, if more than one auditor is present, should meet to consider and evaluate the evidence generated during the audit. The team should analyse any apparent non-conformances or adverse conditions to ensure validity as audit findings. This consideration should also take place where a single auditor is concerned. Objective evidence of a departure from approved procedures, documented requirements and/or other applicable documents should be considered as valid justification for an audit finding. Such audit findings should be recorded and a document known as a Corrective Action Request (CAR) form is a typical vehicle for this. This document has different titles depending upon the industrial or service sector in which it is being used, such as:

— non-conformance report
— outstanding action
— opportunity for improvement
— remedial action report.

An example of a corrective action request form is given in Fig. 16.7.

XYZ COMPANY	CORRECTIVE ACTION REQUEST	CAR No.
COMPANY/DEPARTMENT/DISCIPLINE AUDITED ADDRESS:		AUDIT No. DATE OF AUDIT
BASIS OF AUDIT: QA REQUIREMENTS FOR		
AUDITOR:	COMPANY/DEPARTMENT/ DISCIPLINE REPRESENTATIVE	AREA AUDITED:

NON-CONFORMANCE
SIGNATURE........................   SIGNATURE................. (COMPANY/DEPARTMENT/DISCIPLINE REPRESENTATIVE)   **AUDITOR**
CORRECTIVE ACTION
DATE FOR COMPLETION OF CORRECTIVE ACTION SIGNATURE........................   DATE:- (COMPANY/DEPARTMENT/DISCIPLINE REPRESENTATIVE)
ACTION TAKEN TO PREVENT RECURRENCE OF NON-CONFORMANCE
DATE FOR COMPLETION OF ACTION TO PREVENT RECURRENCE SIGNATURE........................   DATE:- (COMPANY/DEPARTMENT/DISCIPLINE REPRESENTATIVE)
FOLLOW-UP AND CLOSE OUT PROPOSED FOLLOW-UP DATE:- FOLLOW-UP DETAILS
CAR CLOSE OUT DATE   SIGNATURE.................... **AUDITOR**

XYZ-QA-004.1

Fig. 16.7—Corrective action request.

The corrective action request form should be completed by the auditor to show only the nature of the non-conformance. The sections for 'Corrective action', 'Action taken to prevent recurrence of non-conformance' and 'Follow-up and close-out' should be left blank at this stage.

Having reviewed the audit findings and completed any necessary CAR forms, the auditor (or audit team leader) should convene a meeting with the auditee(s) to discuss the outcome of the audit. This meeting, like the entry meeting, is given many titles, such as closing meeting, exit meeting, exit interview, post-audit meeting, and others.

The exit meeting

At this meeting should be present the auditee and, as necessary, management representatives. The names of all persons attending the meeting should again be recorded in the same manner as for the entry meeting.

During this meeting, the auditor (or team leader) should present an overview of the audit results and should present any findings and ensure that such findings are understood by the auditee. At this stage the CARs (if any) should be presented to the auditee and the auditee requested to sign the first section of the form to indicate an understanding of the non-conformance. The signature does not indicate an agreement, only an acknowledgement that the finding is understood. A copy of each CAR is left with the auditee. The auditor (or team leader) should emphasize at this stage that it has not been possible to cover every aspect of the auditee's quality system. It does not follow, therefore, that where no non-conformances have been reported none exist.

The auditor (or team leader) should advise the auditee of the intended issue date of the formal audit report. Generally this should be within ten working days from the date of the exit meeting. It is standard practice to attach the originals of the corrective action requests to the audit report and the auditor (or team leader) should make this clear.

The auditee should be requested to respond to the findings, usually within ten working days of the receipt of the audit report. This response entails the auditee returning the originals of the corrective action requests to the auditing function, indicating on the form:

— the corrective action to be taken to correct the deficiency, the date by which this will be done and signing it in the appropriate place;
— the corrective action to be taken to prevent a recurrence of the deficiency, the date by which this will be done and also signing it in the appropriate place.

It is to be stressed that the response due date is not the date by which the corrective action, and action to prevent recurrence, is expected to be completed but the date by which the corrective action request(s) is (are) to be returned.

Having presented the audit results to senior management and clarified any ambiguities, the audit team should then withdraw. It is not unusual for an auditee to request the auditor to make recommendations to close-out the deficiencies. Internally this could be expected of the auditor but nevertheless it should be made clear that any recommendations made are purely personal and should not be taken as an instruction.

Externally extreme caution must be taken when making recommendations, as the auditor may be taken to account if such recommendations are subsequently found to be ineffective.

It is up to the auditee to determine the extent, the way and the methods for corrective and subsequent preventative actions. At the exit meeting, the auditee may produce objective evidence which may nullify a corrective action. Any such evidence should be evaluated to confirm that not only does it correct the deficiency but also prevents a recurrence of the deficiency. Should it satisfy both counts, then the CAR should not be withdrawn but closed-out in the normal way and recorded accordingly in the audit report.

There may be instances also where the auditee declines to acknowledge a finding on the CAR, in which case the team leader would indicate on the CAR that the auditee declined to sign. This would be recorded in the audit report.

The audit report

The audit report should be prepared by, or under the direction of, the audit team leader who should be responsible for its accuracy and completeness.

The report should contain the following information, as applicable:

— organization/department audited
— scope and objectives of the audit
— details of the audit itinerary or timetable
— identification of the audit team members
— identification of auditee's representatives
— identification of the audit criteria (quality system standard, quality manual, procedures, job instructions, contract workscope, and others)
— record of non-conformances
— the result of the audit
— audit report distribution list.

Audit reports, as for any other series of documents, should be presented in a uniform manner and the formulation of such covered by procedure. A typical audit report would comprise the following:

— lead (or cover) sheet (Fig. 16.8)
— report sheet (Fig. 16.9)
— corrective action requests.

If so required the completed checklists could be included as part of the audit report. This practice, however, is not recommended as it adds to the amount of paper distributed and could lead to disagreements with the auditee regarding the objective evidence listed. The completed checklists should be filed with a copy of the audit report.

The results of the audit should be summarized on the lead sheet and any audit findings (CARs) should be itemized. By giving a summary on the first page this enables management to see at a glance the outcome of the audit. If further information is required, then reference can be made to the details in the body of the report.

An audit summary could read as follows:

Summary of audit—The purpose of this audit was to verify the implementation of document control as covered by procedure(s) No. . . . . . . (here state document number, title and revision status). The audit indicated that generally the requirements of the procedure(s) was/were being implemented but there were certain areas which would appear to require much closer attention.

Deficiencies were identified with regard to the delegation of responsibility, the control of document distribution, the review of documentation and maintaining

XYZ COMPANY	AUDIT REPORT (LEAD SHEET)	AUDIT REPORT No. PAGE 1 OF

AUDITED ORGANISATION   PROJECT/PURCHASE ORDER No.

                                        SCOPE OF SUPPLY
ADDRESS

                                        TYPE OF AUDIT   DATE OF AUDIT

TELEPHONE No.   AUDIT CRITERIA

TELEX No.   AUDIT TEAM

PERSONS CONTACTED

                                        PREVIOUS AUDIT DATE

                                        PREVIOUS AUDIT REFERENCE

SUMMARY OF AUDIT

SIGNATURE..............   SIGNATURE...............
           (AUDIT TEAM LEADER)   (QUALITY MANAGER)
DATE:-   DATE:-

XYZ-QA-002.3

Fig. 16.8—Audit report lead sheet.

XYZ COMPANY	AUDIT REPORT	AUDIT REPORT No. PAGE OF

XYZ-QA-002.4

Fig. 16.9—Audit report sheet.

records up to date. These deficiencies have been addressed by a total of six corrective action requests Nos. 001–006 inclusive.

The body of the report should follow a prescribed format and, as an example, should report on:

1.   The entry meeting
2.   The audit itself
3.   The exit meeting
4.   Designated follow-up
5.   General observations.

Each heading, if this format is used, should always appear in the report and when a heading is not applicable the words 'not applicable' should follow beneath the heading. To explain this more fully:

The entry meeting—Provide a brief summary of the meeting, stating who attended. Avoid too much detail; entry meetings usually follow a very standard pattern. List any specific requests made and/or agreements reached with the auditee.

The audit itself—Give a detailed account of the audit, listing the areas which were found to be satisfactory and in compliance with requirements. Detail the areas which were not in compliance with requirements and which it was necessary to address by corrective action requests. Include as 'observations of concern' activities which were deficient but which were not addressed by corrective action requests. If considered appropriate, make constructive 'recommendations' to the auditee for rectifying the deficiency but do not be dogmatic (auditees will usually find another way of correcting a deficiency in any case).

The exit meeting—Provide a brief summary of the meeting, stating who attended (as for entry meetings, avoid too much detail). Exit meetings usually follow a standard pattern. Record if any correction action request are withdrawn as a result of further discussion and additional information being provided at the exit meeting. Record if the auditee declined to sign a corrective action request (this will also be stated on the corrective action request form by the audit team leader).

Designated follow-up—State the intention to undertake a follow-up audit to verify close-out of each corrective action request, usually within a defined period of the final date stated for the completion of corrective action and the action to prevent a recurrence of the identified deficiencies.

General observations—Include any general observations considered applicable and constructive. As an example:

> Although generally the requirements of the procedures were being implemented, more attention is required adequately to control document distribution, documentation review and the maintenance of up-to-date records.

If there are no 'general observations' add 'not applicable' beneath this heading.

When complete, the audit report should then be signed on the cover sheet by the auditor (or audit team leader) and by the appropriate supervisor (corporate quality assurance manager, senior executive, etc.) after he or she has reviewed the report and the contents have his or her approval.

The original of any corrective action request raised as a result of the audit should accompany the audit report when it is forwarded to the auditee.

It is considered good practice to ensure that the audit report is completed and issued to the auditee, under a covering memo (internal) or letter (external), within 14 days (ten working days) of the final date of the audit. The covering memo/letter should identify the final date by which responses are required for the audit findings—corrective action requests.

Report distribution—It is usual to present the report to the manager of the function under audit with an additional distribution being determined in accordance with the requirements of the company's own quality system.

In the case of external activities, the report will be distributed in accordance with agreements reached with the auditee. Reports containing confidential or proprietary information should be suitably safeguarded by the auditing function.

Report and record retention—Audit documents should be retained in accordance with the requirements of the contract (should there be one) or as determined by legislation, whichever is the greater.

The follow-up

The auditee is responsible for determining and initiating the corrective action necessary to correct a deficiency and to correct the cause of the deficiency. The auditor should be responsible only for identifying the deficiency.

Corrective and preventative actions should be completed within a time-scale determined by the auditee but which is acceptable to the auditing function. Subsequent follow-up actions should also be similarly undertaken to an agreed time-scale.

Following receipt of the responses to the audit findings, the auditor (or audit team leader) should initiate follow-up activities, usually in the form of another audit, to verify the completion of the action to correct the deficiency and the action taken to prevent recurrence.

If the follow-up indicates that the actions taken have corrected and prevented a recurrence of the deficiency, then the corrective action request can be closed-out. This should be stated on the corrective action request form in the appropriate section.

If the follow-up indicates that the action taken does not correct the deficiency or does not prevent a recurrence, then this should be stated on the corrective action request form and the deficiency readdressed by issuing a revision to the corrective action request.

It may be necessary, in the event of a continuing deficiency, for the auditor to call in support from senior management—hence the requirement of all quality system standards that the quality assurance function reports direct to senior management.

Audits, audit reports, corrective action requests and follow-up audits should be controlled and regulated. It is, therefore, prudent to establish and maintain details of all such activities.

Fig. 16.10 is a typical example of an audit report status log, while Fig. 16.11 shows a typical example of a corrective action request status log.

AUDIT REPORT STATUS LOG

AUDIT REPORT NO:	AUDIT TYPE	AUDIT TEAM LEADER	AUDIT DATE	COMPANY/ DEPARTMENT/ DISCIPLINE AUDITED	PROCEDURES/ CRITERIA AUDITED	CONTRACT/ PURCHASE ORDER NO:	DATE AUDIT REPORT ISSUED	CAR's ISSUED

ZYX-QA-002.5

Fig. 16.10—Audit report status log.

CORRECTIVE ACTION REQUEST (CAR) STATUS LOG

CAR SERIAL No.	CAR ISSUED To	DEFICIENCY	AUDIT DATE	INITIALS OF AUDITOR	RESPONSE DUE DATE	DATE REMINDER SENT	CORRECTIVE ACTION COMPLETION DATE	ACTION PREVENT RECURRENCE COMPLETION DATE	PROPOSED FOLLOW-UP DATE	DATE CAR CLOSED

XYZ-QA-004.2

Fig. 16.11—CAR status log.

Traceability of documentation is, once again, most important. It will be necessary, therefore, to develop an identification system to control audit reports and corrective action requests. Provision is made for this in the respective status logs. A typical identification system for internal audits could be a sequence which links the audit to the year during which it was carried out. In the following example the first two numbers represent the year, followed by the audit number:

9201, 9202, 9203 and so on.

For external applications, a supplier identification, purchase order number or contract number could be used as a prefix followed by the sequential audit number.

Any corrective action requests issued during an audit should be cross-referenced to the audit itself to retain traceability. The audit number should be used as a prefix followed by the CAR number, which would commence at 1 (one) for every audit. For example, during audit 9201 three corrective action requests may have been issued and would be identified as follows:

9201–01, 9201–02, 9201–3.

THE AUDIT ROUTE

The complete auditing function has been set out in Fig. 16.12 in the form of a flow chart, which takes each activity step by step from the formulation of the quality system through to implementation and adherence. Each activity is identified with the appropriate responsible department and, where applicable, with the interfacing department.

Following the chart through from the establishment of the quality system (a management responsibility), the procedures and instructions are developed and implemented by the appropriate departments. These procedures and instructions are then audited by the quality assurance function to confirm implementation and effectiveness. If compliant and effective, then the audit report is issued to confirm this. If non-compliant or ineffective then, together with an audit report, corrective action requests should be issued on the department concerned. The department should then determine and implement corrective action and the action to prevent recurrence.

If the discrepancy had been a straightforward operator fault, then the action to correct the deficiency would follow the left-hand route on the flow chart. The follow-up audit would either confirm that the action taken to correct the deficiency and to prevent recurrence was satisfactory, in which case the corrective action request would be closed-out, or the action taken was ineffective, in which case the corrective action request would be reissued.

The discrepancy may be due to a procedural fault. The activity may have been incorrectly documented—the activity itself being perfectly effective (this often occurs when procedures are written by personnel other than those who are familiar with the activity). In such a case, an amendment to the procedure would be required. The revision would then be approved, issued and implemented. A follow-up audit would be carried out to confirm effectiveness, in which case the corrective action request would be closed-out or,

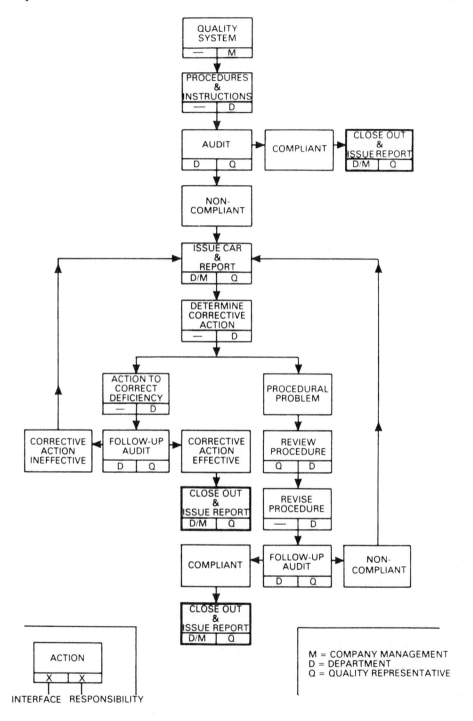

Fig. 16.12—The audit route.

if still non-compliant or ineffective, then the corrective action request would be reissued. Corrective action could go either way, depending on whether the procedure is still ineffective or whether the operator is at fault—thus completing the loop until eventual satisfactory implementation and close-out. In the event of a continuous non-conformance, it will be necessary to refer the problem to senior management for resolution.

THE AUDITOR—GUIDE, PHILOSOPHER AND FRIEND

Throughout the audit activity, particularly in the early stages of the implementation of quality systems, there are bound to be audit findings. Personnel may well have to get used to doing things differently and the new methods may be foreign to them. The auditor should not adopt a belligerent attitude but should be the guide, philosopher and friend. To adopt the so-called 'gotcher' mentality will lead only to antagonism and non-cooperation.

Should a deficiency be found and the auditor asked to make a recommendation regarding corrective action, then by all means assist in this respect but it is prudent to advise the auditee that the advice given is purely personal and should not be taken as 'gospel'. Wherever possible the auditee should be left to determine his or her own corrective action.

Experience has shown that recommending corrective action (particularly in the case of external audits) can create more problems than it solves. The recommended corrective action is invariably taken as an instruction and, when the recommendation is found to be ineffective, the auditor usually finds the blame laid at his or her door.

Corrective action, where a major deficiency is concerned, may involve the auditee in a great deal of time and money. In such instances should the auditee act upon a recommendation which is ineffective in its result, then the auditee could well be inclined to submit an invoice for the costs involved.

An auditor should be aware of the implications when recommending corrective action and, therefore, should be very sure of his or her ground. One must have experience with the activity under audit. In many instances, the recommendation made when a non-compliant action is discovered is to amend the procedure. Amending the procedure is an easy let-out. A follow-up audit by an experienced auditor usually uncovers the truth. The auditee had not read the procedure in the first place and was, therefore, not aware of the requirement. It is a management responsibility to make all personnel aware of their commitments.

Once a deficiency has been discovered and reported upon, it is worth while keeping in touch with the auditee to evaluate the progress of corrective action. This acts as a spur to the auditee and reminds that person of his or her responsibilities. It could also highlight any problems which the auditee may be experiencing with regard to close-out.

As well as being a guide, philosopher and friend, the auditor should also have many other attributes.

AUDITOR QUALIFICATION AND TRAINING

The audit has set out to examine the adequacy of the system for assuring quality. As for a financial audit, one would expect the quality system auditor to be qualified and experienced.

A quality audit is not as simple as it may appear. The auditor must have the right attributes. Apart from the appropriate background, there are other necessary requirements and, in the main, these fall into three distinct categories: education, training and experience.

Education—The requirement here is that auditor candidates should have completed secondary education and should be able to demonstrate competence in reading and writing. Candidates also should be capable of clearly and fluently expressing concepts and ideas orally and in writing in their national language.

Training—Auditor candidates should have undergone training to the extent necessary to ensure their competence in the skills required for carrying out audits and for managing audits.

Training in the following areas is regarded as particularly relevant:

— knowledge and understanding of quality system standards
— auditing techniques of examining, questioning, evaluating and reporting
— the skills required for managing an audit, such as planning, organizing, communicating and directing.

Such competence should be demonstrated by written or oral examination, or other means acceptable to the auditing organization.

Experience—Auditor candidates should have a minimum of five years appropriate practical industrial experience, with a minimum of two years in quality assurance activities.

Industrial experience includes such fields as science, technology, engineering, manufacturing, construction, services, administration, health care, economics etc.

The above requirements are set down in a number of standards and normally refer to personnel carrying out external second or third party activities. They are not requirements for internal auditing, although many organizations are establishing internal auditor requirements utilizing the same criteria.

In the UK a scheme for the Registration of Internal Auditors of Quality Systems has been developed. This is in addition to the Registration Scheme for Assessors of Quality Systems, both of which are controlled by an independent Governing Board and administered by the Institute of Quality Assurance (IQA). Both schemes are recognized by the United Kingdom Government and are independent of any sectional interests.

The internal auditor scheme operates for the qualification and registration of internal auditors engaged in the auditing of quality systems implemented by organizations which satisfy defined and controlled quality criteria. Extracts from the qualification and experience requirements of the scheme (Appendices A, B and C) are reproduced with the kind permission of the Registration Board as Figs. 16.13a, b and c. It should be noted that these requirements are continually under review by the Registration Board and may be subject to change.

APPENDIX A

QUALIFICATIONS AND EXPERIENCE FOR INTERNAL AUDITORS

Criteria for an Internal Auditor

Skills Qualifications and Experience

An Internal Auditor should be familiar with or have experience in the activities being audited, and be familiar with the relevant quality system criteria. Internal Auditors must be able to communicate clearly in writing and orally.

An Internal Auditor shall have the combination of qualifications and experience necessary to assure competence and will normally be expected to hold a minimum of eight credits under the scoring system set out in Appendix B, including a minimum of six credits for experience.

Candidates shall have satisfactorily completed a training course registered by the Board and passed competence evaluation. They must also have completed a number of internal audits as described below.

Three routes are available for candidates applying for registration as Internal Auditors:

(a) Candidates with two or three credits for qualifications are required to have participated in five audits.

(b) Candidates with one credit for qualifications are required to have participated in ten audits.

(c) Candidates with no credits for qualifications are required to have participated in at least twelve audits.

n.b. All audit experience should be reasonably current.

EDUCATION

Auditor candidates should have completed secondary education, that is, that part of the national educational system that comes after the primary or elementary stage but prior to that which qualifies for a degree, or as otherwise determined by the Registration Committee.

EXPERIENCE

Internal Auditor candidates should have a minimum of two years full time appropriate practical workplace experience, in addition to being trained in disciplines appropriate to the business of the organisation and with adequate experience and training in the quality system operated by the organisation.

Prior to assuming responsibility for performing audits, the candidate shall have gained experience in the audit process (For guidance see ISO 10011 parts 1, 2 & 3 1991). For applicants new to Internal Auditing this experience shall have been gained by participating in a minimum of four audits under supervision, the audits taking in total, at least eight audit days for auditing planning, documentation review, actual audit activities and audit reporting.

All relevant experience should be reasonably current.

PERSONAL ATTRIBUTES

Particular personal attributes are required by Internal Auditors which take account of their role in the organisation, and their inter-personal relationships within the organisations. Further guidance is contained in ISO 10011 Part 2, clause 7.

TRAINING (ISO 10011-2 REFERS)

Auditor candidates shall have undergone training to the extent necessary to ensure their competence in the skills required for carrying out audits, and for managing audits. Training in the following areas shall be included:

- Techniques of auditing.

- Interpretation of the quality system requirements.

Training courses must be acceptable to the Board and be registered.

Fig. 16.13a—Appendix A

Notes

1. Applications for registration shall be complete and be supported by documentary evidence of academic and relevant training qualifications. Failure to complete the application form or submit the specified documentary evidence may result in rejection of the application.

2. Audit experience must clearly state date, duration of audit etc and must be verified. Failure to provide this information may result in the rejection of the application.

SCORING SYSTEM FOR EVALUATING QUALIFICATIONS AND EXPERIENCE

The Board retains the right to judge each candidate on all available information and, if necessary, seek confirmation from sources quoted on the application form. This scoring system provides a first measure of a candidate's eligibility for registration. It may be supplemented by information gained from performance on training courses .

A1. Qualifications

1) Higher grade (ONC & above or equivalent)

   score 2 credits ....

   or

2) Craft grade (City and Guilds certificate or equivalent)

   score 1 credit ....

   In addition

3) If a qualification in Quality Assurance is held.

   score 1 additional credit ....

   TOTAL A 1 ....

Fig. 16.13b—Appendix B.

GLOSSARY OF TERMS

For the purposes of Registration the following definitions apply in relation to this Scheme.

Assessment Organisation
An organisation which conducts quality system assessments to a recognised standard.

Internal Audit
A systematic and independent examination to determine whether quality activities and related results comply with planned arrangements and whether these arrangements are implemented effectively and are suitable to achieve objectives.

Internal Auditor
A competent person authorised to manage and perform all or any portion of an Internal audit of a quality system.

Quality System
The organisational structure, responsibilities, procedures, processes and resources for implementing quality management.

Quality System Standards
A Quality System Standard is a document specifying and describing the elements of a quality system.

Registration Agency
A Registration Agency (RA) is a body recognised by the Board as being competent to undertake the authentication of Internal Auditor registration requirements on behalf of the Board and to advise on the development of the Scheme.

A2. Experience

1) Full time experience (other than training) in such fields as science, engineering technology, manufacturing, construction, consultancy and service industries, *score 1 credit* for each year of experience with

    ....

    a maximum of 5 credits

2) If 1 or more years of this experience have been in QA or in carrying out Internal/External Audits, *score 1 additional credit* for each year with

    ....

    a maximum of 3 credits

    TOTAL A 2   ....

    TOTAL A 1 & A 2   ....

Fig. 16.13c—Appendix C.

ROLES AND RESPONSIBILITIES

The roles and responsibilities of the audit team are summarized below:

Auditor

Auditors should be responsible for:

— complying with the audit criteria;
— planning and carrying out assigned responsibilities competently;
— communicating and clarifying audit requirements;
— documenting the objective evidence;
— reporting audit results;
— verifying, as required, the implementation and effectiveness of corrective action;
— retaining and safeguarding documents relevant to the audit;
— ensuring the confidentiality of the audit results;
— co-operating with and supporting the team leader.

Audit team leader

The audit team leader is totally responsible for all phases of the audit and for the conduct of the team under his or her leadership. The team leader should have management capabilities and experience and should have the authority and responsibility to make final decisions regarding the conduct of the audit and of any observations.

The audit team leader also should have the responsibility to:

— assist with the selection of team members;
— prepare the audit itinerary;
— submit the audit report;
— direct follow-up actions as required.

SYSTEM OUTLINE

The audit activities and auditor qualification and training covered in this chapter are summed up in a typical system outline (Appendix A, section 2.15).

CONCLUSION

In conclusion, the results of countless audits undertaken by the author indicate, and continue to indicate, that generally the major problem areas encountered by most companies are caused by:

— insufficient planning
— insufficient or inappropriate training
— inadequate control over documentation
— the absence of a programme of internal quality audits
— inadequate control over purchasing activities.

As will be seen, the above five problem areas constitute 50% of the *ten essential elements* that were described in Chapter 4. This alone must indicate the need for a well-controlled and implemented quality system.

Once the initial quality objectives of the company have been achieved and found to be working effectively and efficiently, with all personnel appreciating the benefits of such a system, the time is ripe to introduce quality improvement techniques. The introduction of quality circles is one such technique, which we shall now consider.

17

Quality circles and problem-solving techniques

Quality circles can play a very important role within a quality system but it is to be emphasized that circles are a part and only a part of the total quality concept. Circles should not be considered an end in themselves but more in the nature of a means to an end.

Many organizations believe, or have been led to believe, that by implementing quality circles all quality problems would be solved. Naturally, such organizations become very disillusioned when it is discovered that such is not the case. Despite this warning, however, quality circles are one aspect of quality management most likely to be adopted by companies who might find the more formalized approach in the rest of this book 'too difficult' whereas a 'circle programme' would appear to be deceptively easy to arrange.

Circles are a method of organizing employee participation in the improvement of a process, the process itself being any activity undertaken by any section of the workforce, even though no tangible product may be produced. The internal product could be described as the result of one's own endeavours and thus everyone concerned in any given process should be given the opportunity to contribute his or her knowledge and experience in a team effort to improve process capability and thus increase job satisfaction.

WHAT ARE QUALITY CIRCLES?

Quality circles are groups of four to twelve people who carry out similar tasks and who generally come from the same work area. The author is of the opinion, however, that circles can be more effective if some members have dissimilar roles and could bring a fresh mind to bear on discussions and, although the exercise should be voluntary, people might be asked (not directed) to join, so as to ensure an interchange of ideas. These people meet on a regular basis to identify and analyse problems and to establish solutions to the problems. The solutions are then presented to management for evaluation and approval. The circle is then often responsible for implementation and effectiveness of the solution.

The quality circle operates in a similar fashion to the quality assurance auditor, whereby a deficiency (problem) is identified, corrective action is taken to correct the deficiency and action taken to prevent recurrence. As for any form of corrective action, there must be management involvement if action is to be effective.

Quality circles relate directly to the quality of the item and/or service and, as with any verification exercise, there is no direct involvement in activities which occurred previously. What is more, a single quality circle would deal only with problems or subjects related specifically to its own area of operation, although some solutions may affect other work areas. It has been widely assumed, quite wrongly, that quality circles will work only in a manufacturing environment. Any organization, where numbers of people are engaged in similar activities, can utilize circle techniques. Indeed, many financial and business organizations have successfully implemented circles as part of their overall quality strategy.

Neither should it be assumed that quality circles are formed to discuss only product- or service-related problems. As the circle members will be experts in their own particular function, their knowledge and experience should be utilized to suggest ways of increasing job satisfaction, which should, in turn, enhance the quality of their working life.

In the preface to the first edition of this book reference was made to Yamanouchi-san as having been instrumental in the author's understanding of the Japanese approach, not only with regard to the quality of the product but also regarding the quality of life—private life as well as working life. Both affect each other.

Yamanouchi-san was, at one time, a circle leader and his particular circle submitted to management many suggestions to improve the product, and others which made the operators' tasks simpler and more effective. Most of the suggestions were accepted by management for implementation and, where they were not accepted, the management went to great lengths to discuss their reasoning with circle members. This attitude, in turn, enhanced operator satisfaction, particularly as the operators themselves felt they had a contribution to make and were, so to speak, masters of their own destiny.

The Japanese are considered to be experts in quality circle applications and, because of their success in this direction, many Western organizations are led to believe that circles are a Japanese invention. This is not entirely the case. Circles certainly developed in Japan following the introduction, from the USA, of statistical quality control methods during the 1950s. The Japanese success has received international acclaim and Western industries are now looking towards achieving similar successes. The author, having worked in Japan for many years, has been able to understand, to a certain extent, the Japanese way of thinking and consequently is convinced that, because of the wide differences between Western and Japanese culture, the West may not achieve the same success in circle implementation. This, however, should not deter Western organizations from adopting circle philosophies, as indeed any success, however small, must be considered worth while, providing implementation costs do not exceed the beneficial results.

THE COMPANY-WIDE APPROACH

Any philosophy which enhances the quality of the product or service should be implemented on a company-wide basis. Quality circles could be considered as one of the tools in the total quality management tool box and, as with any tool, one should acquire the knowledge to use it properly. Such learning would, therefore, require direction. This direction must come from senior management and, as has been said many times before, the commitment must come also from senior management. However, commitment is one thing, support is another! Adequate resources in the way of money, time and people must be made available.

FIRST CONSIDERATIONS

Before embarking on a circle programme, therefore, a number of things should be taken into consideration, such as:

— reasons for introducing a quality circle programme
— associated costs
— methods of establishing the circles programme
— education of management and the workforce in the understanding of, and the benefits and improvements to be derived from, such a programme
— training
— organizational structure for circles
— implementation
— methods of evaluating effectiveness.

Taking each of these in turn:

Reasons for introducing a quality circle programme

An organization should understand that a quality circle programme can produce effective results but it should not be treated as an end to 'quality' problems. Circles are an improvement technique and will not have the desired result without an efficient quality system in place to deal with the results. The programme should be considered as company-wide and not just an isolated technique which can be switched off and on as effectiveness rises or falls. Quality circles are introduced for many reasons and the most generally accepted are for improvements in:

— the quality of the product or service
— employee satisfaction
— communication
— employee effectiveness
— company competitiveness.

It is, therefore, up to each individual organization to establish firmly the reasons before implementing the programme and the reasoning should be made known to the workforce if quality circles are to achieve any success at all. It is, therefore, extremely important that the workforce, together with union representatives, are consulted before any action is taken. The reasons 'why' are important, as has already been established.

Associated costs

Circles are voluntary participation activities but members usually meet in company-paid time. Salaries and wages should, therefore, be taken into account.

It may be considered necessary to employ a consultant to assist in, or even undertake, the development of the circle programme, in which case consultancy fees must be considered and accounted for.

Costs associated with training of personnel in the application of circles, together with training materials, can be substantial. In some instances, the role of the circles' facilitator, whose responsibilities are described later, could be a full-time occupation.

All these costs should be weighed against the expected benefits and savings.

Methods of establishing the circle programme

The methods adopted when developing and implementing a quality system (Chapter 4) are, in many instances, equally applicable here.

A steering committee, or working party, should be established and the responsibility for the formation of this should lie with a senior member of staff who has knowledge of the activities or processes which are considered to be the most likely to receive the most benefit from the introduction of circles. This person is normally given the title 'facilitator'. In general, facilitators can come from any area but experience has shown that, particularly in a manufacturing environment, most come from one of three areas: production departments, training departments or quality control departments. In service companies such appointments are based upon the person's understanding of the business and upon leadership capabilities.

It stands to reason that whoever is appointed to the facilitator position should be totally committed to circle philosophies if the programme is to have any success. It is an important position and that person could well have similar attributes to that of the quality manager and, indeed, there is a very good argument for such an appointment to be made from within the quality assurance group (providing, of course, the organization concerned is operating to the quality assurance philosophies put forward in this book).

In addition to the facilitator, the steering committee should include representatives of management, quality assurance, trade unions and/or other employee representatives.

A circle leader is usually chosen from the supervisory staff to whom, in normal everyday circumstances, the circle members would report. This, however, does not preclude others from the responsibility, providing there is evidence of suitable training and experience to support such an appointment.

The steering committee, or working party, once established, would then:

(1)   determine the requirements for third party (consultancy) assistance in developing the programme, training the participants and the eventual implementation of the scheme;

(2)   define responsibilities and lines of communication between individual circles through to management;

(3)   communicate to all employees the reasons for, and the benefits to be derived from, the implementation of quality circles.

Education of management and the workforce
It is recommended that this be carried out by third party sources—a consultant. Again, experience has shown that, by utilizing the capabilities of someone outside the organization, much more credence is given to the subject. The utilization of third party sources leads to a much greater employee acceptance (the prophet from another land).

Training
Quality circles will never be effective if the workforce is just formed into a collection of departmental or functional groups and told to get on with it. Training in many areas should be given, and these areas would include:

— statistical and quality control techniques
— methods of data collection
— problem-solving techniques
— leadership skills
— brainstorming sessions
— presentation techniques.

The requirement for statistical and quality control techniques is particularly important in production-related circles and is essential where mass production is concerned.

Once a problem has been identified then, of course, the techniques of collecting data and solving the problems do not come automatically—they should be taught. The skills of leadership, as for management, do require training and experience.

Brainstorming sessions have been found invaluable in problem solving but the leader of the session should have had the necessary training to evaluate the results effectively.

Presentation techniques are fundamental to quality circles. The circle leader and his or her team should have the ability to put forward to management, both orally and by means of visual aids, what the problem is, how it was identified and the suggested methods of its solution. The suggested methods must be supported by evidence and by proper costing to substantiate the recommendation. A solution to a problem could be unheeded because of inadequate preparation and poor presentation.

In general, most facilitators receive training from third party sources. The facilitators, in turn, are normally responsible for circle leader training, with the circle members then receiving training from the facilitator, the circle leader or a combination of both.

Some data collection and problem-solving techniques, as outlined above, will be discussed later in this chapter.

Organizational structure for circles
The organizational structure for quality circles has already been touched upon but it is worth while looking at in a little more detail.

As has already been said, quality circles are voluntary participation activities—they are for the members. It is well known that, in most organizations where there are successful circle programmes, the circle members become so identified with their respective circles that they give their circle a club atmosphere by giving it a name such as 'The Cubs', 'The Inner Circle', 'The Family Circle' and so on. One particular circle, operating in the manufacturing sector of industry, whose members worked in very hot and humid conditions, named their circle 'The Devil's Disciples', which was rather apt—and was a very efficient circle that was instrumental in improving working conditions as well as product quality.

The circle objectives are to identify problems, develop solutions and then present the complete case to management for consideration with the view to eventual approval and implementation. The philosophy of quality circles has been called 'management from the bottom upwards'.

Management is, in effect, delegating some of its responsibilities to the workforce. This should, therefore, relieve management of some of the mundane but time-consuming and important tasks, thus giving more time to the solving of company policy issues. Another advantage of such a form of delegation is that it leads to a better and more open form of communication, which can, in turn, lead only to an enhancement in employee—management relationships.

The organization should, therefore, start with the circle members themselves. Membership should be strictly voluntary with no enforced membership. Conversely, no one should be banned from membership.

Each circle should appoint a circle leader and it is usual for this leader to be a supervisor in normal everyday circumstances. Circles, to be effective, should liaise with each other, so that related problems can be discussed. There is, therefore, the need for a co-ordinator—the co-ordinator is the facilitator already referred to. The facilitator provides the link not only between individual circles but also between the circles and management. As such, the facilitator would be instrumental in overseeing the development of the circle programme and assisting with, and co-ordinating, the circle meetings. This person will also watch over circle activities with regard to problem identification and solving and the eventual implementation of solutions. Obtaining the necessary funding for the circle programme will also be within the realm of the facilitator.

In some large organizations where circle programmes are identified for several locations with two or more facilitators, there would be a requirement for an upper structure co-ordinator to bring it all together. A 'senior facilitator' perhaps!

The circle leaders are primarily responsible for the effectiveness of the meetings and should ensure that all circle members are adequately trained in the problem-solving techniques which were previously touched upon.

Implementation
Areas or activities which can benefit from quality circle participation are areas where people work together and experience similar problems. Typically these could cover:

Accounts
Administration
Design/Engineering
Production
Sales and marketing

and there will be other examples.

Each circle within any of these areas should set itself a project. Initially, until circle members are practised in problem solving, the projects should be small in nature. It is a well-known fact that the smaller problems, which can be quickly solved and which are generally overlooked by management, can have a much greater impact upon the well-being of the workforce and the company as a whole than the solutions to major problems which involve considerable expenditure in cost, time and resources and affect only a small part of the business with limited beneficial results.

Some examples of activities for circle consideration are:

— office administration control
— repair/reworking of rejected items
— maintenance
— productivity improvements
— design changes
— document control
— invoicing
— customer complaints.

A schedule should be developed for circle meetings. Invariably the type of project chosen will dictate the frequency of meetings. On average these will probably be once a week at a predetermined time. The length of the meeting should be limited and experience has shown that one hour is usually adequate. A well 'chaired' meeting of one hour can usually achieve far more than a two-hour free for all. Hence the need for a well-trained leader; otherwise the circle might degenerate into a time-wasting talking shop.

Good chairmanship is a difficult art but the first essential, in the author's experience, is preparation. The chairperson should know reasonably well in advance the topics that are to be raised; should have some clear idea about what he or she hopes the meeting will achieve; and should give a guide from the chair without suppressing good contributions. At the end of the discussion the findings should be summarized and approval sought before proceeding to the next item on the agenda. This makes the note-taker's job easy and obviates future wrangling over the minutes. (This applies to any meeting of course; a good secretary will state what he or she intends to record and ask the chair for comments.)

A systematic approach should be made to problem solving. The causes should be investigated and solutions discussed and tested. Documentary evidence should be developed to support the anticipated effectiveness of the proposed solution.

Circle leaders should consider also whether the project will have an effect on other circles. In such cases, there could be a need to invite the other 'affected' circle's leader to the meeting.

Problems can, in many instances, be solved more quickly if experts or specialists are invited. For example, if the project under review related to welding, it would be prudent to invite someone from the metallurgical department to give some expert advice.

Methods of evaluating effectiveness

The methods of evaluating effectiveness can be many and varied. A lot will depend on the nature of the project. Production-related problems, which have been 'solved' by circle members, could result in tangible savings in areas such as:

— reduction in scrap
— reduction in repairs/reworking
— speed-up in unit assembly.

In the main, experience has shown that the benefits resulting from the introduction of quality circle programmes are:

— improvements in quality and efficiency
— improvements in communication and co-operation
— improvements in management–employee relationships
— enhanced job satisfaction.

Improvements in quality and efficiency can be measured in monetary terms provided management is aware of quality costs. Improvements in communication and co-operation are difficult to measure in monetary terms but their effect can be seen in the improvements in management–employee relationship. Enhanced job satisfaction should lead to a greater feeling of 'belonging' and should result in a reduction of absenteeism with increased efficiency.

PROBLEM SOLVING

Quality circles, as has been said, are set up to identify and analyse problems and establish solutions to the problems. Identifying a problem is the easiest part of a circle's activity. We are all very good at identifying problems and would be only too anxious to air them, but do we have sufficient information to analyse what causes them?

In order to discuss and evaluate a problem, which can be either product or service related, it will be necessary, in the first instance, to collect all the available pertinent information pertaining to that problem and, having obtained all the associated data, it will then be possible to analyse these data and to discuss and evaluate methods of disposing of, or reducing the effects of, the problem. Assessment of available data is, therefore, the first stage of the analysis. The second stage is to determine what further data should be collected and how these data should be presented and evaluated.

Brainstorming sessions are an ideal method of obtaining a large number of ideas and always work better than individual thought. These sessions are usually undertaken at a quality circle meeting when a problem associated with that circle's activities is presented for discussion. At these sessions each member of the circle is, in turn, given the opportunity to present his or her ideas of the possible causes of the problem with suggested solutions. A time limit is placed on these contributions—usually one minute. If a member has no contribution to make then that person will 'pass' and the next member will 'take up the baton', so to speak. This part of the brainstorming session should be limited to putting forward individual ideas. It should be an uninhibited session and no other member should interrupt the flow. Members should be encouraged to contribute no matter how 'way-out' the contribution may be. A seemingly idiotic suggestion may well initiate a good one from someone else. The circle leader will list for all to see, usually on a flip-chart or white board, the proffered problem causes and suggested remedies. The session continues until everyone has run out of ideas.

In some instances brainstorming sessions are not completed at the first meeting as the members get a mental block with the number of ideas put forward being very limited. If such is the case, then it is better to postpone the session until the next meeting, which will permit the members to 'sleep on it'. This postponement will not only give the members a chance to think further about the subject but also a chance to obtain suggestions from other members of staff.

Once all ideas are exhausted and listed, the circle members will then evaluate the possible causes of the problem under discussion. After full consideration of all possible contributory factors, the circle members then have the task of investigating the most likely cause(s) for the problem's existence.

Once these probable causes have been determined the remedies listed can then be evaluated to decide on the most appropriate solution. Some of the remedies suggested will be most obvious and others may border on the trivial, but nevertheless all should be considered and evaluated. Most quality problems are due to a combination of causes which can be categorized under the following four headings (known as the 'four Ms'): machines, methods, materials and manpower, so the solution may range over the whole area of these 'four Ms'.

Under the category of *machines* would be included such items as production equipment, computers/word processing, vehicles, cleaning equipment or any type of equipment associated with the business.

Under the category of *methods* would be the procedures or routines associated with carrying out a task.

Under the category of *materials* would be included such things as raw materials (metal, wood, etc.), software, stationery, cleaning material and others.

Under the category of *manpower* would of course be the operator skills, which would include training requirements.

Perhaps the solution may involve just one of these categories or a combination of them. It may well be that the solution will involve nothing more than a change in a process procedure.

DATA COLLECTION

Having decided on the possible solution to the problem, it will then be necessary to collect all the data associated with the problem area.

Checklists and defect charts are usually the best means of collecting data but certain decisions must first be made, such as:

— whether the data are to be organized around the type of defect, employee, shift, or machine (equipment);
— the period over which the data are to be collected.

The check sheet should be designed in order that information can be collected with the minimum of effort. It should be borne in mind that the degree of success in solving problems will rely on the value of the information one collects. The most effective method is to break down the activity into a number of sub-activities and to evaluate each accordingly. On the checklist should be recorded the faults, the reasons for rejection and a brief description of the nature of the fault at each sub-activity stage. The faults can then be summated to produce defect data for the entire process.

The information required will have a bearing on where the information can be collected. In the first instance it will be worth while examining any records which may be available rather than starting from scratch.

When all the pertinent information is collected it must then be arranged into an easily read manner. There are a number of methods of presenting information, such as the use of:

— histograms
— Pareto diagrams
— scatter diagrams
— cause and effect diagrams (sometimes called fishbone diagrams or Ishikawa diagrams).

Some of these were introduced in Chapter 5. Suffice to say that a number of publications dealing with the subject of quality circles and problem solving are included in the bibliography. However, the process does not finish there. Once a solution, or solutions, have been agreed upon the circle must then evaluate the cost of implementing the solution, together with the anticipated savings, and present the findings to management in a convincing manner.

PRESENTING THE SOLUTIONS TO MANAGEMENT

It is an unfortunate fact of quality circle life that many hours can be spent by a circle in evaluating and solving a problem with the results being rejected by management because of inadequate presentation. The importance of good presentation cannot be overstressed, but what should be borne in mind is that the recommendations of a quality circle might be regarded by management as a criticism of management effectiveness—which, in fact, they probably are. Therefore:

1.   The report must be presented with extreme tact and care. Being right is not enough!
2.   Management must be receptive to new ideas.

The presentation of the results not only gives management the information required to assess the viability of the recommended corrective action but it also assists with other important aspects of circle activity such as the development of communication and leadership skills.

The presentation of results to management is most effective if use is made of visual aids in the form of overhead slides or large diagrams. Such visual aids, however, should not contain wordy information; diagrams, drawings, pictures and charts hold the attention much better than a list of words.

It should also be borne in mind that, in many cases, the circle members themselves are the experts in the activity and know far more about the subject than the audience. If this is realized then the presenter will have the confidence to talk from a position of strength.

It makes a great deal of sense to rehearse the presentation before giving it to management. Try it out on one's colleagues first.

THE STEPS TO EFFECTIVE PRESENTATION

There are a number of steps to effective presentation and these are:

1. Take time to plan and prepare for the presentation.
2. Think carefully about the audience.
3. Tailor the presentation to the type of audience.
4. Check all equipment and materials before the presentation.
5. Be positive.
6. Prepare for awkward questions and negative attitudes.
7. Put forward the points in a logical order.
8. Keep the presentation short and to the point.
9. Use innovative visual aids.
10. Speak up and slowly.
11. Avoid jargon which may be unfamiliar to the audience.
12. Maintain eye contact with the audience.
13. Be natural but avoid informality.
14. Distribute any hand-outs after the presentation.

CONCLUSION

The implementation of a quality circle programme should be given great consideration, particularly in the circumstances previously discussed.

The UK National Society for Quality Circles gives the following essential factors for success (reprinted with the kind permission of the NSQC from its publication *Circle Programme Guidelines*):

Voluntary participation
Members and leaders must be volunteers.

Top management support
The most senior manager of the unit must be committed to the programme— making it clear by example that all the management team are expected to give their active support.

Operational management support
Management must be seen to be interested by committing the employee time for regular circle meetings, attending circle meetings when invited and helping with the implementation of approved solutions.

Facilitator guidance
At least one suitable individual must be able to devote sufficient time to the circle programme. This activity can be combined with other duties, but a programme of around 15 circles is likely to be a full-time job.

Training
Facilitators, leaders and members must be properly trained in team-work, in problem-solving and in presentation skills. At the beginning of a programme, at least the facilitator (and often the first leaders) are trained by a consultant or other professionally competent resource. The facilitator can subsequently train leaders and help them in turn to train their circle members.

Shared work background
Circles should initially be formed from people from the same work area. Shared work knowledge helps a faster development of the essential team-work and also helps the circle to contain problems to those under its members' direct control.

Solution orientated
Circles must work in a systematic way on solving problems—not just discussing them—investigating causes, testing solutions and whenever possible being involved in their implementation.

Recognition
Circles are not paid directly for their solutions but management should arrange for recognition by means of visits or special events, or by contribution to social functions.

A quality circle programme will not solve all problems. Management should also get its own house in order. Circles, where they can be implemented, should be only a part of a company's quality system—an integral part where no activity is subservient to the other. Each activity—administration, sales, marketing, finance, design, procurement, manufacture, installation, maintenance, after-sales service, and so on—forms part of the total presentation (*Gesamtkunstwerk*).

18

An introduction to computer software control

With computer-aided design (CAD) becoming more and more common-place, the ability to assure the quality of the related software has presented, and indeed is still presenting, many problems. It is worth while, therefore, taking a brief look into the subject, if only to verify how closely computer software control relates to design control, as discussed in Chapter 12.

WHAT IS SOFTWARE?

A start should be made by defining what software is. The *Penguin Dictionary of Computers* defines it as follows:

> In its most general form, software is a term used in contrast to hardware to refer to all programs which can be used on a particular computer system.

(In computer software parlance, 'program' rather than 'programme' is used.)

It is, therefore, an intangible item representing information stored on disk, tape or punched card.

Software systems may be more easily understood if looked upon as containing a number of communicating processes which run independently of one another. Each independent communication process represents a single activity.

THE COMMUNICATING PROCESSES

The software design activity identifies, integrates and co-ordinates these various communicating processes by means of selection. The selection of such processes is determined by the application i.e. design, document control, data storage, etc. The more processes which are selected, the more interfaces are involved.

To explain this more fully it is worth while extending the Wagnerian philosophy of *Gesamtkunstwerk* still further. After the initial planning of the total presentation of the music drama, it is then written down, or designed, by the composer. Wagner would have written the orchestral part on the musical score. The vocal parts would be written within the appropriate section of the score.

Instructions would have also been documented by him regarding the costumes and the scenery. In all, there are four communicating processes involved in *Gesamtkunstwerk*: music, voice, costume and scenery. All of these need to be brought together so that the final result is what the composer intended.

It is the bringing together of these four art forms at the right place and at the right time which compares with the interfacing of the communicating processes in software design. These software interfaces must be designed to occur also at the right place at the right time if the desired result (or fitness for purpose of the software design) is to be achieved. It is the initial planning and eventual control of these interfaces which are fundamental to software design.

Assuming the music drama is to be transferred to video tape from an actual performance, then the performance must be fault-free (or as near fault-free as possible) if the recording is to be acceptable. This means that the composer's interpretation of the orchestral and vocal scores must be understood by the conductor.

Scenery and costume details are easily documented and would be quite easily interpreted.

Once the video recording is made, it is too late to change any details, unless those sections requiring change are re-enacted, rerecorded and edited into the original tape. In order to do this, the changes should be documented, or identified, in the score.

The same thing applies to computer software. Changes should be documented.

Inspection of a piece of hardware has always been possible to verify conformance to a given requirement or specification, even though at the time of inspection the hardware may have been unsuitable for service requirements. For software, however, there is nothing to inspect because, as has already been said, it is invariably in the form of information stored on a magnetic tape or disk.

If there is nothing to inspect, then the only assurance of quality is with the selection, integration and interfacing of the processes themselves.

As with design control, software control requirements will be seen to be very similar.

The computer industry is a rapidly expanding industry. The hardware manufacturers are many and varied, and software languages are just as numerous. The computer differs enormously from other man-made items in its versatility in coping with countless applications.

SOFTWARE LANGUAGES

These various applications are generally tied to software design techniques which are known as languages. Most languages are identified by their acronyms and, as an example, a few languages are identified to give an idea of the variations:

FORTRAN   FORmula TRANslation. A language for scientific and mathematical applications.

ALGOL   Originally known as IAL or International Algebraic Language. It is the European equivalent to Fortran which was developed in the USA at the same time.

BASIC   Beginner All-purpose Symbolic Code. A high-level language principally
               designed for developing programs in conversational mode.
COBOL   COmmon Business Oriented Language. A language internationally ac-
               cepted for general commercial use,

and so on.

With all these languages and the associated hardware, it is imperative that the user
specifies exactly what the requirements are. These requirements should be specified in
basic terms and the software design engineers will then translate them into the appropriate design technique.

THE MAJOR ACTIVITIES

Upon receiving the software requirement or contract, it is therefore most necessary to
review the requirements in detail.

Referring to the table in design control (Fig. 12.1), the first activity will be found to be
contract review. It goes without saying that this is an equally, if not more, important
activity for software quality assurance.

Contract review (planning)

This activity is identical to that for design control and will require the establishment of a
review team to consider, in detail, the customer requirements and to verify a complete
understanding of the software applications.

A quality plan should be developed in a manner described in Chapter 10 and should
detail the procedural controls to cover the contract requirements. These controls should
include as a minimum:

Document preparation, control and retention
Discipline check
Interdiscipline check
Internal design review
Change control
External design review
Audit and corrective action

The action by quality assurance should be to verify, either by attendance at or by the
evidence of minutes, that the contract review meeting was carried out and that actions
arising from the meeting were satisfactorily closed out.

Document preparation, control and retention

Initially, the software design requirements and applications will be documented and the
methods of preparation, checking, approval and distribution are the same as for hardware
design.

The method of documenting software design activities should be agreed, defined and
communicated to all concerned.

Documentation identification should be standardized and controlled and should include any customer requirements.

Document approval procedures should be established and the appropriate approval responsibilities (signatories) registered.

Document checking routines, including the routines for amending documents, should be formalized.

Document issue and distribution should be controlled on the 'need to know' basis with a formal reproduction system as described in Chapter 12.

In addition to standard design documentation, there will be the requirement for a software system manual, programmer's and operator's manuals, specifications for tests and trials, and so on. All such documents should be covered by formal controls, which will ensure that the format and contents of the documents are in accordance with contract requirements.

The methods of retaining documents during design activities, together with retrieval methods, storage facilities and eventual handover to the customer, should be established.

The action by quality assurance would be to verify the formulation of all necessary procedures to cover the document control activities and to confirm implementation and the effectiveness of the document control system.

Discipline and interdiscipline checking:
These should follow the same pattern as that described in Chapter 12.

Internal design reviews
This is one area where much greater control is required than for hardware design. In order to develop the software design, the various communicating processes have to be brought together. This bringing together is where interface, or communication, control is paramount. With formal design review meetings these interfaces should be identified in the minutes of meetings and actions can be monitored through to close out.

It is the 'informal' review meetings which are more difficult to audit. By an 'informal' review is meant a meeting held spontaneously between two, possibly three, software design engineers to discuss applications and interfaces. Experience has shown that generally, in such instances, no minutes are kept and sometimes important conclusions are reached. It is, therefore, imperative that all personnel involved in software design keep 'action logs' which notate the actions they take and identify decisions made. These action logs are auditable documents.

An action log would normally comprise a book or day by day diary. It requires considerable self-discipline to maintain an action log but such can become an invaluable document should problems subsequently arise.

Design interface control
There could be situations in the design of computer software where more than one design contractor is utilized or where part of the design is subcontracted. The methods of interfacing, together with interface areas, should be clearly defined.

Again, this activity is executed and controlled in the same manner as for hardware design.

Change control
In software parlance, this is generally known as configuration control. Many organizations have great problems in this area, yet if changes are controlled in a formalized manner, the problems should be few.

Experience has shown that generally too many personnel are allowed access to design information stored in computers and these same people have the ability to amend or modify a design. During such a modification exercise, little thought is given to the impact that such a modification may have on other disciplines and a simple act of making what is thought to be a minor modification could present enormous problems later on.

Design changes or modifications should be agreed by all involved disciplines before the software is amended. The changes should be documented, as for engineering design control, and the necessary approval for the change to be implemented should be obtained. Access into the computer program to undertake changes should be strictly controlled by utilizing confidential entry codes. It is considered prudent to limit this access to possibly two people and these people should make changes only with the signed approval of designated responsible personnel.

Access to view the design could, of course, be made available to personnel on the 'need to know' basis.

There could be a facility within the software system for changes or modifications to be stored and, say once a week, reviewed by the appropriate personnel to consider their implications and to authorize implementation as necessary. This storage system should be independent of the main software program.

Whatever method is used, either hard copy or software storage, details of changes of modifications should be retained on file, in order that there is the objective evidence of the change in the event of subsequent problems. This leaves what is generally known as an audit trail.

External design reviews
These are, once again, the same as for engineering design.

Audit and corrective action
All in all, the bases for auditing computer software design activities are straightforward, provided the documentary evidence of quality is maintained by all concerned. The production of a quality plan should be, therefore, a fundamental requirement.

This has been just a brief look into computer software control and further reading on the subject is referenced in the bibliography.

19

Management review

No system, however effective, will remain current indefinitely. As has been said, internal audits will verify whether or not the quality system is adequate and effective, but audits alone will not tell the complete story. There are many other factors which can affect the integrity of the system and, in the main, these emanate from outside the company. Some examples will be discussed later.

The market orientation of much of industry is dynamic. In many instances, instead of working to a specification the work is often directed at satisfying subjective needs of the market. The importance of constant market monitoring is therefore paramount and a company must always be aware of its competition.

Management must have the ability to anticipate change and be receptive to change. The entire management system should be devised so as to respond rapidly to change as dictated by the market or proposed by internal means, such as quality circles. It is therefore important that a method of reacting rapidly to such changes is incorporated into the quality system.

SCHEDULING OF REVIEWS

Management should, therefore, make a point of scheduling a regular and systematic review and evaluation of the entire quality system. This review is carried out to ensure the continued adequacy and effectiveness of all the elements within the system. The responsibility for undertaking such a review could well lie with the working party, who should meet at appropriate intervals to discuss and evaluate the impact of change as it concerns the company and its quality system.

THE REVIEW PROCEDURE

In order that a management review is carried out in a systematic and effective manner, it will be necessary to develop a documented procedure which should identify the following:

—frequency of reviews
— initiation of reviews
— those attending
— the review itself
— documentation of results
— implementation of any changes.

Let us take each in turn:

Frequency of reviews
It should be the responsibility of management to determine how frequently the review of the total system is to be carried out. During the early stages of implementation, reviews are likely to occur quite frequently—say every three months. In the main, these early reviews will tend to concentrate on the results of internal audits. However, as the workforce becomes accustomed to working in a regularly monitored environment, the internal requirements for change decrease. External sources, however, will continue to exert pressure for change and it is these that must be regularly considered. Experience has shown that, in such instances, management reviews should be carried out at least once a year but preferably every six months. There may, of course, be instances where immediate change is required and the review should be initiated on a priority basis.

Initiation of reviews
Management will determine who is to be responsible for calling a review meeting. In many companies this is the quality manager. There may be instances, however, where other members of the management team may consider there is justification in calling for an urgent review. The procedure is such cases should be for the request to be channelled through the quality manager.

Those attending
As has previously been mentioned, the attendees at a management review meeting could well be the working party, with the senior executive as chairman and the quality manager as co-ordinator. It is recommended that all members of the working party attend such reviews, with the addition of any others who may be able to contribute to the discussion.

The review itself
There are a number of items which could be considered at the review. The following are not meant to be exhaustive:

— results of internal audits
— customer feedback (complaints)
— results of market research
— changes in economic situations
— new or updated legislation
— new business methods
—new technology.

Let us take each in turn:

Results of internal audits

There may be instances where audits have indicated a trend towards consistent non-conformances, which may mean a complete management reappraisal in a given area or department. On the other hand, it may well be that audits have shown the system to be continuously effective and that the time is now right to consider quality improvement techniques, such as quality circles, statistical process control, inventory control, and others.

Customer feedback (complaints)

The ability to respond rapidly to customer complaints and to implement corrective action is the hallmark of a well-run company. Customers may also make comment on an aspect of the product or service which could indicate a requirement to amend some aspect of the system in order to retain a competitive edge. All such feedback should be analysed and acted upon accordingly.

Results of market research

As has been said, a company must keep up to date with customer expectations and have the ability to anticipate market changes. It is important, therefore, that the results of constant market monitoring are reviewed regularly.

Changes in economic situations

Fluctuations in currency exchange rates may need to be evaluated to determine impact on the price of the product or service. Fluctuating interest rates may also have to be considered in a similar light.

New or updated legislation

New legislation may have been issued that applies to the company's activities and which may have an impact on the safety aspects or certification requirements.

New business methods

New business or marketing techniques may have been developed. On occasions, if the company is part of a group, instructions could emanate from group headquarters stipulating new business techniques are to be followed.

New technology

New machinery or equipment may have come on to the market which should be considered as appropriate to the company.

Documentation of results

Whatever the outcome of the review, the results should be documented. Normally, minutes of meetings are quite sufficient provided they are developed to indicate the subject under discussion, the outcome of the discussion and the person(s) responsible for any action which is to be taken.

Documentary evidence should exist to confirm that the review took place, even if the decisions made were to change nothing.

Implementation of any changes

The person, or persons, responsible for implementing any changes should be advised and the appropriate action taken by them. Subsequent internal audits will verify the implementation and effectiveness of such changes.

Fig. 19.1 is a summation of such a review process. It will be seen that there is no finite end to the application of a quality system. We have now come full circle and, in the interests of continuous improvement, the entire process will have to be repeated. In other words:

Plan   what is required to improve the business.
Train   personnel in quality improvement techniques.
Action   the improvement process.
Monitor   the implementation and effectiveness of improvement techniques.
Improve   yet again.
Review   the entire process.

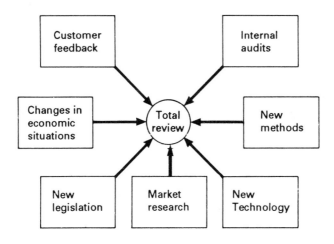

Fig. 19.1—Management review of quality system.

By continually reviewing methods of working and ceaselessly improving the way things are done, the outcome can lead only to enhanced customer satisfaction with the product or service which, in turn, must reflect in increased productivity, efficiency, higher profitability and increased competitiveness. All this can be summed up in eight C's:

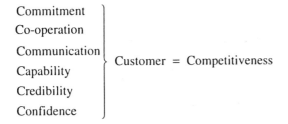

Commitment
Co-operation
Communication
Capability   Customer = Competitiveness
Credibility
Confidence

Any form of quality system will work only if it has the *commitment* of management and the *co-operation* of all concerned. To co-operate one must have *communication*. Thus comes the *capability* in the work we do which must give *credibility* and *confidence*, not only to the senior executive but to the most important person of all—the *customer*. If customers are happy then this must enhance *competitiveness*.

20

Future trends

The principles and practices of the total presentation described in this book are ideal. As was established in the early pages, any quality system should be developed to suit the individual workings of an organization. What has been written in these pages can be used only as a foundation on which to build quality systems.

MASTER THE THEORY BEFORE BREAKING THE RULES!

The author is reminded in this instance, when studying the composition of music, of his introduction to harmony. It was instilled into him that the theory of harmony harboured certain fundamental rules with regard to harmonic progression, such as the avoidance of consecutive thirds, fifths and octaves; the leading note should always rise to the tonic; the end of a phrase always marked by a certain harmonic formula, and many, many others.

Having learnt the theory and practised it true to its rules, one was then given licence to break the rules to suit musical taste and application. The same could be said of the contents of this book. Here is the theory which has been found to work well in practice. The 'rules' could well be broken to suit individual company needs. Take what is required and adapt to suit!

In general, it is the high-technology industries that have taken the lead in adopting these principles of quality assurance and not unnaturally expect and demand their suppliers to employ the same principles. The requirement has, therefore, been imposed upon the supplier by the buyer rather than the supplier recognizing for himself the need for the implementation of a company-wide policy of total application, which could, and would, be 'good for him'. This is unfortunate. If a home-based high-technology company cannot obtain the product it requires, to an appropriate specification and to proper quality standards from a home-based supplier, it will look elsewhere. As many industries know to their cost, this has happened all too frequently.

WHICH DIRECTION?

Industry, in general, is slowly beginning to realize the benefits of quality assurance as discussed in this book. Its importance is increasingly recognized at government level as many governments have introduced schemes for its promotion. A number of trends may be mentioned:

First, the national schemes which many countries are adopting which take the form of financial assistance to enable a company to obtain the services of a management consultant. Such schemes are admirable and many companies are benefiting from them. Unfortunately, such schemes necessarily rely on the abilities of the consultants who are involved, and abilities of consultants are rather like the 'curate's egg'—good in parts.

Secondly, reciprocal product certification schemes are being developed. These schemes serve to assess the product and to verify compatibility with mutually agreed standards. Such schemes can lead only to a greater interchange of marketing between the countries involved in them and must inevitably lead to a wider variety of choice to the benefit of the customer. As has already been said, certification confirms that a product meets certain minimum requirements laid down in a standard or statutory documents; what it does not reveal, however, are the problems encountered in getting the product certified. A well thought out quality system, implemented with management support and commitment, will lead to the reduction and eventually the total elimination of such problems. Certification and quality systems should go hand in hand.

Thirdly, government imposition of quality systems upon contractors is now the rule in certain industries in some countries. This is coercion rather than persuasion but if it takes legislation to make industry realize the potential of an effective quality system, then perhaps one should not object to its imposition, although force is not necessarily effective. 'He that complies against his will is of his own opinion still' (Samuel Butler, 1613–1680, *Hudibras III*: 3:547).

Fourthly, training in quality assurance/management systems applications is now making headway. Many engineering, scientific and business degree courses are including quality assurance concepts but there is still a long way to go in this respect. Unfortunately, many of the engineering disciplines still seem to view quality assurance as a new name for inspection and testing and have yet to realize its significance in its total management aspects.

Degree courses in quality-related subjects have been in vogue in the USA for some years and the benefits of such education are now beginning to be realized in many other countries. Universities and colleges are beginning to take note and are developing suitable courses. Unfortunately, however, many of these courses are being conducted by engineering faculties which implies that quality assurance is an engineering/production philosophy only. Quality assurance would attain greater acceptance if such courses were developed on an inter-faculty basis with management in prominence.

The fact still remains that, regardless of the type of 'quality' education, in general the students are from 'quality' departments. It is the exception rather than the rule to see a senior executive at a seminar or training course, which leads one to believe that senior executives still normally feel that they can delegate their quality responsibilities, which they most certainly cannot. The commitment must come from the top if all are to get it right first time, every time.

Finally, an effective quality system, as has been shown, can lead only to increased productivity, efficiency, higher profitability and increased competitiveness.

Appendix A: Typical quality manual for a Part 1 or Category 1 quality system

XYZ COMPANY LIMITED

DOCUMENT NUMBER

XYZ–MN–001

DOCUMENT TITLE

QUALITY MANUAL

Edition A
Rev. 1
October 1992

TABLE OF CONTENTS

1 COMPANY POLICY
1.1   Policy statement
1.2   General statement
1.3   Amendments, reissue and distribution
1.4   Authority and responsibility/organization

2 SYSTEM ELEMENT OUTLINES
2.1   Contract review
2.2   Design control
2.3   Document control
2.4   Purchasing
2.5   Purchaser supplied product
2.6   Product identification and traceability
2.7   Process control
2.8   Inspection and testing
2.9   Inspection, measuring and test equipment
2.10 Inspection and test status
2.11 Control of non-conforming product
2.12 Corrective action
2.13 Handling, storage, packaging and delivery
2.14 Quality records
2.15 Internal quality audits
2.16 Training
2.17 Servicing
2.18 Statistical techniques
2.19 Quality costs
2.20 Management review

3 PROCEDURES INDEX

Document no. XYZ–MN–001
Edition A
Rev. 1
October 1992

PART 1

COMPANY POLICY

Document no. XYZ–MN–001
Edition A
Rev. 1
October 1992

1.1 POLICY STATEMENT

The XYZ Company Limited specializes in the design, procurement, manufacture and installation of specialized equipment, supplying mainly to high technology markets. The nature of the company's activities places particular emphasis upon experience, expertise, capability, reliability and quality.

The management of the XYZ Company Limited has adopted the policy of providing only equipment and associated services which have the requisite quality to merit customer satisfaction throughout the effective life of the equipment.

In order to achieve this objective, it is the policy of the XYZ Company Limited to establish and maintain an efficient and effective quality system, planned and developed in conjunction with all management functions. Determination of conformance of work to contract and regulatory requirements is verified on the basis of objective evidence of quality.

This policy is issued, therefore, to indicate clearly the attitude of company management with regard to quality and related matters. Such a policy is essential for the long-term success of the company in a competitive marketplace, as well as achieving employee satisfaction.

The XYZ Company Limited's quality manual and the system elements outlined therein describe how the quality system of the XYZ Company Limited is designed to ensure that all quality and regulatory requirements are recognized and that a consistent and uniform control of these requirements is adequately maintained. The XYZ Company Limited's quality manual also defines how effective control is established.

A. PERSON
Managing Director
January 1992

[It is recommended that this policy statement be issued on company headed paper]

Document no. XYZ–MN–001
Edition A
Rev. 1

October 1992

1.2   GENERAL STATEMENT

The assurance of quality is fundamental for all work undertaken by the XYZ Company Limited and is practised by all personnel in their daily activities.

Quality is enhanced by working in a systematic manner to formalized procedures designed to eliminate the occurrence of deficiencies.

To promote a uniformity of work method throughout, irrespective of customer requirements, certain procedures fundamental to the XYZ Company Limited shall be implemented at all times, without significant deviation.

It shall be the responsibility of the individual department and discipline managers to compile, implement and integrate the requirements of these procedures into their regular working methods and to ensure that all such methods are clearly defined and documented.

It shall be the responsibility of the XYZ Company Limited's management to ensure that these procedures are implemented and consistently and regularly reviewed to reflect current customer and company philosophies.

It shall be the responsibility of the quality assurance function to monitor constantly the implementation of the current quality system in order to verify that the necessary procedures and instructions exist or, in the absence of such, to determine that they are developed and to verify implementation and adherence by regular auditing.

The quality assurance function shall be so organized as to be free of commercial/contractual restraints and to represent the XYZ Company Limited on all matters relating to quality assurance.

1.3   AMENDMENTS, REISSUE AND DISTRIBUTION

The quality assurance function reviews this manual periodically with other departments to reaffirm its adequacy and conformance to current requirements of the Company. The maximum period between reviews of the manual is once yearly.

Amendments to the manual are made as required to reflect the current quality system. The amendments are made by replacement of the applicable page(s). Each amended page is identified by amendment number and date of amendment.

Amendments are numbered consecutively until such time as a new edition incorporates all such changes. When changes affect a considerable number of pages, and in any case after not more than ten amendments to one edition, the manual is reissued. Editions are identified in alphabetical order. Each edition cancels and replaces all previous editions and amendments.

The amendment list indicates all the amendments to the latest edition of the manual.

A complete list of quality manual holders, together with the amendment records, are retained by the quality assurance function. Amendments and new editions of the manual are automatically distributed to all registered holders.

It shall be the responsibility of all registered manual holders to update the manual assigned to them and to destroy obsolete copies of all amended pages.

1.3.1 Definitions and terminology used within the XYZ Company Limited's quality system are as ISO 8402:1986 unless otherwise stated.

Document no. XYZ–MN–001
Edition A
Rev. 1
October 1992

Page 6 of 48

1.4   AUTHORITY AND RESPONSIBILITY/ORGANIZATION

1.4.1   Departmental managers

With regard to quality, all departmental managers shall be responsible for:

— the quality of work carried out by personnel within their respective departments;
— verifying that approved procedures are adopted within their department and that any necessary complementary procedures are established, implemented, reviewed and updated as required;
— ensuring that all staff are adequately qualified and experienced in their relevant technical discipline to perform the duties of their position in a satisfactory manner;
— ensuring that all staff are familiar with company procedures and have ready access to them.

1.4.2   Quality manager (management representative)

The quality manager is the final authority and represents the Company on all quality matters pertinent to the quality system as established by contract requirements, regulatory requirements and company quality policies and procedures. The quality manager reports directly to the managing director.

The quality manager has the primary responsibility to structure the quality system, which will involve all Company departments in a focused effort to ensure compliance with quality requirements.

Specifically, the quality manager is involved in areas such as:

— drafting the Company policy on quality
— setting the Company quality objectives
— reviewing the organizational relationships as they affect quality and developing proposals for improvements
— determining and reporting the principal causes of quality losses and non-conformances
— monitoring the Company's system to determine where improvements are needed and recommending, as necessary, the appropriate corrective action.

Document no. XYZ–MN–001
Edition A
Rev. 1
October 1992

1.4.3 Organization

The organization charts show the relationship of the various functions within the company and the various elements of the quality assurance function.

Company organization

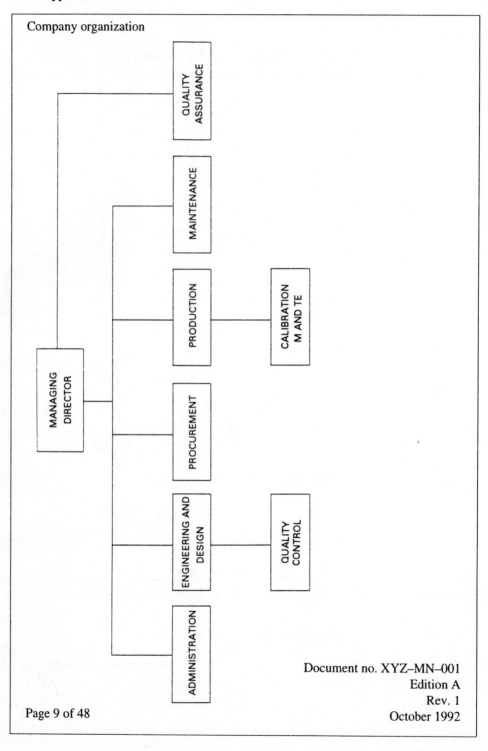

Document no. XYZ–MN–001
Edition A
Rev. 1
October 1992

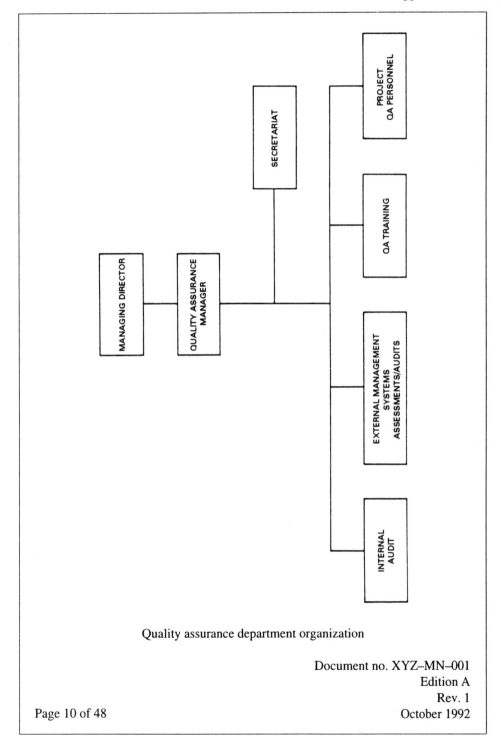

Quality assurance department organization

Document no. XYZ–MN–001
Edition A
Rev. 1
October 1992

PART 2

SYSTEM ELEMENT OUTLINES

Document no. XYZ–MN–001
Edition A
Rev. 1
October 1992

2.0   GENERAL

2.0.1   This section contains a brief outline of the primary functions of the XYZ Company Limited (XYZ–CL) to support the current quality system as determined by in-house and contract requirements.

It includes the controls to be exercised on those aspects of a function which have an effect on quality to ensure conformance to contractural requirements. The system elements herein outlined reflect not only current quality policies but also take into consideration the requirements of national and international standards and regulations related to quality systems, such as:

— ISO 9001
— AS 3901
— AS 2990
— ANSI/ASME NQA-1
— BS 5750.1
— BS 5882
— CAN 3 Z299.1
— NS 5801

Document no. XYZ–MN–001
Edition A
Rev. 1
October 1992

Page 12 of 48

2.0.2   The XYZ–CL quality system includes as applicable, but is not limited to, written procedures for controlling the following:

Function	*Element outline number*
Contract review	2.1
Design control	2.2
Document control	2.3
Purchasing	2.4
Purchaser-supplied product	2.5
Product identification and traceability	2.6
Process control	2.7
Inspection and testing	2.8
Inspection, measuring and test equipment	2.9
Inspection and test status	2.10
Control of non-conforming product	2.11
Corrective action	2.12
Handling, storage, packaging and delivery	2.13
Quality records	2.14
Internal quality audits	2.15
Training	2.16
Servicing	2.17
Statistical techniques	2.18
Quality costs	2.19
Management review	2.20

Document no. XYZ–MN–001
Edition A
Rev. 1
October 1992

Page 13 of 48

2.1 CONTRACT REVIEW

2.1.1 All enquiry documents received from prospective customers shall be reviewed to ensure that the requirements are understood and all necessary information is available prior to developing the quotation and before its submission to the prospective customer.

2.1.2 Upon receipt of contract/order and prior to commencement of any work, provision shall be made by the relevant personnel for a detailed internal review of all contract documents.

2.1.3 This review shall confirm the following criteria:

— work scope
— customer specifications
— regulatory requirements
— relevant national and XYZ–CL standards and procedures.

2.1.4 As a result of the review, should any of the above items require clarification or amplification, the XYZ–CL contract manager shall inform the customer and maintain an action log until the queries are satisfactorily resolved.

2.1.5 Following the review of contract requirements, all assigned personnel shall prepare a statement of all criteria for their function prior to the start of project (contract) activities. In the case of single person functions, the statement shall be prepared by that person.

2.1.6 Each statement shall contain details of the work scope and lists of the specific applicable customer specifications and philosophies, regulatory requirements and national and XYZ–CL standards and procedures.

2.1.7 The XYZ–CL contract manager shall ensure the criteria from each function meet the requirements of the contract.

Page 14 of 48

Document no. XYZ–MN–001
Edition A
Rev. 1
October 1992

2.1.8   It shall be the responsibility of XYZ–CL management to ensure that all documents referred to in clause 2.1.3 above are maintained up to date by the document control function, with adequate copies to enable them to be accessible to all relevant members of the XYZ–CL project (contract) team.

2.1.9   Each function shall maintain a file or have access to each of the referenced documents in clause 2.1.3 above which are applicable to their scope of work.

2.1.10 Details of WHO, WHAT and HOW are defined in XYZ–CL written procedures and job instructions index in Part 3 of this manual.

2.2   DESIGN CONTROL

2.2.1   Methods of control

2.2.1.1   Design activities shall be controlled by the establishment and maintenance of detailed procedures for the implementation of a documented design and development system.

2.2.1.2   The design and development system shall provide for: the investigation of new techniques used in or specified for the design; the evaluation of new materials under the environmental conditions in which they will be used; and the consideration of life cycle costs.

2.2.1.3   All design activities shall be undertaken in accordance with established procedures and codes of design practice to control the safety aspects of the design and physical and functional tolerances to avoid the use of irrational limits and ensure interchangeability of parts.

2.2.1.4   Reliability, maintainability and value engineering analyses shall be undertaken on a regular basis utilizing defect data feedback from previous designs whenever possible.

2.2.1.5   Design reviews shall be undertaken during the design process to identify progress and to assure adequacy of the design and the inclusion of specified requirements. Responsibilities and general methods whereby design documents are reviewed shall be defined.

2.2.2   Design input

2.2.2.1   Prior to commencing any design activities, XYZ–CL shall review all design information made available with an order or contract, including: product specifications; regulatory requirements; operational and environmental conditions; and design support data, to ensure that adequate information is available to complete the design.

2.2.2.2   Incomplete, ambiguous or conflicting requirements shall be resolved prior to commencing the design.

2.2.3   Design output

2.2.3.1   Design output shall be documented by means of calculations, drawings, specifications, procedures, etc., which are compatible with, and traceable to, the design input, to provide, in a complete and unambiguous form, the information necessary to implement the design. The design output shall include reference to the relevant acceptance criteria.

2.2.3.2   Characteristics of the design, essential to the safe and proper function of the product, shall be identified and the design shall comply with the appropriate regulatory requirements.

2.2.4   Design verification

2.2.4.1   Procedures shall be established and implemented to ensure that design output meets design input by undertaking the following:

(a)   Initial checking of design documents—which shall define the responsibilities and general methods whereby such documents are subjected to a systematic initial check within the originating disciplines.

(b)   Interdiscipline checking—which shall define the responsibilities and general methods whereby documents with design interfaces are checked by the interfacing disciplines.

(c)   Authorization and revision status/identification of documents—which shall define the necessary authorization of documents including standard methods of adding and identifying revisions.

(d)   Design interface control—which shall define the methods and responsibilities to control the interfaces between systems, contractors, regulatory authorities, etc., to ensure compatibility of the respective designs.

(e)   Design feedback—which shall ensure that problems reported at all stages of a project from manufacturing through assembly, installation, commissioning and servicing, receive attention in such a way as to avoid repetition of past problems and promote future improvements.

2.2.5   Design changes

2.2.5.1   Following approval of any design document, subsequent changes shall require approval by the same authority that initiated and approved the original design document.

2.2.5.2   The engineering department of XYZ–CL shall implement and operate a system which shall control changes from wherever they originate and which shall ensure they are channelled through one recording area both in and out.

2.2.5.3   The system shall also ensure that all changes are correctly documented and have received authorization from the original design source to be actioned.

2.2.5.4   Engineering change control shall provide for four categories of change, which are as follows:

(a)   Category 1, being additions to the contracted scope of work and which result in changes to the specifications.

(b)   Category 2, being changes to technical specifications that become necessary to maintain the design integrity.

(c)   Category 3, being changes to technical specifications that are proposed as desirable to meet new or additional requirements relating to safety, efficiency, cost and schedule, and also those which become necessary to meet customer requirements resulting from market research.

(d)   Category 4, being changes to the original scope of work due to the activities of other third party sources which result in excess variations to cost, time and resources.

2.2.6   Details of WHO, WHAT and HOW are to be defined in XYZ–CL written procedures and job instructions indexed in Part 3 of this manual.

2.3   DOCUMENT CONTROL

2.3.1   General

2.3.1.1 Provision shall be made adequately to control all documents.

2.3.1.2 XYZ–CL shall acknowledge acceptance of customer imposed requirements and standards which shall be included under the above controls.

2.3.1.3 'As built' documents shall be similarly controlled.

2.3.1.4 The issue, control and recall of all documents shall be under the jurisdiction of the document control manager.

2.3.1.5 Inspection and test plans, and other related instructions, shall be prepared and issued as required by contract. Test reports shall be prepared and issued, also as required by contract.

2.3.1.6 The system of documentation control shall ensure that essential drawings, technical requirements, contract change information, contract instructions, specifications or any other documents are available at the point of use.

2.3.1.7 Procedures of the latest issue shall be distributed by the document control function to all locations where required for the effective functioning of the quality system.

2.3.1.8 All documents shall be reviewed and approved for release by the manager of the responsible department in co-ordination with the quality assurance function.

2.3.2   Change to documentation

2.3.2.1 All changes to documents shall be implemented in writing and processed in a manner which ensures prompt action at the specified locations. Records shall be maintained of changes as they are made. Documents shall be revised and reissued, as a new edition, after a practical number of changes have been issued. Written notations on documents shall not be permitted.

2.3.2.2 A master list shall be established to identify the current revision of documents in order to preclude the use of non-applicable documents.

2.3.2.3 Provision shall be made to remove and recall all obsolete documents from all points of issue and activity locations.

Document no. XYZ–MN–001
Edition A
Rev. 1
October 1992

Page 19 of 48

2.3.2.4   Requests for changes to customer controlled documents shall be prepared and submitted as prescribed by the customer.

2.3.3   Retention of documentation

2.3.3.1   When required for traceability purposes a copy of each superseded document, established in accordance with the requirements of the XYZ–CL quality system, shall be retained in a suitable environment.

2.3.4   Details of WHO, WHAT and HOW are defined in XYZ–CL written procedures and job instructions index in Part 3 of this manual.

2.4   PURCHASING

2.4.1   General

2.4.1.1   A purchase requisition, containing all relevant information and validated by an authorized person, shall be issued prior to any purchasing activity taking place.

2.4.2   Assessment of supply sources

2.4.2.1   Sources selected by the purchasing department for procurement of material and services shall be evaluated and approved by the engineering department and the quality manager prior to including them on a list of acceptable/approved suppliers.

2.4.2.2   Whenever possible, a minimum of three acceptable/approved suppliers shall be required to submit bids and each bid shall be evaluated by the appropriate functions. The managing director shall be the final authority on which bidder shall receive a purchase order.

2.4.2.3   Supply of material, services, assemblies and finished items shall be processed from acceptable/approved suppliers. Records shall be maintained to substantiate supplier quality performance.

2.4.2.4   The extent of control over the purchasing activity shall include subsequent quality audits and monitoring at a supplier's facility as required.

2.4.2.5   A current list of acceptable/approved suppliers for parts, processes and services shall be maintained by the purchasing department.

2.4.3   Purchasing data

2.4.3.1   Purchase orders shall be reviewed by the appropriate functions to ensure that all pertinent drawings, specifications and complete information relative to the item and/or services to be procured are listed and the sources of supply have all necessary data, including designation of appropriate quality requirements.

2.4.3.2   The extent of traceability requirements to be applied to materials, components and equipment shall be specified also in the purchase order. Such requirements shall be controlled in accordance with Section 2.6 of this manual.

Document no. XYZ–MN–001
Edition A
Rev. 1
October 1992

2.4.3.3 All purchase orders and associated reference data shall be available for review by the customer as required.

2.4.4 Verification of purchased product

2.4.4.1 The inspection function shall evaluate all purchase items where any of the following conditions apply:

(a) Inspection of quality characteristics cannot be verified during subsequent processing or would require destructive testing.

(b) Inspection is necessary to verify that specific processes, tests or inspections required of the supplier were adequately accomplished.

(c) Inspection at any other point would destroy or require the replacement of costly packaging materials.

2.4.4.2 Amendments to a purchase order shall be processed in the same way as the original, with reference made to the original purchase order.

2.4.5 Customer facilities

2.4.5.1 When required, a customer shall be afforded the right to verify at source, or upon receipt, that purchased items conform to specified requirements. This right of access shall extend to a subcontractor's facility to permit verification at source.

2.4.5.2 Details of WHO, WHAT and HOW are defined in XYZ–CL written procedures and job instructions index in Part 3 of this manual.

Document no. XYZ–MN–001
Edition A
Rev. 1
October 1992

Page 22 of 48

2.5   PURCHASER-SUPPLIED PRODUCT

2.5.1   All products supplied by the customer for use on a given contract shall be inspected on receipt for condition, completeness and contract requirements. They shall be stored and handled in accordance with instructions specified by, or agreed with, the customer.

2.5.2   Special care shall be taken on receipt of all purchaser-supplied product to ensure that documentation received with the product is correct and that all deficiencies and defects are reported immediately to the customer for verification and action.

2.5.3   Functional or non-destructive testing shall be conducted on receipt, or prior to issue, as required by the contract.

2.5.4   A separate storage area shall be maintained for all purchaser-supplied products, with records maintained for proper accountability of the products received and issued, in accordance with contract requirements.

2.5.5   Periodic inspection shall be conducted during storage to confirm the condition of the product and adequacy of storage. Reports shall be issued detailing the results of all such inspections, which shall be analysed and actioned as necessary. Purchaser-supplied products shall be reinspected for damage during preparation for use. Investigation shall be carried out, where required, to determine the cause of damage or malfunction. The customer shall be advised of all cases where a product is found unsuitable for use.

2.5.6   Details of WHO, WHAT and HOW are defined in XYZ–CL written procedures and job instructions indexed in Part 3 of this manual.

2.6   PRODUCT IDENTIFICATION AND TRACEABILITY

2.6.1   XYZ–CL shall implement and operate a system to trace certain materials, components and equipment to their specific source and to identify such with their respective material and test certificates.

2.6.2   Where traceability is required by contract, codes or regulations, items shall be identified and traceable to a specified point of origin. Such traceability shall be operable throughout the design, manufacture, installation and operational life of the product as applicable.

2.6.3   XYZ–CL shall, where contracted to do so, be responsible for determining which items, materials, components or equipment require traceability and to operate such in accordance with a system which shall provide for:

(a)   the traceability of such items, materials, components or equipment which may contribute to an accident, resulting in loss of life, injury or loss of production;

(b)   the identification, with certainty, of the number and location of all material, components and equipment items which, if found to be defective, shall be replaced;

(c)   the data and information necessary for the preparation of the most efficient installation and maintenance procedures;

(d)   the data and information necessary for generating future design modifications and improvements.

2.6.4   Each item (batch, component or part) shall be traceable to the applicable drawing and manufacture procedure card through all stages of manufacture, installation, repair or modification.

2.6.5   Separate batches of identical items shall be assigned a unique identification consisting of, but not necessarily limited to, manufacture procedure card number.

2.6.6   Where applicable, a unique identification shall be recorded on all documents such as process and inspection and test records.

2.6.7   Details of WHO, WHAT and HOW are defined in XYZ–CL written procedures and job instructions indexed in Part 3 of this manual.

Document no. XYZ–MN–001
Edition A
Rev. 1
October 1992

Page 24 of 48

2.7 PROCESS CONTROL

2.7.1 General

The company shall ensure that processes which directly affect quality shall be carried out under controlled conditions.

2.7.2 Control of special processes

2.7.2.1 Special processes shall be performed by qualified personnel using approved written procedures and controlled equipment.

2.7.2.2 The following list identifies some special processes:

— welding
— plastic moulding
— magnetic particle inspection
— penetrant inspection
— radiography
— ultrasonic examination
— heat treating
— brazing
— galvanizing.

2.7.2.3 Special working environments such as humidity and temperature control, clean room and clean station shall be provided when required.

2.7.2.4 Qualification results for processes, equipment and personnel shall be kept current and available for verification by authorized personnel.

2.7.2.5 All control gauges used for special processes (i.e. measuring equipment, NDT equipment, temperature controls) shall be initially certified by an approved laboratory and thereafter shall be included in XYZ–CL's calibration system (section 2.9 refers).

2.7.2.6 Any special processing carried out by a supplier shall require engineering department concurrence prior to placement of order.

2.7.3 Details of WHO, WHAT and HOW are defined in XYZ–CL written procedures and job instructions indexed in Part 3 of this manual.

Page 25 of 48

Document no. XYZ–MN–001
Edition A
Rev. 1
October 1992

2.8   INSPECTION AND TESTING

2.8.1   Receiving inspection and testing

2.8.1.1   All products received shall be verified upon receipt for condition, completeness, identification and general compliance with procurement document requirements, including availability of required documentation. Any deficiencies identified shall be handled in accordance with section 2.11—Control of non-conforming product.

2.8.1.2   Products in compliance with procurement requirements shall be released to the storage area.

2.8.1.3   The documentation received in support of purchased items substantiating acceptance shall be filed with the purchase order.

2.8.1.4   Items shall be withheld from production pending completion of inspection and test or receipt of reports. Release of withheld items shall be permitted only when under positive recall control.

2.8.1.5   Items rejected on receipt shall be clearly identified as being on 'hold' and shall be placed in a quarantined area pending implementation of a non-conformance report.

2.8.1.6   Resulting from an evaluation of the non-conformance, corrective action shall be agreed with the supplier, e.g.

— accept without repair by concession
— rework or repair to meet specified requirements
— regrade for alternative application
— scrap
— return to supplier for rework/repair/replacement.

2.8.2   In-process inspection and testing

2.8.2.1   Detailed written instructions to ensure conformance of items to all applicable requirements shall be available in all manufacturing and installation areas.

2.8.2.2   The control of quality during manufacture and installation shall be maintained by monitoring the processes and the results of inspections.

Document no. XYZ–MN–001
Edition A
Rev. 1
October 1992

2.8.2.3   Except when released under a positive recall procedure, products shall not be released for further processing until all the required inspections and tests have been completed and reported.

2.8.2.4   Each complete inspection and test shall be recorded on the relevant route or stage inspection and test card with the date and identity of the inspector, tester and operator. As each inspection point is cleared on the relevant route card, previous inspection results shall be verified.

2.8.2.5   Inspection points and the requirements for special instructions shall be detailed on route cards with an assigned operations number.

2.8.2.6   Where traceability is required by order, codes or regulations, this shall be handled in accordance with the procedures for 'Identification and traceability'.

2.8.2.7   Procedures for identifying and handling non-conforming items, together with procedures for general workmanship and material handling, shall be available in the respective work areas.

2.8.2.8   Non-conforming items shall be processed in accordance with the written procedure established for this activity.

2.8.2.9   Test specifications and data shall be verified, recorded and accepted on forms compatible with contractual requirements.

2.8.2.10   All production operations shall be performed using the most appropriate equipment, with special tooling requirements as required.

2.8.3   Final inspection and testing

2.8.3.1   The inspection function shall prepare a check-list of inspection and test records and data required to substantiate that goods, manufactured items and installations were inspected in accordance with the specified requirements.
Records and data shall include the following:

— compliance with material specification
— compliance with drawing requirements
— inspection records to substantiate acceptance of items in-process, and acceptability and certification of processing operations
— identification of non-conforming items for rejection, rework or non-conforming item review action.

Document no. XYZ–MN–001
Edition A
Rev. 1
October 1992

Page 27 of 48

2.8.3.2   The inspection function shall certify the acceptability of the items by affixing the appropriate identification stamp to the item and documentation.

2.8.3.3   Acceptable items shall be identified with part number, drawing issue, acceptance stamp and lot number, in the manner prescribed by the drawing or applicable specification.

2.8.3.4   Acceptance of finished items shall be indicated by the inspection function authorizing the final inspection operation on the route card, after verifying that all previous inspection and process stages have been accepted and authorized.

2.8.3.5   Inspection stamps, where used as an authorizing process, shall be designed to indicate company identity and the inspector.

2.8.4   Details of WHO, WHAT and HOW are defined in XYZ–CL written procedures and job instructions indexed in Part 3 of this manual.

Document no. XYZ–MN–001
Edition A
Rev. 1
October 1992

Page 28 of 48

2.9 INSPECTION, MEASURING AND TEST EQUIPMENT

2.9.1 General

2.9.1.1 All measuring and test equipment (including privately owned) used in inspection shall be calibrated in accordance with an approved written calibration and maintenance schedule. The schedule shall include, as applicable, equipment location, number or type, frequency of checks, check method, acceptance criteria and the action to be taken in case of unsatisfactory results.

2.9.1.2 Primary master standards, where utilized, shall be certified by approved facilities having standards traceable to 'national standards'.

2.9.1.3 Records shall be evaluated periodically to ascertain adequacy of calibration inspection intervals presently in use.

2.9.1.4 All measuring and test equipment shall bear a tag, sticker or other identification indicating calibration status. Where this is not possible, calibration status shall be traceable through a master indexing system.

2.9.1.5 Equipment used as a medium for inspection shall require an initial inspection for accuracy, or shall be proven prior to release for use on production.

2.9.1.6 Where equipment is found to be out of calibration, the validity of previous inspection and test results shall be assessed, documented and, where necessary, appropriate recall action taken.

2.9.1.7 At all times, during both handling and use of equipment, care shall be taken to ensure that damage is not sustained and calibration affected.

2.9.1.8 All equipment shall be safeguarded to avoid unauthorized adjustments which would invalidate the calibration setting.

2.9.1.9 Details of WHO, WHAT and HOW are defined in XYZ–CL written procedures and job instructions indexed in Part 3 of this manual.

Document no. XYZ–MN–001
Edition A
Rev. 1
October 1992

Page 29 of 48

2.10   INSPECTION AND TEST STATUS

2.10.1   A system shall be maintained to indicate positively the status of inspection and/or test by utilizing manufacturing route cards, tags or stamped impressions.

2.10.2   Other control devices may be used to show the inspection and/or test status of items processed through a facility as the need arises.

2.10.3   Manufacturing route cards shall be issued to control the production of items. Inspection and/or test status shall be indicated by the inspection authority applying a stamp on the manufacturing route card adjacent to the operation performed.

2.10.4   Acceptance of finished items shall be indicated by the inspection authority validating the final inspection operation on the card after verifying that all previous inspection and process stages have been accepted and validated.

2.10.5   Inspection stamps shall be designed to identify the company and the inspection authority concerned.

2.10.6   Items shall be validated beside the operation or part number, with care being taken to ensure that any stamped impression does no damage. When direct use of an inspection stamp is not possible, the impression shall be placed on the package, tag, label or nameplate.

2.10.7   The authority for application or removal of any inspection status indicators such as tags, labels, stamps, etc., is the quality control manager.

2.10.8   Details of WHO, WHAT and HOW are defined in XYZ–CL written procedures and job instructions indexed in Part 3 of this manual.

2.11   CONTROL OF NON-CONFORMING PRODUCT

2.11.1   Non-conforming goods

2.11.1.1   Non-conforming items shall be identified and segregated from the production flow to prevent unauthorized use, shipment or inclusion with conforming items.

2.11.1.2   Applicable repair or rework forms shall be completed which shall identify the item, the deviation or discrepancy and shall be forwarded to the engineering department for review. The item shall then be appropriately classified to meet one of the following criteria:

— rework to meet the specified requirements
— accept with or without repair by concession
— regrade for alternative application
— scrap.

2.11.1.3   Non-conforming items received from suppliers shall be handled in the same manner as in clause 2.11.1.2 above.

2.11.1.4   Personnel responsible for dispositioning non-conforming items shall ascertain that the deviation or discrepancy is clearly described relative to its acceptance criteria.

2.11.1.5   Decision on subcontractors' non-conforming items shall be subject to approval by XYZ–CL and the customer's representative.

2.11.1.6   XYZ–CL shall maintain objective evidence to substantiate that repaired and reworked items have been reinspected or retested according to applicable procedures.

2.11.2   Non-conforming services

2.11.2.1   Non-conforming services shall be identified and documented. Corrective action shall be initiated to correct the condition and prevent recurrence.

2.11.2.2   Where non-conforming services result in the production of non-conforming goods the control of these goods shall be as described in clause 2.11.1.1.

2.11.2.3   Details of WHO, WHAT and HOW are defined in XYZ–CL written procedures and job instructions indexed in Part 3 of this manual.

2.12   CORRECTIVE ACTION

2.12.1   The responsibility and authority for initiating corrective action shall be defined.

2.12.2   When non-conforming products are identified, the cause of the discrepancy shall be investigated, corrective action taken and preventative measures initiated.

2.12.3   When corrective action is necessary, controls shall ensure that the specified corrective action has been undertaken and is effective.

2.12.4   A system shall be implemented to ensure that any changes to existing procedures are recorded.

2.12.5   All system activities, and the associated objective evidence of product conformance, shall be analysed to ensure that potential causes of non-conforming products are detected and eliminated.

2.12.6   In order to detect and eliminate potential causes of non-conforming products, a continuous analysis of service reports and customer complaints, shall be implemented.

2.12.7   Details of WHO, WHAT and HOW are defined in XYZ–CL written procedures and job instructions indexed in Part 3 of this manual.

2.13   HANDLING, STORAGE, PACKAGING AND DELIVERY

2.13.1   Handling

2.13.1.1   A system shall be maintained for the preservation, segregation and handling of all items through the entire manufacturing and installation process. All precautions shall be taken to protect products from abuse, misuse, damage, deterioration and unauthorized use.

2.13.1.2   Items subject to deterioration or corrosion due to environmental conditions shall be cleaned and preserved for full protection at all times.

2.13.1.3   Handling and storing of parts during manufacture shall be monitored by the responsible inspection authority.

2.13.1.4   Unsatisfactory conditions shall be brought to the attention of the quality control manager for corrective action.

2.13.1.5   Suspect items shall be placed on 'hold' and transferred to a restricted storage area until acceptability is established or other disposition arranged.

2.13.2   Storage

2.13.2.1   Secure storage areas shall be made available for the isolation and protection of accepted products prior to use or shipment.

2.13.2.2   A system shall be implemented for authorizing receipt and despatch to and from such storage areas.

2.13.2.3   Preservation instructions for all items shall be referenced on the manufacturing route cards.

2.13.2.4   Items in storage shall be inspected periodically to verify condition and, where applicable, shelf-life currency. Non-conforming situations shall be dealt with as in 2.13.1.4 above.

2.13.3   Preservation, packing and delivery

2.13.3.1   Adequate packing of completed products shall be undertaken to assure cleanliness, prevention of damage and preservation during shipment to destination.

2.13.3.2   Prior to shipment, the acceptability of the product, proper documentation, preservation, packaging, load-out and tie-down requirements, as determined by the contract, shall be verified.

2.13.3.3   Packaging shall be carried out in accordance with customer requirements. Where no requirements are indicated, then XYZ–CL's standard practices shall be used.

2.13.3.4   Satisfactory load-out details shall be established to ensure safe arrival at destination.

2.13.4   Installation and/or contractual services

2.13.4.1   Where installation and/or contractual services after delivery are required, adequate documentation and procedures shall be provided to achieve and maintain such requirements.

2.13.5   Details of WHO, WHAT and HOW are defined in XYZ–CL written procedures and job instructions indexed in Part 3 of this manual.

Document no. XYZ–MN–001
Edition A
Rev. 1
October 1992

2.14   QUALITY RECORDS

2.14.1   General

2.14.1.1   Legible records shall be generated and maintained to support and substantiate all quality-related activities. These records shall provide evidence of the quality of the item or service and testify directly or indirectly that the product is in compliance with contractual requirements.

2.14.1.2   Records shall be maintained for all applicable activities such as:

    (a)   system and compliance audits
    (b)   inspections performed in accordance with the inspection and test plan
    (c)   reliability of procurement sources
    (d)   raw material certification
    (e)   acceptability of precision tools and gauges
    (f)   control of non-conforming items
    (g)   corrective action on repetitive discrepancies
    (h)   inspection of stores area
    (i)   tests, approvals and audits by agencies, prime contractors and other clients
    (j)   certifications for approval of personnel and processes
    (k)   functional test reports and data
    (l)   installation and commissioning test reports
    (m)   design calculations and drawings.

2.14.1.3   Accumulated records shall be reviewed and evaluated by responsible personnel for the purpose of improving systems, records, etc.

2.14.1.4   Inspection records shall identify the item, applicable requirements, inspections performed, date of inspection, inspection authority, result obtained and the feedback of corrective action generated by the records. Where measurements are not practical, the results shall include the number of conforming items, the number rejected and the nature of the defects. Results of inspections for interchangeability of parts or components shall be recorded.

2.14.1.5   Quality records shall include analyses of data resulting from inspections. Associated records shall demonstrate the use of these data for corrective action.

Document no. XYZ–MN–001
Edition A
Rev. 1
October 1992

2.14.2   **Retention of records**

2.14.2.1   Records shall be retained for the period required by legislation or as specified by contract, whichever is the greater.

2.14.2.2   Records shall be stored in a suitable environment to minimize deterioration or damage and to prevent loss.

2.14.2.3   Where required by contract, records shall be made available for evaluation by the customer or the customer's representative.

2.14.3   **Traceability of design**

2.14.3.1   Records shall be retained to enable traceability of the design process and the review of design procedures to provide for effective design approval.

2.14.4   **Disposal of records**

2.14.4.1   A formal system for the disposal of records shall be also established.

2.14.5   Details of WHO, WHAT and HOW are defined in XYZ–CL written procedures and job instructions indexed in Part 3 of this manual.

2.15   INTERNAL QUALITY AUDITS

2.15.1   The quality manager shall establish, document and implement a pro-gramme for audits, which shall evaluate objectively the adequacy of the procedures and instructions as referenced in this manual.

2.15.2   The audit programme shall define:

— the functions, procedures and instructions to be audited;
— the personnel qualified to perform audits;
— the frequency of audits;
— the methods of reporting findings;
— the means for having corrective actions agreed upon and implemented.

2.15.3   Audits shall include an evaluation of:

— activities, processes, work areas, items and services being produced;
— quality practices, procedures and instructions;
— certification, documents and records.

2.15.4   Audits shall be carried out by appropriately trained and qualified person-nel who are not directly responsible for the area being audited.

2.15.5   Audits shall be performed in accordance with documented audit proce-dures utilizing checklists which identify essential characteristics.

2.15.6   Management responsible for the area audited shall review, agree and correct deficiencies revealed in the documented audit results and shall implement corrective action to prevent a recurrence of the deficiency.

2.15.7   All action taken to correct deficiencies shall be re-audited to verify com-pliance and a close-out report issued.

2.15.8   Details of WHO, WHAT and HOW are defined in XYZ–CL written procedures and job instructions indexed in Part 3 of this manual.

Document no. XYZ–MN–001
Edition A
Rev. 1
October 1992

2.16   TRAINING

2.16.1   All functions that require acquired skills and which could be adversely affected by the lack of such skills shall be identified, categorized and documented.

2.16.2   Documented evidence of personnel competence shall be retained and, at regular intervals through review, examination or other means, an evaluation shall be undertaken to determine whether personnel carrying out such functions require additional training or experience to rectify any shortfall.

2.16.3   Training shall be undertaken utilizing in-house courses or by training schemes operated by recognized third party organizations.

2.16.4   Satisfactory completion of training shall be demonstrated by methods such as:

— examination
— testing
— certification
— letter of attendance.

2.16.5   All records of competence shall be maintained and related to the identified training needs.

2.16.6   Details of WHO, WHAT and HOW are defined in XYZ–CL written procedures and job instructions indexed in Part 3 of this manual.

Document no. XYZ–MN–001
Edition A
Rev. 1
October 1992

2.17   SERVICING

2.17.1   Comprehensive instructions covering on-site servicing activities shall be developed and issued.

2.17.2   The design and utilization of all special tools and equipment, including measuring and test equipment, used for on-site servicing activities shall be validated. The validation process shall include, where appropriate, identification, traceability, calibration, maintenance and inspection.

2.17.3   All elements of XYZ–CL's internal quality system shall apply, as appropriate, to on-site activities.

2.17.4   The responsibility for the provision of backup services shall be clearly defined in a servicing specification.

2.17.5   Details of WHO, WHAT and HOW are defined in XYZ–CL written procedures and job instructions indexed in Part 3 of this manual.

Page 39 of 48

Document no. XYZ–MN–001
Edition A
Rev. 1
October 1992

2.18 **STATISTICAL TECHNIQUES**

2.18.1   Statistical techniques adopted by XYZ–CL shall be as documented in established procedures or as defined by contract.

2.18.2   The conditions necessary for the proper implementation of such techniques shall be defined.

2.18.3   Analyses of results shall be used to verify the acceptability of process capability and product techniques. Such results shall be documented and evaluated to identify causes of defects.

2.18.4   Details of WHO, WHAT and HOW are defined in XYZ–CL written procedures and job instructions indexed in Part 3 of this manual.

Document no. XYZ–MN–001
Edition A
Rev. 1
October 1992

Page 40 of 48

2.19   QUALITY COSTS

2.19.1   General

2.19.1.1 The quality manager shall be responsible for the collection of quality cost data for analysis and for the establishment of a programme to extract and provide quality costs on a periodic basis.

2.19.2   Quality cost data

2.19.2.1 The collection of quality cost data shall include:

— the identification of quality cost elements
— the categorization of quality cost elements into preventative, appraisal and failure costs
— the cost accounting methods
— the collection of quality cost data for those elements not previously costed.

2.19.3   Quality cost data sources

2.19.3.1 Quality cost data shall be obtained from such sources as:

— budgets
— estimates
— wages and salary sheets
— time sheets
— scrap/reject reports
— rework data
— process costs
— production and personnel performance data
— inspection and test records
— internal quality audit reports
and others

2.19.4   Recording

2.19.4.1 Quality cost data shall be recorded by computer and shall be tabulated according to quality cost contributors.

Document no. XYZ–MN–001
Edition A
Rev. 1
October 1992

2.19.5 Analysis of quality cost data

2.19.5.1 In order to establish costing trends, a regular analysis shall be undertaken by the quality manager which shall be reviewed by management with a view to the reduction or optimization of such costs.

[*N.B.* Generally, standards defining quality systems do not address the subject of quality costs. As the control of quality costs is an integral part of assuring quality and the prevention of failure, it is recommended that this subject be addressed.]

Document no. XYZ–MN–001
Edition A
Rev. 1
October 1992

2.20   MANAGEMENT REVIEW

2.20.1   General

2.20.1.1 XYZ–CL management shall undertake a regular and systematic review and evaluation of the entire quality system. The maximum period between reviews shall be one year.

2.20.1.2 Reviews shall be initiated by the quality manager in liaison with appropriate members of the management team.

2.20.2   Review agenda

2.20.2.1 The management review shall include, but not be limited to, the following aspects:

— results of internal audits
— customer feedback (complaints)
— changes in economic situations
— new or updated legislation
— new business methods
— new technology
— market research analyses.

2.20.3   Documentation of results

2.20.3.1 The results of management reviews shall be documented and the implementation of any changes verified by the quality function.

PART 3

PROCEDURES INDEX

Document no. XYZ–MN–001
Edition A
Rev. 1
October 1992

3.0   PROCEDURES

3.1   XYZ–CL has documented procedures for all activities that apply to this quality system.

3.2   Each procedure identifies, as applicable, such things as its purpose and scope; 'who' is responsible for 'what', 'how', 'when' and 'where' all steps are to be performed. 'What' materials, equipment, devices, special processes, documentation, etc., are to be used and 'how' it is all controlled.

3.3   An index of XYZ–CL procedures is incorporated in section 3.4.

3.4   PROCEDURES INDEX

Title	*Document number*
Quality manual	XYZ–MN–001
Planning (contract review)	XYZ–MN–002
Management review	XYZ–MN–003
Work instructions	XYZ–MN–004

Design control

Design criteria control	XYZ–DE–001
Design input	XYZ–DE–002
Design output	XYZ–DE–003
Design verification	XYZ–DE–004
Design changes	XYZ–DE–005
Design review	XYZ–DE–006

Document control

Document preparation	XYZ–DC–001
Document changes	XYZ–DC–002
Document distribution	XYZ–DC–003

Purchasing

Vendor assessment	XYZ–PR–001
Tender package development	XYZ–PR–002
Bid package review and evaluation	XYZ–PR–003
Supplier selection	XYZ–PR–004
Purchase orders	XYZ–PR–005
Incoming inspection	XYZ–PR–006

Purchaser supplied product

Incoming inspection	XYZ–CP–001
Corrective action	XYZ–CP–002

Product identification and traceability

General	XYZ–PD–001

Process control

Inspection and test plans	XYZ–PC–001
Control of special processes	XYZ–PC–002

Inspection and testing
In-process inspection   XYZ–QC–001
Final inspection and test   XYZ–QC–002

Inspection, measuring and test equipment
General   XYZ–EC–001
Design data   XYZ–EC–002
Changes in measurement methods   XYZ–EC–003
Assistance to customer   XYZ–EC–004
Subcontractor-used devices   XYZ–EC–005
(including privately owned)

Inspection and test status
General   XYZ–IT–001
Methods of identification   XYZ–IT–002

Control of non-conforming product
Non-conforming items   XYZ–NC–001
Non-conforming services   XYZ–NC–002

Corrective action
Procedure   XYZ–QA–001

Handling, storage, packaging and delivery
Handling   XYZ–HS–001
Storage   XYZ–HS–002
Preservation and packaging   XYZ–HS–003
Delivery   XYZ–HS–004

Quality records
General   XYZ–RC–001
Retention of records   XYZ–RC–002

Internal quality audits
Procedure   XYZ–QA–002

Training
Policy   XYZ–MN–005

Document no. XYZ–MN–001
Edition A
Rev. 1
October 1992

Page 47 of 48

Servicing
General   XYZ–SV–001
Installation   XYZ–SV–002
Maintenance   XYZ–SV–003

Statistical techniques
Procedure   XYZ–ST–001

Quality costs
Procedure   XYZ–FI–001

Appendix B: Typical procedure for the development of activity documents

Document Number
XYZ–DOC–002

Document Title

PROCEDURES—PREPARATION, STYLE AND FORMAT

Cover page/Revision status

1	5/10/92	Issued for Use	LES	FMC	MTV
0	20/8/92	For Comment	LES	—	—
REV	DATE	REVISION DESCRIPTION	BY	CHK	APP

Page 1 of 5

CONTENTS

1.0 PURPOSE
2.0 SCOPE
3.0 REFERENCES
4.0 DEFINITIONS
5.0 ACTIONS
    5.1 Authorization to proceed
    5.2 Procedure format
    5.3 Procedure content
    5.4 Variations
6.0 DOCUMENTATION

XYZ–DOC–002
Rev. 1

1.0   PURPOSE

    1.1   The purpose of this procedure is to describe the method of preparation, style and format of all procedures established for use by the XYZ Company Limited departments and/or disciplines.

        This procedure shall be used as an example of such preparation, style and format.

2.0   SCOPE

    2.1   This procedure shall apply to all documents which identify the activities and functions of a department or group and shall be observed by all XYZ Company Limited departments and disciplines without exception.

3.0   REFERENCES

    3.1   XYZ–DOC–001   Numbering system for XYZ Company Limited documents.

    3.2   XYZ–DOC–003   Procedure for development, approval and implementation of activity documents.

    3.3   XYZ–DOC –004   Procedures index.

4.0   DEFINITIONS

    4.1   Procedure

        A document that details the purpose and scope of an activity and specifies how it is to be properly carried out.

5.0   ACTIONS

    5.1   Authorization to proceed

        The need for a procedure shall be identified by the department or discipline Manager concerned and the development of such agreed with the appropriate discipline Head (refer document XYZ–DOC–003).

    5.1.1 Once the requirement has been agreed and an author delegated, the author shall obtain a definitive procedure number from the document control centre (refer document XYZ–DOC–001). This procedure number shall be unique for the procedure to which it is to be applied and shall not be used to identify any other document. In the event that the decision to proceed with the procedure is rescinded, then the document control centre shall be so advised and the number reinstated for future use.

5.2 Procedure format

    5.2.1 The cover page of the procedure shall be in accordance with form DOC–0021 (see attachment number 6.1) and completed with the following information:

        — Document number
        — Document title
        — Cover page/revision status
        — Revision and approval box

        Refer to the cover page of this procedure for standard format. The cover page shall always be identified as page 1 of —.

    5.2.2 The procedure contents list shall always appear as page 2 of —.

    5.2.3 The contents page and all subsequent pages of the procedure shall be completed using XYZ standard bordered stationery (see attachment number 6.2). Each page shall be identified by number and shall carry the appropriate document identification and revision in the bottom right-hand corner.

5.3 Procedure content

All procedures shall carry the same content which shall be as follows:

    5.3.1 Purpose—which outlines the object or intention of the document.

    5.3.2 Scope—which outlines the area, department, group, or personnel to which the procedure is applicable.

    5.3.3 References—which detail other documents which have a bearing on the activities within the procedure.

    5.3.4 Definitions—which explain a word or action not generally understood, or which may have a specific interpretation in the procedure.

    5.3.5 Actions—which details the actions of those personnel involved in the activity. This section shall identify wherever possible who does what and also how, when, where and why the activity is carried out.

    5.3.6 Documentation—which list any documentation referred to within the procedure. Samples of such documentation shall be attached.

5.4 Variations

    5.4.1 The procedure index shall always include the content as detailed in clause 5.3 above (see attachment number 6.3). There shall be no variation. In the event that, for example, there are no references or definitions, then under the applicable heading the word NONE shall be inserted.

    5.4.2 In the event that additional details are required to be incorporated as a supplement to the procedure, then these shall be incorporated as an appendix to the procedure.

6.0 DOCUMENTATION

    6.1 Procedure cover page.

    6.2 XYZ Company Limited standard border stationery.

    6.3 Procedure contents page.

XYZ–DOC–002
Rev. 1

Document number

_____

Document title

_____

Cover Page/Revision Status

0					
REV	DATE	REVISION DESCRIPTION	BY	CHK	APP

Page 1 of
Form No. DOC–0021

XYZ–DOC–002
Attachment No. 6.1

Form No. DOC–0022

XYZ–DOC–002
Attachment No. 6.2

CONTENTS

1.0 PURPOSE
2.0 SCOPE
3.0 REFERENCES
4.0 DEFINITIONS
5.0 ACTIONS
6.0 DOCUMENTATION

Appendix C: Glossary of terms

Unless otherwise indicated the definitions given in the International Standard ISO 8402–1986 (Quality—Vocabulary) apply.

Audit checklist   A document which guides the continuity and depth of an audit. (Author)

Corrective action request   A document which addresses a non-conformance to a system element, procedure or job instruction. (Author)

Customer   This term applies in both the internal and external sense and means the recipient of an item or service. (Author)

Inspection   Activities such as measuring, examining, testing, gauging one or more characteristics of a product or service and comparing these with specified requirements to determine conformity.

Inspection and test plan   A document which describes the inspections and tests to be performed on a given item. (Author)

Job instructions   A document which directs personnel in a specific task. (Author)

Non-conformance   The non-fulfilment of specified requirements.

Organization   A company, firm, enterprise or association, or part thereof, whether incorporated or not, public or private, that has its own function(s) and administration. (Australian Standard DR 89201:R)

Procedure   A document which describes what is to be done and by whom, and how, when, where and why an activity is to be carried out. (Author)

Product (1)   The result of activities or processes (tangible product; intangible product, such as a service, a computer program, a design, directions for use), or: An activity or process (such as the provision of a service or the execution of a production process).

Product (2)   The result of one's own endeavours. (Author)

Quality   The totality of features and characteristics of a product or service that bear upon its ability to satisfy stated or implied needs.

Quality assurance   All those planned and systematic actions necessary to provide adequate confidence that a product or service will satisfy given requirements for quality.

Quality audit   A systematic and independent examination to determine whether quality activities and related results comply with planned arrangements and whether these arrangements are implemented effectively and are suitable to achieve objectives.

Quality control   The operational techniques and activities that are used to fulfil requirements for quality.

Quality management   That aspect of overall management function that determines and implements the quality policy.

Quality manual   A document which describes, in general terms, the quality policies, procedures and practices of an organization. (Author)

Quality plan   A document setting out the specific quality practices, resources and sequence of activities relevant to a particular product, service, contract or project.

Quality policy   The overall quality intentions and direction of an organization as regards quality, as formally expressed by top management.

Quality system   The organizational structure, responsibilities, procedures and resources for implementing quality management.

Quality system element   The administrative activities affecting quality that need to be implemented and controlled to ensure that the product or service meets specified requirements. (Source: Australian Standard 2990–1987)

Quality system review   A formal evaluation by top management of the status and adequacy of the quality system in relation to quality policy and new objectives resulting from changing circumstances.

Supplier   This term applies in both the internal and external sense and means the producer of an item or service.

Total quality management   The management policies, objectives and operations of an organization which involve all functions of its entire business activities in order to sustain a competitive advantage by consistently exceeding the 'current and future' expectations of customers based on continuous improvement in all processes, goods and services, through the creative involvement of all people. (Author—derived from various sources)

Appendix D: Standards associated with quality assurance

(Although all titles are given in English, it should not assumed that the related document is published in the English language.)

GENERAL STANDARDS

International

ISO 8402–1986	Quality—Vocabulary.
ISO 9000–1987	Quality management and quality assurance standards—Guidelines for selection and use.
ISO 9001–1987	Quality systems—Model for quality assurance in design/development, production, installation and servicing.
ISO 9002–1987	Quality systems—Model for quality assurance in production and installation.
ISO 9003–1987	Quality systems—Model for quality assurance in final inspection and test.
ISO 9004–1987	Quality management and quality system elements—Guidelines.
ISO 9004–2:1991	Quality management and quality system elements, Part 2—Guidelines for services.
ISO 10011:1990	Generic guidelines for auditing quality systems, Part 1—Auditing. Part 2—Qualification criteria for auditors. Part 3—Managing audit programmes.

Published by the International Organization for Standardization, Geneva.

Australia

AS 2000–1987	Guide to AS 1821–1823—Suppliers Quality Systems.
AS 3900–1987	Identical with ISO 9000–1987
AS 3901–1987	Identical with ISO 9001–1987
AS 3902–1987	Identical with ISO 9002–1987
AS 3903–1987	Identical with ISO 9003–1987
AS 3904–1987	Identical with ISO 9004–1987
AS 2561–1982	Guide to the determination of quality costs.
SAA QS1–1988	Guide to the preparation of quality manuals.
SAA QS5–1988	Guide to the assessment and auditing of quality management systems.
AS 3991.1	Identical with ISO 10011:1.
AS 3991.2	Identical with ISO 10011:2.
AS 3991.3	Identical with ISO 10011.3.

Published by the Standards Australia, North Sydney.

Austria

Currently reviewing the International Standards ISO 9000–9004 which have been issue in draft from as:

OE NORM–PREN 29000
OE NORM–PREN 29001

OE NORM–PREN 29002
OE NORM–PREN 29003
OE NORM–PREN 29004

To be published by Öesterreichisches Normungsinstitut, Vienna.

Belgium
NBN X 50–002–1 (1988)   Identical with ISO 9000–1987.
NBN X 50–003   (1988)   Identical with ISO 9001–1987.
NBN X 50–004   (1988)   Identical with ISO 9002–1987.
NBN X 50–005   (1988)   Identical with ISO 9003–1987.
NHN X 50–002–2 (1988)   Identical with ISO 9004–1987.

Published by Institut belge de normalisation, Bruxelles.

Canada
CAN 3 Z299.0–96   Guide for Selecting and Implementing the CAN3 Z299.85 Quality
                   Assurance Program Standards.
CAN3 Z299.1–85   Quality Assurance Program—Category 1.
CAN3 Z299.2–85   Quality Assurance Program—Category 2.
CAN3 Z299.3–85   Quality Assurance Program—Category 3.
CAN3 Z299.4–85   Quality Assurance Program—Category 4.
CAN3 Q395–81   Quality Audits.

Published by the Canadian Standards Association, Rexdale, Ontario.

Denmark
DS/EN 29000 (1988)   Identical with ISO 9000–1987.
DS/EN 29001 (1988)   Identical with ISO 9001–1987.
DS/EN 29002 (1988)   Identical with ISO 9002–1987.
DS/EN 29003 (1988)   Identical with ISO 9003–1987.
DS/EN 29004 (1988)   Identical with ISO 9004–1987.

Published by Dansk Standardiseringsraad, Hellerup.

Finland
SFS–ISO 9000–1988   Identical with ISO 9000–1987.
SFS–ISO 9001–1988   Identical with ISO 9001–1987.
SFS–ISO 9002–1988   Identical with ISO 9002–1987.
SFS–ISO 9003–1988   Identical with ISO 9003–1987.
SFS–ISO 9004–1988   Identical with ISO 9004–1987.

Published by Suomen Standardisoimisliitto, Helsinki.

France
NF.X.50–121:1987   Identical with ISO 9000–1987.
NF.X.50–131:1986   As ISO 9001–1987 but with minor differences.

NF.X.50–132:1986   As ISO 9002–1987 but with minor differences.
NF.X.50–133:1986   As ISO 9003–1987 but with minor differences.
NF.X.50–133:1986   As ISO 9004–1987 but with minor differences.

Published by Association Française de Normalisation, Paris.

Germany
DIN ISO 9000–1987   Identical with ISO 9000–1987
DIN ISO 9001–1987   Identical with ISO 9001–1987
DIN ISO 9002–1987   Identical with ISO 9002–1987
DIN ISO 9003–1987   Identical with ISO 9003–1987
DIN ISO 9004–1987   Identical with ISO 9004–1987

Published by DIN Deutsches Institut für Normung, Berlin.

Hungary
MI 18990–1988   Identical with ISO 9000–1987.
MI 18991–1988   Identical with ISO 9001–1987.
MI 18992–1988   Identical with ISO 9002–1987.
MI 18993–1988   Identical with ISO 9003–1987.
MI 18993–1988   Identical with ISO 9004–1987.

Published by Magyar Szabványügyi Hivatal, Budapest.

India
ISO 1021
    Part 1–1988   Identical with ISO 8402–1986.
    Part 2–1988   Identical with ISO 9000–1987.
    Part 3–1987   Equivalent to ISO 9004–1987.
    Part 4–1988   Identical with ISO 9001–1987.
    Part 5–1988   Identical with ISO 9002–1987.
    Part 6–1988   Identical with ISO 9003–1987.
IS 10708–1985   Guidelines for analysis of quality costs.
IS 12040–1987   Guidelines for development of vendor rating systems.

Published by Bureau of Indian Standards, New Delhi.

Ireland
I.S. 300
    Part 0–1987   Identical with ISO 9000–1987
    Part 1–1987   Identical with ISO 9001–1987
    Part 2–1987   Identical with ISO 9002–1987
    Part 3–1987   Identical with ISO 9003–1987
    Part 4–1987   Identical with ISO 9004–1987
I.S. 302:1984   Quality Manual Preparation Guide.
I.S. 304:1984   Quality Audit.

I.S. 305:1985   Guide to Quality Management in the Service Industries.

Published by National Standards Authority of Ireland, Dublin.

Italy

UNI/ISO 8402–1987	Terminology
UNI/EN 29000–1987	Identical with ISO 9000–1987
UNI/EN 29001–1987	Identical with ISO 9001–1987
UNI/EN 29002–1987	Identical with ISO 9002–1987
UNI/EN 29003–1987	Identical with ISO 9003–1987
UNI/EN 29004–1987	Identical with ISO 9004–1987

Published by Ente Nazionale Italiano di Unificazione, Milano.

Japan

Currently there are no Japanese Industrial Standards on quality assurance or any which correspond to the ISO 9000 series.

The Japanese Industrial Standards Committee have, however, published a Japanese translation of ISO 9000–9004:1987.

Malaysia

MS 985   Code of practice for suppliers quality control systems. (This code of practice specifies three levels of quality systems, which are generally in line with ISO 9001–9003:1987.)

Published by the Standards and Industrial Research Institute of Malaysia, Selangor.

Netherlands

ISO 9000–9004:1987 accepted by the Nederlands Normalisatie Instituut and a Dutch version issued.

New Zealand

NZS 9000 – 1990	Identical with ISO 9000–1987.
NZS 9004 – 1990	Identical with ISO 9004–1987.
NZS 9001 – 1990	Identical with ISO 9001–1987.
NZS 9002 – 1990	Identical with ISO 9002–1987.
NZS 9003 – 1990	Identical with ISO 9003–1987.
NZS 9004 – 1990	Identical with ISO 9004–1987.

Published by Standards Association of New Zealand, Wellington.

Norway

NS–EN 29000:1988	Identical with ISO 9000:1987.
NS–EN 29001:1988	Identical with ISO 9001:1987.
NS–EN 29002:1988	Identical with ISO 9002:1987.

NS–EN 29003:1988   Identical with ISO 9003:1987.
NS–EN 29004:1988   Identical with ISO 9004:1987.

Published by Norges Strandiseringsforbund, Oslo.

Singapore
SS 308 Part 1:1985   Inspection programme requirements.
SS 308 Part 2:1986   Quality verification requirements.

Published by Singapore Institute of Standards and Industrial Research.

South Africa
SABS 0157 Part 0:1987   Equivalent to ISO 9000–1987.
SABS 0157 Part 1:1987   Equivalent to ISO 9001–1987.
SABS 0157 Part 2:1987   Equivalent to ISO 9002–1987.
SABS 0157 Part 3:1987   Equivalent to ISO 9003–1987.
SABS 0157 Part 4:1987   Equivalent to ISO 9004–1987.

Published by South African Bureau of Standards, Pretoria.

Spain
UNE 66 900–1987   Equivalent to ISO 9000–1987.
UNE 66 901–1987   Equivalent to ISO 9001–1987.
UNE 66 902–1987   Equivalent to ISO 9002–1987.
UNE 66 903–1987   Equivalent to ISO 9003–1987.
UNE 66 904–1987   Equivalent to ISO 9004–1987.
UNE 66 905 (1)–1987   Instructions for the application of UNE 66 901.
UNE 66 905 (2)–1987   Instructions for the application of UNE 66 902.
UNE 66 905 (3)–1987   Instructions for the application of UNE 66 903.

Published by Asociación Española de Normalización y Certificación, Madrid.

Sweden
SS—ISO 9000:1988   Identical with ISO 9000–1987.
SS—ISO 9001:1988   Identical with ISO 9001–1987.
SS—ISO 9002:1988   Identical with ISO 9002–1987.
SS—ISO 9003:1988   Identical with ISO 9003–1987.
SS—ISO 9004:1988   Identical with ISO 9003–1987.
SS—02 01 04   Quality vocabulary.

Published by Standariserings Kommissionen i Sverige, Stockholm.

Tunisia
NT 110.17–1987   Identical with ISO 8402–1986
NT 110.18–1987   Identical with ISO 9000–1987
NT 110.19–1987   Identical with ISO 9001–1987
NT 110.20–1987   Identical with ISO 9002–1987

NT 110.21–1987   Identical with ISO 9003–1987
NT 110.22–1987   Identical with ISO 9004–1987

Published by National Institute for Standardization and Industrial Property, Tunis–Belvedere.

United Kingdom

BS 4778 Part 1:1987   Quality vocabulary and International terms.
                      Identical with ISO 8402:1986.
BS 4778 Part 2   National terms.
BS 4778 Part 3   Reliability and maintainability terms.
BS 5750 Part 0
   Section 0.1:1987   Identical with ISO 9000–1987.
BS 5750 Part 0
   Section 0.1:1987   Identical with ISO 9004–1987.
BS 5750 Part 1:1987   Identical with ISO 9001–1987.
BS 5750 Part 2:1987   Identical with ISO 9002–1987.
BS 5750 Part 3:1987   Identical with ISO 9003–1987.
BS 5750 Part 4:1990   Guide to the use of BS 5750 Parts 1, 2 and 3.
BS 6143:1992   The determination and use of quality related costs.
BS 7229 Part 1:1991   Identical with ISO 10011:1.
BS 7229 Part 2:1991   Identical with ISO 10011:2.
BS 7229 Part 3:1991   Identical with ISO 10011:3.

Published by British Standards Institution, London.

USA

ANSI/ASQC Q90:1987   Identical with ISO 9000–1987.
ANSI/ASQC Q91:1987   Identical with ISO 9001–1987.
ANSI/ASQC Q92:1987   Identical with ISO 9002–1987.
ANSI/ASQC Q93:1987   Identical with ISO 9003–1987.
ANSI/ASQC Q94:1987   Identical with ISO 9004–1987.
ANSI/ASQC C1   Specifications of general requirements for a quality program.
ANSI/ASQC Z–1.15:1979 Generic guidelines for quality systems.

Published by American National Standards Institute, New York.

Yugoslavia

JUS A.K1.011–1987   Identical with ISO 9000–1987.
JUS A.K1.011–1987   Identical with ISO 9004–1987.
JUS A.K1.012–1987   Identical with ISO 9001–1987.
JUS A.K1.013–1987   Identical with ISO 9002–1987.
JUS A.K1.014–1987   Identical with ISO 9003–1987.
JUS A.K1.015   Guide to the use of JUS A.K1.012.
JUS A.K1.016   Guide to the use of JUS A.K1.013.

JUS A.K1.017   Guide to the use of JUS A.K1.014.
JUS A.K1.018   Guide for the development of a quality manual.

Published by Savezni zavod za standardizaciju, Belgrade.

The following countries have indicated acceptance of the ISO 9000 series of standards for eventual publication:

China
Columbia
Greece
Hong Kong
Indonesia
Jamaica
Papua New Guinea
Philippines
Poland
Syria

INDUSTRY-RELATED STANDARDS

Engineering and Construction
Australia
AS 2990–1987   Quality Systems for Engineering and Construction Projects.

Published by the Standards Australia, North Sydney.

Nuclear
Canada
CAN3–N2860.82

Published by Canadian Standards Association.

International
ISO.6125:1980   Nuclear power plants: Quality Assurance.

Published by International Organization for Standardization.

United Kingdom
BS.5882:1980 Specification for a total quality assurance programme for nuclear power plants.

Published by British Standards Institution.

USA

ANSI/ASME.NQA-1 1983   Quality Assurance Program Requirements for Nuclear Facilities.

ANSI/ASME.NQA 1983   Quality Assurance Requirements for Nuclear Power Plants.

Published by American Society of Mechanical Engineers.

Military
International

AQAP-1   NATO Quality Control System Requirements for Industry.

AQAP-4   NATO Inspection System Requirements for Industry.

AQAP-9   NATO Basic Inspection Requirements for Industry.

Published by Allied Quality Assurance Publications.

United Kingdom

Adoption of AQAP Standards.

Published by Her Majesty's Stationery Office.

USA

MIL-Q-9858A   Quality Program Requirements.

Published by US Military.

Bibliography

Burgess, J. A. (1984) *Design assurance for engineers*, New York: Marcel Dekker Inc.

Crosby, P. B. (1979) *Quality is free*, New York: McGraw-Hill Book Company.

Crosby, P. B. (1984) *Quality without tears*, New York: McGraw-Hill Book Company.

Deming, W. (1982) *Quality, productivity and competitive position*, Massachusetts: Institute of Technology.

Department of Trade and Industry (1983) *The case for quality*, London: Her Majesty's Stationery Office.

Department of Trade and Industry (1983) *Quality management: A guide for chief executives*, London: Her Majesty's Stationery Office.

Dunn, R., and Ullman, R. (1982) *Quality assurance for computer software*, New York: McGraw-Hill Book Company.

Feigenbaum, A. V. (1983) *Total quality control*, 3rd edition, New York: McGraw-Hill Book Company.

Fukuda, R. (1983) *Managerial engineering: techniques for improving quality and productivity in the workplace*, Stamford, Connecticut: Productivity Inc.

Hayes, G. E. (1983) *Quality assurance; Management and technology*, Revised edition.

Hongo, T. (1980) *Management by objectives: a Japanese experience*, Tokyo: Asian Productivity Organization.

Johnson, L. M. (1982) *Quality assurance program evaluation*, Santa Fe Springs: Stockton Trade Press.

Juran, J. M. (1964) *Managerial breakthrough*, New York: McGraw-Hill Book Company.

Juran, J. M., and Gryna, F. M. (1980) *Quality planning and analysis*, New York: McGraw-Hill Book Company.

McConnell, J. (1986) *The seven tools of TQC*, Sydney: Enterprise, Australia Publications.

Peters, T. J., and Waterman, R. H. (1982) *In search of excellence*, New York: Harper and Row.

Roberts, G. W. (1983) *Quality assurance in research and development*, New York: Marcel Dekker Inc.

Rogerson, J. H. (1986) *Quality assurance in process plant manufacture*, London: Elsevier Applied Science.

Sayle, A. J. (1988) *Management audits*, 2nd edition, London: McGraw-Hill Book Company.

Stebbing, L. (1990) *Quality management in the service industry*, Chichester: Ellis Horwood Limited.

Taguchi, G. (1986) *Introduction to quality engineering: designing quality into products and processes*, Tokyo: Asian Productivity Organization.

QUALITY CIRCLES

Barra, R. (1983) *Putting quality circles to work*, New York: McGraw-Hill Book Company.

Department of Trade and Industry (1985) *Quality circles*, London: Her Majesty's Stationery Office.

Hutchins, D. (1985) *The quality circle handbook*, London: Pitman Publishing Limited.

Mohr, W., and Mohr, H. (1983) *Quality circles: Changing images of people at work*, Reading, Mass.: Addison Wesley.

NSQC (1985) *Circle programme guidelines*, London: National Society of Quality Circles.

Robson, M. (1982) *Quality circles: A practical guide*, Aldershot: Gower Publishing Company.

QUALITY CONTROL AND STATISTICS

Burr, I. (1976) *Statistical quality control methods*, New York: Marcel Dekker Inc.

Caplen, R. H. (1983) *A practical approach to quality control*, 4th edition, London: Business Books Limited.

Cochran, W. G. (1977) *Sampling techniques*. 3rd edition.

Dodge, H. F., and Romig, H. G. (1959) *Sampling inspection tables: Single and double sampling*.

Freund, J. E., and Williams, F. J. (1982) *Elementary business statistics*, 4th edition, Englewood Cliffs, New Jersey: Prentice-Hall.

Grant, E. L., and Leavenworth, R. S. (1980) *Statistical quality control*, 5th edition, New York: McGraw-Hill Book Company.

Ishikawa, K. (1982) *Guide to quality control*, 2nd revised English edition, Tokyo: Asian Productivity Organization.

Juran, J. M., Gryna, F. M., and Bingham, R. S. (1979) *Quality control handbook*, 3rd edition. New York: McGraw-Hill Book Company.

Oakland, J. S. (1986) *Statistical process control: a practical guide*, London: Heinemann.

Price, F. (1984) *Right first time*, Aldershot: Gower Publishing Company.

Rosander, A. C. (1985) *Applications of quality control in the service industries*, New York: Marcel Dekker Inc.

Shapiro, S. S., and Gross, A. J. (1981) *Statistical modeling techniques*.

Schilling, E. S. (1982) *Acceptance sampling in quality control*, New York: Marcel Dekker Inc.

Taguchi, G. (1981) *On-line control during production*, Tokyo: Japanese Standard Association.

Index